GREATER BRUSSELS

0 km 3

0 miles 3

THE UPPER TOWN
Pages 54–75
Street Finder maps 2, 3, 4

VILLA GERMAINE

THE UPPER
TOWN

0 metres 500

0 yards 500

Vista of a tree-lined path in the Parc du Cinquantenaire

Basilique National du Sacré-Coeur

Gilt statue on façade of a Guildhouse in Antwerp

Belgian oysters

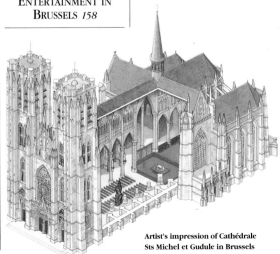
Artist's impression of Cathédrale Sts Michel et Gudule in Brussels

INTRODUCING BRUSSELS

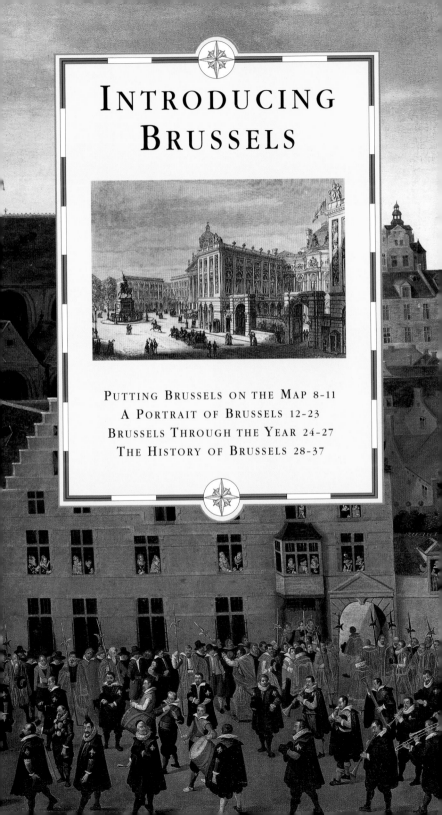

Putting Brussels on the Map

BRUSSELS IS THE capital of Belgium and the centre of govern-ment for the European Union. Although Belgium is one of Europe's smallest countries, covering 30,500 sq km (11,580 sq miles), it has one of the continent's highest population densi-ties, with 10 million inhabitants (300 people for every square kilometre). Belgium is a bilingual country (Flemish and French). Although Brussels falls geographically in the Flemish half, it is largely French-speaking. Belgium's largest city, with almost one million inhabitants, Brussels is also the most visited, receiving some six million visitors a year, although 70 per cent of these come for business. Today, Brussels' excellent communications make it an ideal place from which to explore historic Belgian cities such as Antwerp, Ghent and Bruges.

Satellite photograph of Brussels: buildings appear as light blue, red represents green vegetation

WESTERN EUROPE

NORWAY
SWEDEN
DENMARK
REPUBLIC OF IRELAND
UNITED KINGDOM
NETHERLANDS
Brussels
BELGIUM
GERMANY
LUXEMBOURG
CZECH REPUBLIC
FRANCE
SWITZERLAND
AUSTRIA
SLOVENIA
ITALY
CROATIA
PORTUGAL
SPAIN

Western Europe
Brussels is known for its efficient road and rail systems, linking the city to the Netherlands Germany, France and the United Kingdom.

Hull

Harwich

NORTH SEA

Vlissingen

Zeebrugge
N58
N34
Dover
Oostende
Bruges
N49
E40
A17
Ghent
N43
E40
Ijzer
Kortrijk
E17
A19
Escaut
N62
Lille
E429
E42
A26
A16
Lille
A1
A
Lens
E19
E17
N43

KEY

□	Greater Brussels
□	Area below sea level
✈	Airport
⛴	Ferry port
━	Motorway
━	Major road
━	Railway
▪▪	Country boundary

FRANCE

St Quentin
N2
E17

BRUSSELS AND ENVIRONS

Mechelen

A12

E19

N26

E314

Aalst

Vilvoorde

N47

E40

Nationale

E40

Leuven

BRUSSELS

N8

Woluwe

Anderlecht

N5

E411

Wavre

Halle

E19

Waterloo

A8

Brussels and its Environs

The sights in Brussels are covered in detail on pages 40–83
and a Street Finder map is provided on pages 174–7.
Attractions beyond Brussels can be found on pages 86–121.

AMSTERDAM

Schiphol

Leiden

E19

DEN HAAG

E30

Rotterdam

Hoek van
Holland

Lek

Rotterdam

E31

A59

Dordrecht

NETHERLANDS

N59

A17

A58

Breda

A59

Maas

E34

Mönchengladbach

A61

ANTWERP

Antwerpen

Albert Kanaal

N74

A46

E17

E19

A12

E313

E314

Scheldt

Mechelen

E314

GERMANY

A4

Nationale

N2

Maastrict

Maastricht

BRUSSELS

Leuven

N3

Aachen

N8

Dijle

E40

N3

E40

Waterloo

N29

Liège

Verviers

E42

N6

Meuse

E42

BELGIUM

N90

Mons

E42

Namur

N5

Charleroi

Ourthe

E25

Sambre

N97

Dinant

E411

N4

Bastogne

N7

Meuse

N5

N95

N4

N43

LUXEMBOURG

Charleville-
Mézières

Arlon

E44

A34

N4

Luxembourg

A13

Luxembourg

N43

0 km   20

0 miles   20

Central Brussels

C ENTRAL BRUSSELS is divided into two main areas, each of which has its own chapter in the guide. Historically the poorer area where workers and immigrants lived, the Lower Town contains the exceptional 17th-century heart of the city, the Grand Place, as well as the cosmopolitan Place de Brouckère, and the historic workers' district, the Marolles. The Upper Town, traditional home of the aristocracy, is an elegant area which encircles the city's green oasis, the Parc de Bruxelles. Running up through the area is Rue Royale, which ends in the 18th-century Place Royale, home to the city's finest art museums.

Hôtel de Ville
The focus of the Grand Place, Brussels' historic Town Hall dates from the early 15th century. Its Gothic tracery façade features the famous needle-like crooked spire (see pp44–5).

KEY

▢	Major sight
▢	Place of interest
▢	Other building
P	Parking
ⓘ	Tourist information
▣	Police station
✚	Hospital
▦	Bus terminus
▦	Tram stop
▤	Train station
Ⓜ	Metro station
✝	Church

La Bourse façade
Overlooking the city from busy Boulevard Anspach in the Lower Town, Brussels' Stock Exchange was built in 1873 in ornate style (see p47).

Place du Petit Sablon
*This square is a jewel
of the Upper Town.
Originally a horse market,
the central area became
a flower garden in 1890,
surrounded by wrought-
iron railings decorated
with stone statuettes.
Each figure represents a
medieval trade or craft
that brought prosperity to
the capital (see p68–9).*

0 metres   500

0 yards   500

Palais Royal
*The official home of the
Belgian monarch, this is one
of the finest 18th-century
buildings in the Upper Town.
A highlight of Neo-Classical
architecture, it overlooks Parc
de Bruxelles (see pp58–9).*

Brussels' Best: Architecture

REFLECTING Brussels' importance in the history of northern Europe, the city's architecture ranges from grand medieval towers to the glittering post-modern structures of European institutions. With a few examples of medieval Brabant Gothic still on show, the capital of Europe has the best Flemish Renaissance architecture in the world in the Baroque splendour of the Grand Place, as well as elegant Neo-Classical churches and houses. The quantity and quality of Art Nouveau *(see pp16–17)*, with its exquisite interiors and handmade features, are highlights of 19th- and 20th-century residential building. The cutting-edge designs in the Parliament Quarter, planned by committees of European architects, take the tour up to date.

Basilique du Sacré-Coeur
Begun in 1904 and only completed in 1970, this huge Art Deco edifice is the world's fifth-largest church (see p81).

BASILIQUE DU
SACRÉ-COEUR

Grand Place
Almost entirely rebuilt by merchants after French bombardment in 1695, this cobbled square is one of the world's best Baroque ensembles (see pp42–3).

Palais de Justice
Bigger in area than St Peter's in Rome, the city's law courts were built in Neo-Classical style using the profits of colonialism, and completed in 1883 (see p69).

Lower Town

Porte de Hal
This imposing 14th-century tower is the only remaining trace of the city's solid, thick second perimeter wall. It owes its survival to its use as an 18th-century prison and latterly as a museum (see p79).

0 metres 500

0 yards 500

Cathédrale Sts Michel et Gudule
The white stone façade from 1250 is an outstanding example of Brabant Gothic style (see pp70–71).

Palais de la Nation
The home of the Belgian Parliament since the country's independence in 1830, this magnificent building was constructed in the late 18th century by the Neo-Classical architect Guimard, who also designed the expansive stone façade and many of the surrounding state buildings.

Upper Town

Palais d'Egmont
This 18th-century ducal mansion bears the name of a Flemish count executed for defending his countrymen's civil rights in 1568.

European Parliament
Named "Les Caprices des Dieux" ("The Whims of the Gods"), this glassy postmodern construction serves 626 politicians.

Belgian Artists

BELGIAN ART ROSE to the fore when the region came under Burgundian rule in the 15th century. Renaissance painters produced strong works in oil, characterized by intricate detail and lifelike, unidealized portraiture. The quest for realism and clarity of light was heavily influenced by the new Dutch schools of art. Yet, in contrast, Belgium's second golden artistic age, in the 20th century, moved away from these goals, abandoning reality for surrealism in the challenging work of artists such as René Magritte.

Belgium is justifiably proud of its long artistic tradition. Rubenshuis in Antwerp *(see pp96–7)*, Brussels' Musée Wiertz *(see p72)* and Musées Royaux des Beaux-Arts *(see pp62–7)* are fine examples of the respect Belgium shows to its artists' homes and their works.

Portrait of Laurent Froimont by Rogier van der Weyden

THE FLEMISH PRIMITIVES

ART IN BRUSSELS and Flanders first attracted European attention at the end of the Middle Ages. **Jan van Eyck** (c.1400–41) is considered to be responsible for the major revolution in Flemish art. Widely credited as the creator of oil painting, van Eyck was the first artist to use the oil medium to fix longer-lasting glazes and to mix colour pigments for wood and canvas. As works could now be rendered more permanent, the innovation spread the Renaissance fashion for panel paintings. However, van Eyck was more than just a practical innovator, and can be seen as the forefather of the Flemish Primitive school

with his lively depictions of human existence in an animated manner. Van Eyck is also responsible, with his brother, for the striking polyptych altarpiece *Adoration of the Holy Lamb*, displayed in Ghent Cathedral *(see p110)*.

The trademarks of the Flemish Primitives are a lifelike vitality, enhanced by realism in portraiture, texture of clothes and furnishings and a clarity of light. The greatest interpreter of the style was Rogier de la Pasture (c.1400–64), better known as **Rogier van der Weyden**, the town painter of Brussels, who combined van Eyck's light and realism with work of religious intensity, as in *Lamentation (see p66)*. Many in Belgium and across Europe were schooled and inspired by his work, continuing and expanding the new techniques. **Dieric Bouts** (1415–75) extended

the style. With his studies of bustling 15th-century Bruges, **Hans Memling** (c.1433–94) is considered the last Flemish Primitive. Moving towards the 16th century, landscape artist **Joachim Patinier** (c.1475–1524) produced the first European industrial scenes.

THE BRUEGHEL DYNASTY

IN THE EARLY years of the 16th century, Belgian art was strongly influenced by the Italians. Trained in Rome, **Jan Gossaert** (c.1478–1533) brought mythological themes to the art commissioned by the ruling Dukes of Brabant.

But it was the prolific Brueghel family who had the most influence on Flemish art throughout the 16th and 17th centuries. **Pieter Brueghel the Elder** (c.1525–69), one of the greatest Flemish artists, settled in Brussels in 1563. His earthy rustic landscapes of village life, peopled with comic peasants, are a social study of medieval life and remain his best-known work. **Pieter Brueghel the Younger** (1564–1638) produced religious works such as *The Enrolment of Bethlehem* (1610). In contrast, **Jan Brueghel the Elder** (1568–1625) painted intricate floral still lifes with a draped velvet backdrop, becoming known as "Velvet Brueghel". His son, **Jan Brueghel the Younger** (1601–78) also became a court painter in Brussels and a fine landscape artist of note.

The Fall of Icarus by Pieter Brueghel the Elder

Self-portrait by Rubens, one of many from his lifetime

THE ANTWERP ARTISTS

IN THE 17TH century, the main centre of Belgian art moved from the social capital, Brussels, to Antwerp, in the heart of Flanders. This move was largely influenced by **Pieter Paul Rubens** (1577–1640), who lived in Antwerp. He was one of the first Flemish artists to become known through Europe and Russia. A court painter, Rubens was also an accomplished landscape artist and interpreter of mythology, but is best known for his depiction of plump women, proud of their figures. Rubens was so popular in his own time that his bold and large-scale works were translated by Flemish weavers into series of tapestries.

Anthony van Dyck (1599–1641), a pupil of Rubens and court portraitist, was the second Antwerp artist to gain world renown. The Brueghel dynasty continued to produce notable figures: Jan Brueghel the Elder eventually settled in Antwerp to produce art with Rubens, while his son-in-law, **David Teniers II** (1610–90) founded the Antwerp Academy of Art in 1665.

THE EUROPEAN INFLUENCE

THE INFLUENCE OF Rubens was so great that little innovation took place in the Flemish art scene in the 18th century. In the early years of the 19th century, Belgian art was largely dominated by the influence of other European schools. **François-Joseph Navez** (1787–1869) introduced Neo-Classicism to Flemish art. Realism took off with **Constantin Meunier** (1831–1905) and Impressionism with **Guillaume Vogels** (1836–96). The Brussels-based **Antoine Wiertz** (1806–65) was considered a Romantic, but his distorted and occasionally disturbing works, such as *Inhumation précipitée* (c.1830) seem to have early surrealist leanings. **Fernand Khnopff** (1858–1921) was influenced by the German Romantic Gustav Klimt. An early exponent of Belgian Symbolism, Khnopff's work is notable for his portraits of menacing and ambiguous women. Also on a journey from naturalism to surrealism, **James Ensor** (1860–1949) often used eerie skeletons in his work, reminiscent of Bosch. Between 1884 and 1894, the artists' cooperative **Les XX (Les Vingt)** reinvigorated the Brussels art scene with exhibitions of famous foreign and avant garde painters.

SURREALISM

THE 20TH CENTURY began with the emergence of Fauvism led by **Rik Wouters** (1882–1916), whose bright sun-filled landscapes show the influence of Cézanne.

Surrealism began in Brussels in the mid-1920s, dominated from the start by **René Magritte** (1898–1967). The movement had its roots back in the 16th century, with the phantasmagoria of Bosch and Pieter Brueghel the Elder. Fuelled by the chaos of World War I, much of which took place on Flemish battlefields, Magritte defined his disorientating surrealism as "[restoring] the familiar to the strange". More ostentatious and emotional, **Paul Delvaux** (1897–1989) produced elegant, freakish interiors occupied by ghostly figures. In 1948 the **COBRA Movement** promoted abstract art, which gave way in the 1960s to conceptual art, led by installationist **Marcel Broodthaers** (1924–76), who used daily objects, such as a casserole dish full of mussels, for his own interpretation.

Sculpture by Rik Wouters

UNDERGROUND ART

Notre Temps (1976) by Expressionist Roger Somville at Hankar station

Some 58 Brussels metro stations have been decorated with a combination of murals, sculptures and architecture by 54 Belgian artists. Although none but the most devoted visitor to the city is likely to see them all, there are several notable examples. **Annessens** was decorated by the Belgian COBRA artists, Dotremont and Alechinsky. In the **Bourse**, surrealist Paul Delvaux's *Nos Vieux Trams Bruxellois* is still on show with *Moving Ceiling*, a series of 75 tubes that move in the breeze by sculptor Pol Bury. At **Horta** station, Art Nouveau wrought ironwork from Victor Horta's now destroyed People's Palace is displayed, and **Stockel** is a tribute to Hergé and his boy hero, Tintin *(see pp18–19)*.

Brussels' Best: Art Nouveau

AMONG EUROPE'S most important architectural move-ments at the start of the 20th century, Art Nouveau in Belgium was led by Brussels architect Victor Horta (1861–1947) and the Antwerp-born interior designer Henry van de Velde (1863–1957). The style evolved from the Arts and Crafts Movement in England and the fashion for Japanese simplicity, and is characterized by its sinuous decorative lines, stained glass, carved stone curves, floral frescoes and elaborately curled and twisted metalwork. As new suburbs rose up in the 1890s, over 2,000 new houses were built in the style. Although many were demolished, details can still be seen in almost every Brussels street.

Hôtel Métropole
The high-vaulted lobby and bar of this luxurious 1894 hotel recall the city's fin-de-siècle heyday (see p49).

Old England
This former department store uses glass and steel rather than brick, with large windows and twisted metal turrets (see p60).

Hôtel Ciamberlani
Architect Paul Hankar designed this redbrick house in rue Defacqz for the sgraffiti artist Albert Ciamberlani, with whom he worked.

The Lower Town

Musée Horta
Curved window frames and elaborate metal balconies mark this out as the home and studio of Art Nouveau's best-known architect (see p78).

Hôtel Hannon
This stylish 1902 townhouse was built by Jules Brunfaut (1852–1942). One of its metal-framed windows has striking stained-glass panes (see p79).

Maison Cauchie
*Restored in 1989,
architect Paul Cauchie's
home in rue des Francs
has examples of sgraffiti,
a technique in which
designs are incised onto
wet plaster to reveal
another colour beneath.*

Maison Saint Cyr
*Horta's disciple Gustave
Strauven was keen to out-
do his mentor with this
intricate façade, only 4 m
(14 ft) wide* (see p72).

The Upper Town

Hôtel Solvay
*An early Horta creation
of 1894, this home was
built for a wealthy family.
Horta designed every
element of the building,
from the ochre and yellow
cast-iron façade columns
and glass front door to
the decorative but func-
tional doorknobs* (see p79).

0 metres   500
0 yards   500

Belgian Comic Strip Art

Tintin's dog Snowy

BELGIAN COMIC STRIP art is as famous a part of Belgian culture as chocolates and beer. The seeds of this great passion were sown when the US comic strip Little Nemo was published in French in 1908 to huge popular acclaim in Belgium. The country's reputation for producing some of the best comic strip art in Europe was established after World War II. Before the war, Europe was awash with American comics, but the Nazis called a halt to the supply. Local artists took over, and found that there was a large audience who preferred homegrown comic heroes. This explosion in comic strip art was led by perhaps the most famous Belgian creation ever, Tintin, who, with his dog Snowy, is as recognizable across Europe as Mickey Mouse.

demonstrated by his work before and during the war, where he expressed a strong sense of justice in such stories as *King Ottakar's Sceptre*, where a fascist army attempts to seize control of a central European state. Hergé took great care in researching his stories; for *Le Lotus Bleu* in 1934, which was set in China, he wrote: "I started... showing a real interest in the people and countries I was sending Tintin off to, concerned by a sense of honesty to my readers."

Spirou cover

Hergé at work in his studio

HERGÉ AND TINTIN

TINTIN'S CREATOR, Hergé, was born Georges Remi in Brussels in 1907. He began using his pen name (a phonetic spelling of his initials in reverse) in 1924. At the young age of 15, his drawings were published in the *Boy Scout Journal*. He became the protégé of a priest, Abbot Norbert Wallez, who also managed the Catholic journal *Le XXe Siècle*, and was swiftly given the

responsibility of the children's supplement, *Le petit Vingtième*. Eager to invent an original comic strip, Hergé came up with the character of Tintin the reporter, who first appeared in the story *Tintin au Pays des Soviets* on 10 January 1929. Over the next 10 years the character developed and grew in popularity. Book-length stories began to appear from 1930.

During the Nazi occupation in the 1940s *Tintin* continued to be published, with political references carefully omitted, in an approved paper *Le Soir*. This led to Hergé being accused of collaboration at the end of the war. He was called in for questioning but released later the same day without charge. Hergé's innocence was amply

Statue of Tintin and Snowy

POST-WAR BOOM

BELGIUM'S OLDEST comic strip journal *Spirou* was launched in April 1938 and, alongside the weekly *Journal de Tintin* begun in 1946, became a hothouse for the artistic talent that was to flourish during the postwar years. Many of the country's best-loved characters were first seen in *Spirou*, and most of them are still in print. Artists such as Morris, Jijé, Peyo and Roba worked on the journal. Morris (b.1923) introduced the cowboy parody, *Lucky Luke* in *Spirou* in 1947, a character who went on to feature in several live-action films and many US television cartoons.

COMIC STRIP CHARACTERS

Some of the world's best-loved comic strip characters originated in Belgium. *Tintin* is the most famous, but *Lucky Luke* the cowboy, the cheeky children *Suske en Wiske* and *The Smurfs* have also been published worldwide, while modern artists such as Schueten break new ground.

Tintin by Hergé

Lucky Luke by Morris

During the 1960s, the idea of the comic strip being the Ninth Art (after the seventh and eighth, film and television) expanded to include adult themes in the form of the comic-strip graphic novel.

PEYO AND THE SMURFS

BEST KNOWN for *The Smurfs*, Peyo (1928–92) was also a member of the team behind the *Spirou* journal which published his poetic medieval series *Johan et Pirlouit*, in 1952. *The Smurfs* first appeared as characters here – tiny blue people whose humorous foibles soon eclipsed any interest in the strip's supposed main characters. Reacting to their popularity, Peyo created a strip solely about them. Set in the Smurf village, the stories were infused with satirical social comment. *The Smurfs* were a popular craze between 1983 and 1985, featuring in advertising and merchandising of every type. They spawned a feature-length film, TV cartoons and popular music, and had several hit records in the 1980s.

Modern cover by Marvano

WILLY VANDERSTEEN

WHILE SPIROU and *Tintin* were French-language journals, Willy Vandersteen (1913–90) dominated the Flemish market. His popular creation, *Suske en Wiske* has been translated into English and appears as *Bob and Bobette* in the UK, and *Willy and Wanda* in the US. The main characters are a pair of "ordinary" kids aged between 10 and 14 years who have extraordinary adventures all over the world, as well as travelling back and forth in time. Today, Vandersteen's books sell in their millions.

COMIC STRIP ART TODAY

COMIC STRIPS, known as *bandes dessinées* or *beeldverhaal*, continue to be published in Belgium in all their forms. In newspapers, children's comics and graphic novels the Ninth Art remains one of the country's biggest exports. The high standards and imaginative scope of a new generation of artists, such as Schueten and Marvano, have fed growing consumer demand for comic books. Both French and Flemish publishers issue over 22 million comic books each year. Today, Belgian cartoons are sold in more than 30 countries, including the US.

Larger-than-life cartoon by Frank Pé adorns a Brussels building

STREET ART

THERE ARE currently 18 large comic strip images decorating the sides of buildings around Brussels' city centre. This outdoor exhibition is known as the Comic Strip Route and is organized by the Centre Belge de la Bande Dessineé (the Belgian Centre for Comic Strip Art) *(see pp50–51)* and the city of Brussels. Begun in 1991 as a tribute to Belgium's talent for comic strip art, this street art project continues to grow. A free map of the route is available from tourist information offices, as well as from the comic museum itself.

Suske en Wiske by Vandersteen

The Smurfs by Peyo

Contemporary comic-strip artists at work in their studio

Contemporary cartoon strip by Schueten

Tapestry and Lace

Lacemaker's studio sign

F OR OVER SIX CENTURIES, Belgian lace and tapestry have been highly prized luxury crafts. Originating in Flanders in the 12th century, tapestry has since been handmade in the centres of Tournai, Brussels, Arras, Mechelen and Oudenaarde, while the lace trade was practised from the 1500s onwards in all the Belgian provinces, with Bruges and Brussels particularly renowned for their delicate work. The makers often had aristocratic patrons; intricate lace and fine tapestries were status symbols of the nobility and staple exports throughout Europe from the 15th to 18th centuries. Today Belgium remains home to the very best tapestry and lace studios in the world.

Tapestry weavers *numbered over 50,000 in Flanders from 1450–1550. With the ruling Dukes of Burgundy as patrons, weavers prospered, and hangings grew more elaborate.*

Tapestry designs *involve weaver and artist working closely together. Painters, including Rubens, produced drawings for a series of weavings of six or more on grand themes (detail shown).*

The texture of the weave was the finest ever achieved; often 12 threads to the inch (5 per cm).

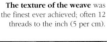

Weavers working today *still use medieval techniques to produce contemporary tapestry, woven in Mechelen and Tournai to modern designs.*

TAPESTRY

By 1200, the Flemish towns of Arras (now in France) and Tournai were Europe-wide known centres of weaving. Prized by the nobility, tapestries were portable and could be moved with the court as rulers travelled their estates. As trade grew, techniques were refined; real gold and silver were threaded into the fine wool, again increasing the value. Blending Italian idealism with Flemish realism, Bernard van Orley (1492–1542) revolutionized tapestry designs, as seen above in *The Battle of Pavia 1525*, the first of a series. Flemish weavers were eventually lured across Europe, where ironically their skill led to the success of the Gobelins factory in Paris that finally stole Flanders' crown in the late 1700s.

The lace trade rose to the fore during the early Renaissance. Emperor Charles V decreed that lace-making should be a compulsory skill for girls in convents and béguinages (see p53) throughout Flanders. Lace became fashionable on collars and cuffs for both sexes. Trade reached a peak in the 18th century.

Classical myths were popular themes for tapestry series.

Lace makers are traditionally women. Although their numbers are dwindling, many craftswomen still work in Bruges and Brussels, centres of bobbin lace, creating intricate work by hand.

Victorian Lace heralded a revival of the craft after its decline in the austere Neo-Classical period. Although men no longer wore it, the growth of the status of lace as a ladies' accessory and its use in soft furnishing led to its renewed popularity.

Belgian Lace is bought today mainly as a souvenir, but despite the rise in machine-made lace from other countries, the quality here still remains as fine as it was in the Renaissance.

Brussels: Political Capital of Europe

Manneken Pis statue

HOME TO MOST of the European Union's institutions and the headquarters of NATO, Brussels is one of Europe's most important political and business centres. Since the 1950s, the sense of Brussels as an international powerhouse has drawn an influx of people from around the world. The city has proved itself a fine host to the thousands of Eurocrats and business people that both visit and live here, with its celebrated hotels and restaurants, as well as with its cultural heritage, reflected in its historic buildings and museums. The people of Brussels are proud of their role in the new Europe. Despite the intricate and separatist-torn nature of Belgian politics, the country is unified in its support for a united Europe.

The signing of the European Common Market Treaty, Rome, 1957

HISTORICAL BEGINNINGS

THE EUROPEAN Union has its origins in the aftermath of World War II. The spirit of postwar reconciliation led France and West Germany to join forces to create the European Coal and Steel Community (ECSC). The project to continue the consolidation of Europe as a single political and financial entity began with the signing of the Treaty of Rome in 1957. This inaugurated the creation of a common market, the European Economic Community (EEC). Initially, six countries joined the EEC *(see opposite)* and the organization came into being on January 1, 1958.

The EEC was made up of two bodies, the Council of Ministers and the Commission, and coexisted with the ECSC and the atomic energy commission, Euratom. In 1967, however, these three groups merged, later becoming known as the European Community (EC). By this time the economic benefits of membership were evident, with intra-Community trade increasing by almost 30 per cent each year. The six founder members had also made an agreement on a common agricultural policy (CAP), which fixed prices and offered grants to EEC farmers. With economic improvement came calls for political union. As early as 1961, member states discussed the possibility of collaborative government. The larger states were less enthusiastic than smaller countries, and obstructed agreements over union.

The UK, Denmark and Ireland joined the EC in 1973, increasing its population by 25 per cent. The expectation of a return to profitable trade was crushed by the world recession of the mid-1970s which brought economic hardship to each of the member states.

Nonetheless this decade saw two important innovations: the creation of the European Regional Development Fund, which offers aid to the poorest areas of the EC, including major beneficiary, Ireland, and the European Monetary System (EMS), established in 1979. Otherwise known as the Exchange Rate Mechanism or ERM, this system was designed to protect member states from the vicissitudes of world markets. The European Currency Unit or ECU, a forerunner to the single currency (the Euro), was also initiated, despite the problem of a budget deficit in the 1980s.

MAASTRICHT

AFTER THE BUDGET issue was resolved in 1988 by the then Commission President Frenchman Jacques Delors, the 12 member states began to discuss the creation of a single European currency. The foundations were laid by the Maastricht Treaty of 1992, which changed the EC into the European Union (EU) and which set out a detailed timetable for economic and monetary union (EMU). The treaty imposed stringent economic criteria on states which wanted to participate. At the 1992 summit held in Edinburgh, Brussels' position as the focus city of the EU was also confirmed.

Euro coin

Denmark and Britain were among those most reluctant to commit themselves to the single currency, a situation reflecting Britain's great wariness of the far-reaching consequences of the idea and its ambivalence towards the European project in general. This was further illustrated by the fact that Britain is one of only two European Community countries (the other being Ireland) not to have signed up to the EU's Schengen Agreement, under which border controls between EU member states have been removed. This means that travellers can now journey around all of the other member states without once showing their passports.

THE FUTURE

THE EU HAS developed throughout the 1990s, with the arrival of Sweden, Finland and Austria in 1995 and, on January 1, 1999, the establishment of a single European currency in 11 of the EU's member states. Despite this, criticism of the EU escalated in the 1990s. Its bureaucracy was seen as a source of irritation by many of its 375 million citizens. The EU's executive body, the Commission has also been the focus of resentment. EU President Jacques Santer was forced to resign in 1999 after allegations of mismanagement, incompetence and fraud.

Former Italian Prime Minister Romano Prodi replaced Jacques Santer in 1999. Debate continues about the accession of central and eastern European states, as well as the long-term goal of increased political unity.

THE EUROPEAN COMMISSION

THE COMMISSION is the EU's executive arm, responsible for formulating policies which are then ratified or rejected by the Council of Ministers. There are twenty Commissioners, including the President, each with a specific area of responsibility ranging from transport to technology. The Commission

is responsible for ensuring that policies are carried out, and that member states do not violate EC law.

Once based in the star-shaped Berlaymont building, the Commissioners have been rehoused while asbestos is removed from the building.

THE COUNCIL OF MINISTERS

THE COUNCIL of Ministers is composed of representatives of each member state: each nation has a block of votes depending on its size. The Council must approve all legislation for the EU, often a difficult task to accomplish given that most Europe-wide laws will seldom be to the liking of every state; most laws require a "qualified majority" of 62 out of 87 votes before they are passed. The Council of Ministers meets behind closed doors, and its members are answerable only to their national governments, which has led to calls for reform.

THE EUROPEAN PARLIAMENT

THE EUROPEAN Parliament is responsible for approving the EU's annual budget, as well as monitoring the Commission's performance.

The Parliament is the only European institution subject to election by the general public. There are 626 MEPs, elected by proportional

representation. The Parliament sits in Brussels, Strasbourg and Luxembourg. In Brussels, the glass-and-steel Parliament building on Rue Wiertz is nicknamed *Le Caprice des Dieux* (The Whims of the Gods) *(see p73).*

BRUSSELS' POLITICS

BELGIUM'S system of government is complex as regional interests are powerful. The country is divided into three federal regions, Flanders Wallonia and Brussels, and conflict between separatist Walloon and Fleming factions threatens Belgian unity.

The Brussels' regional government oversees the city's 19 communes. Each one has its own powers, including a police force. Separate French and Flemish organizations rule on cultural matters.

Contemporary geometric bridge in Brussels' Quartier Européen

BRUSSELS THROUGH THE YEAR

THE TEMPERATE climate of Brussels is typical of Northern Europe and means that a range of activities throughout the year take place both inside and out. Mild damp winters and gentle summers allow the city's strong artistic life to flourish in historic buildings and modern stadiums alike. The Belgians make the most of their seasonal changes. Theatre, dance and film start their season in January, with evening venues

Revellers at Ommegang

that range from ancient abbeys lit by the setting sun to drive-in cinemas. The city's flower festival launches the summer in highly colourful style, with the Grand Place literally carpeted in millions of blooms every other August. Through the year, festivals in Brussels range from energetic, exuberant historic processions that have taken place yearly since medieval times, to innovative European experimental art.

SPRING

BRUSSELS' LIVELY cultural life takes off as the crisp spring days lengthen and visitors begin to arrive in the city. Music festivals take place in a wide variety of open-air venues. As the city's parks burst into bloom, the world-famous tropical greenhouses at Laeken are opened to the public and Brussels' chocolatiers produce delicious creations for Easter.

The Royal Glasshouse at Laeken, famed for its rare exotic orchids

MARCH

International Fantasy Film Festival *(middle fortnight)*. Lovers of the weird and wonderful will find new and vintage work here in cinemas all over the city.
Ars Musica *(mid-Mar to early Apr)*. This celebration of modern music is one of Europe's finest festivals, boasting famous performers and beautiful venues, often the Musée d'art ancien *(see pp62–3)*. The festival is now a must for connoisseurs of the contemporary music world.
Eurantica *(last week)*. The Baudouin Stadium at Heysel plays host to hundreds of traders and members of the public anxious for bargains in the world of antiques.
Easter *(Easter Sunday)*. The annual Easter Egg hunt, with eggs allegedly hidden by the bells of churches in Rome. Over 1,000 brightly coloured

Easter eggs are hidden by adults in the Parc Royal, and Belgian children gather to forage among the flowerbeds.

APRIL

Sablon Baroque Spring *(third week)*. The Place du Grand Sablon hosts new classical ensembles in a gathering of young Belgian talent performing 17th-century music.
The Royal Greenhouses at Laeken *(12 days, dates vary)*. The private greenhouses of the Belgian Royal family are opened to the public as their numerous exotic plants and cacti start to flower. Breathtaking 19th-century glass and wrought ironwork shelters hundreds of rare species *(see pp82–3)*.
Flanders Festival *(mid-Apr to October)*. A celebration of all things musical, this

classical medley offers more than 120 performances by internationally renowned choirs and orchestras.
Scenes d'Ecran *(third weekend)*. Over 100 new European films draw crowds in cinemas across the city.

MAY

Europe Day Festivities *(7–9 May)*. As the capital of Europe, Brussels celebrates its role in the European Union – even Manneken

Runners taking part in the Brussels twenty-kilometre race

AVERAGE DAILY HOURS OF SUNSHINE

Climate
Belgium has a fairly temperate Northern European climate. Although not often freezing, winters are chilly and a heavy coat is required. Summers are warmer and much brighter, though you will still need a jersey for the evenings. Rainwear is always a necessity.

Pis is dressed as a Euro-supporter, in a suit of blue, decorated with yellow stars.
Kunsten FESTIVAL des Arts *(9–31 May)*. This innovative festival covers theatre and dance and is the forum for much exciting new talent.
Queen Elisabeth Music Contest *(May to mid-June)*. Classical fans will flock to the prestigious musical competition, now in its fifth decade. Young singers, violinists and pianists gather in front of well-known conductors and soloists to determine the champion among Europe's finest student players.
Brussels Twenty-Kilometre Race *(last Sunday)*. As many as 20,000 keen professional and amateur runners race round the city, taking in its major landmarks.
Jazz Marathon *(last weekend)*. Bistros and cafés are the venues for myriad small jazz bands, with some well-known artists playing anonymously.

SUMMER

THE SEASON OF pageantry arrives with Ommegang in July, one of Europe's oldest and best-known processions, which takes place in the Grand Place and the surrounding streets. Multicultural music runs throughout the summer, with classical, jazz and avant-garde US and European performers playing in venues ranging from tiny beer cafés to the great King Baudouin stadium in Heysel. Independence is celebrated

on Belgian National Day. Families enjoy the Foire du Midi, the huge fairground over 2 km square (1 sq mile) covered with rides and stalls.

JUNE

City of Brussels Summer Festival *(early June to Sep)*. Classical concerts take place in some of the city's best-known ancient buildings.
Festival of Wallonia *(Jun–Oct)*. Covering Brussels and Flanders, this series of gala concerts showcases the best in young Belgian classical orchestral and soloist talent.
Couleur Café Festival *(last weekend)*. Spread over three summer evenings in the Tour et Taxis renovated warehouse, the fashionable and funky programme includes salsa, African drummers, acid jazz and multicultural music.
Fête de la Musique *(last weekend)*. Two days of concerts and recitals featuring world music take place in the halls and museums of the city.

African drummer performing at the Couleur Café Festival

JULY

Ommegang *(first weekend in July)*. This festival has been celebrated in Brussels since 1549, and now draws crowds from around the world. Translated as "a tour", the procession revolves around the Grand Place and the surrounding streets. Over 2,000 participants dress up and become members of a Renaissance town; jesters, courtiers, nobles and soldiers; they go on to parade before Belgian dignitaries. Tickets have to be booked months in advance.

The Ommegang pausing in front of dignitaries in the Grand Place

AVERAGE MONTHLY RAINFALL

MM		Inches
300		12
240		9
180		6
120		
60		3
0		0

Jan Feb Mar Apr May Jun Jul Aug Sep Oct Nov Dec

Rainfall chart
On the whole Belgium is rather a rainy country, with Brussels experiencing constant low rainfall throughout the year. Spring is the driest season, but summers can be damp. In winter, rain may turn to snow and sleet.

Brosella Folk and Jazz Festival *(second weekend)*. Musicians from all over Europe play informal gigs in the Parc d'Osseghem in the shadow of the Atomium.
Festival d'Eté de Bruxelles *(Jul–Aug)*. Classical concerts take place through the high summer in venues around the Upper and Lower Town.
Foire du Midi *(mid-Jul–mid-Aug)*. Brussels' main station, Gare du Midi, is host to this month-long funfair, which attracts people in their thousands. Especially popular with children, it is one of the biggest fairs in Europe, and includes an enormous Ferris wheel.
Belgian National Day *(21 Jul)*. The 1831 declaration of independence is commemorated annually with a military parade followed by a firework display in the Parc de Bruxelles.
Palais Royal Open Days *(last week in Jul–second week of Sep)*. The official residence of the Belgian Royal family, the opulent staterooms of the Palais Royal, including the huge throne room, are open to the public for six weeks during the summer *(see pp58–9)*.

AUGUST

Plantation du Meiboom *(9 Aug)*. This traditional festival dates from 1213. Parading crowds dressed in huge puppet costumes parade around the Lower Town and finally reach the Grand Place where a maypole is planted as a celebration of summer.

Costumed revellers at the Plantation of the Meiboom

Tapis des Fleurs *(mid-Aug, biannually, for four days)*. Taking place on even-numbered years, this colourful celebration pays tribute to Brussels' long-established flower industry. The Grand Place is carpeted with millions of fresh flowers in patterns echoing historical scenes. The beautiful flower carpet measures 2,000 sq m (21,000 sq ft).

AUTUMN

FRESH AUTUMN days are the cue for many indoor events; innovative jazz is performed in the city's cafés and the French cultural centre in Le Botanique. Architecture is celebrated in the heritage weekend where the public can tour many private houses and personal art collections.

SEPTEMBER

The Birthday of Manneken Pis *(last weekend)*. Brussels' celebrated mascot is clothed in a new suit by a chosen dignitary from abroad.
Lucky Town Festival *(first weekend)*. Sixty concerts take place in over 30 of some of Brussels' best-known and atmospheric cafés.
Les Nuits Botaniques *(last week)*. Held in the former greenhouses of the Botanical gardens, now the French cultural centre, this series of musical events is a delight.

The Grand Place, carpeted in millions of fresh flowers

AVERAGE MONTHLY TEMPERATURE

Temperature chart
This chart gives the average maximum and minimum temperatures for Brussels. Generally mild, Brussels' climate does produce chilly weather and cold winters from October to March. Spring sees milder temperatures and is followed by a warm summer.

Journées du Patrimoine/ Heritage Days *(second or third weekend)*. Private homes, listed buildings and art collections are opened for a rare public viewing to celebrate the city's architecture.

OCTOBER

Audi Jazz Festival *(mid-Oct–mid-Nov)*. All over Belgium informal jazz concerts bring autumnal cheer to country towns and the capital. Performers are mainly local, but some European stars fly in for performances in Brussels' Palais des Beaux-Arts. Ray Charles and Herbie Hancock have appeared in past years.

WINTER

S NOW AND RAIN typify Brussels' winter weather, and attractions move indoors. Art galleries launch world-class exhibitions and the Brussels Film Festival showcases new and established talent. As the festive season approaches, the ancient Lower Town is brightly lit and families gather for Christmas with traditional Belgian cuisine.

NOVEMBER

Nocturnes des Sablons *(last weekend)*. Shops and galleries stay open until 11pm around the Place du Grand Sablon. Horse-drawn carriages transport shoppers around the area, with mulled wine on offer in the festively decorated main square.

DECEMBER

Fête de Saint Nicolas *(6 Dec)*. The original Santa Claus, the patron saint of Christmas, is alleged to arrive in the city on this day. Children throughout the country are given their presents, sweetmeats and chocolate.
Reveillon/Fête de Noel *(24–25 Dec)*. In common with the rest of mainland Europe, Christmas is celebrated over a feast on the evening of 24 December. Gifts are given by adults on this day, and 25 December is traditionally for visiting extended family. The city's Christmas decorations provide a lively sight until 6 January.

Christmas market in the Grand Place around the traditional Christmas Pine

JANUARY

Fête des Rois *(6 Jan)*. Epiphany is celebrated with almond cake, the *galette des rois*, and the search for the bean inside that declares its finder king for the night.
Brussels Film Festival *(mid–late Jan)*. Premières and film stars are adding weight to this European film showcase.

FEBRUARY

Antiques Fair *(middle fortnight)*. Brussels' crossroads location is useful here as international dealers gather in the historic Palais des Beaux-Arts *(see p60)*.
International Comic strip and Cartoon Festival *(middle fortnight)*. Artists and authors, both new and established, arrive for lectures and screenings in this city with its comic strip heritage.

PUBLIC HOLIDAYS

New Year's Day (1 Jan)
Easter Sunday (variable)
Easter Monday (variable)
Labour Day (1 May)
Ascension Day (variable)
Whit Sunday (variable)
Whit Monday (variable)
Belgian National Day (21 July)
Assumption Day (15 Aug)
All Saints' Day (1 Nov)
Armistice Day (11 Nov)
Christmas Day (25 Dec)

THE HISTORY OF BRUSSELS

A S THE CULTURAL AND CIVIC *heart of Belgium since the Middle Ages, Brussels has been the focus of much political upheaval over the centuries. But, from the battles of the 17th century to the warfare of the 20th century, it has always managed to re-create itself with vigour. Now, at the start of a new millennium, Belgium's capital is prospering as the political and economic centre of Europe.*

When Julius Caesar set out to conquer the Gauls of northern Europe in 58 BC, he encountered a fierce tribe known as the Belgae (the origins of the 19th-century name "Belgium"). Roman victory led to the establishment of the region they called Gallia Belgica. The earliest mention of Brussels itself is as "Broucsella", or "settlement in the marshes" and dates from a 7th-century manuscript.

15th-century Flemish tapestry showing the stars

Following the collapse of the Roman Empire in the 5th century, a Germanic race known as the Franks came to rule the region and established the Merovingian dynasty of kings, based in their capital at Tournai. They were followed by the Carolingian dynasty, which produced one of the most important figures of the Middle Ages – Charlemagne (AD 768–814). His noted military expertise ensured that invaders such as the Northern Saxons and the Lombards of Italy were repelled. He was also credited with establishing Christianity as the major religion across western Europe. The pope rewarded him by crowning him Emperor of the West in AD 800; effectively he was the first Holy Roman Emperor, ruling a vast area extending from Denmark to Italy. By the 10th century, the inheritance laws of the Franks meant that the empire was divided up among Charlemagne's grandsons, Louis, Charles the Bald and Lothair. Lothair's fortress, founded in 979, marks the official founding of Brussels. The period had brought a measure of stability to the area's volatile feudal fiefdoms, leading to a trading boom in the new towns of the low countries.

INDUSTRIAL BEGINNINGS

At the start of the 12th century, commerce became the guiding force in western Europe and the centres of trade quickly grew into powerful cities. Rivers and canals were the key to the growth of the area's trading towns. Ghent, Ypres, Antwerp and Bruges became the focus of the cloth trade plied across the North Sea between France, Germany, Italy and England. Brussels, with its skilled craftsmen, became a trade centre, and impressive buildings such as the Cathédrale Sts Michel et Gudule *(see pp70–71)*, built in 1225, demonstrated its stature.

TIMELINE

Charlemagne

600 AD	750	900	1050

58–50 BC Gauls defeated by Julius Caesar and Roman occupation begins

768 Charlemagne is born and goes on to rule most of Europe as the Holy Roman Emperor

1106 Dukes of Louvain become the Dukes of Brabant

695 First mention of Brussels as "Broucsella" in the Bishop of Cambrai's papers

843 Emperor Otto II gives the region of Lower Lotharingia to Charlemagne's grandson, Lothair

1000 Lotharingia now under the rule of the Holy Roman Emperor

1005 Henry II, Count of Louvain, builds town walls around Brussels

◁ *Philip the Good*, Duke of Burgundy (c.1500) by Rogier van der Weyden

Nineteenth-century painting of the Battle of the Golden Spurs

economy. The subsequent depression marked the beginning of decades of conflict between the craftsmen and merchant classes. In 1356, Jeanne, Duchess of Louvain, gained control over Brussels, and instituted the workers' Charter of Liberties. Craftsmen were finally given some political powers in the city. Trade resumed, attracting new people to Brussels. As the population grew, new streets were built outside the city walls to accommodate them. Between 1357 and 1379 a second town wall was constructed around these new districts.

THE CRAFTSMEN'S REBELLION

Over the next two hundred years Brussels became one of the foremost towns of the Duchy of Brabant. Trade here specialized in fine fabrics that were exported to lucrative markets in France, Italy and England. A handful of merchants became rich and exercised political power over the towns. However, conflict grew between the merchants, who wanted to maintain good relations with England, and their autocratic French rulers who relied upon tax revenue from the towns.

The 14th century witnessed a series of rebellions by the craftsmen of Bruges and Brussels against what they saw as the tyranny of the French lords. In May 1302, Flemish craftsmen, armed only with spears, defeated the French at the Battle of the Golden Spurs, named for the humiliating theft of the cavalry's spurs. Encouraged by this success, the Brussels craftsmen revolted against the aristocracy who controlled their trading economy in 1356. They were also angered by the Hundred Years' War between England and France, which began in 1337. The war threatened wool supplies from England which were crucial to their cloth-based

THE HOUSE OF BURGUNDY

The new town walls were also built in reply to the invasion of Brussels by the Count of Flanders. However, in 1369 Philip, Duke of Burgundy, married the daughter of the Count of Flanders, and when the count died in 1384 the Low Countries and eastern France came under the couple's Burgundian rule.

In the 1430s Brussels became the capital of Burgundy, a situation that was to change the city forever. Brussels

Richly detailed Brussels tapestries such as this
Allegory of Hope **(1525) were prized commodities**

TIMELINE

1225 Construction of Cathédrale Sts Michel et Gudule	*Medieval helmet*	1302 Battle of the Golden Spurs – Flemish defeat of French cavalry	1356 Craftsmen's leader Everard 't Serclaes expels Flemish from Brussels
1200	**1250**	**1300**	**1350**
St-Michel statue	1229 Brussels granted its first charter, and relations between England and Flanders break down	1338 Flemish towns become allied to England for the Hundred Years' War	
		1356 Duchess Jeanne of Louvain grants Charter of Liberties	

Painting of the family of the Hapsburg King of
Austria, Maximillian I and Mary of Burgundy

was now an administrative and cultural
centre, famous for its grand architecture, in the form of mansions and
churches, and its luxury crafts trade.

THE HAPSBURG DYNASTY

In 1477 Mary of Burgundy, the
last heir to the duchy, married
Maximillian of Austria. Mary
died in 1482, leaving Maximillian and the Hapsburg
dynasty rulers of the city at
a time when Brussels was
experiencing serious eco-
nomic depression. In 1488
Brussels and the rest of
Flanders rebelled against this
new power which had rein-
stated relations with France.
The Austrians held on to
power largely because of the
plague of 1490 which halved Brussels'
population. Maximillian passed his rule
of the Low Countries to his son, Philip
the Handsome in 1494 the year after he
became Holy Roman Emperor. When

Portrait of Charles V,
Holy Roman Emperor

Maximillian died, his daughter, Regent
Empress Margaret of Austria, moved
the capital of Burgundy from Brussels
to Mechelen, where she educated her
nephew, the future emperor Charles V.

SPANISH RULE

In 1515, at the age of 15, Charles
became Sovereign of Burgundy. The
following year he inherited the
Spanish throne and, in 1519, became
the Holy Roman Emperor. As he was
born in Ghent, and considered Flanders
his real home, he restored Brussels as
the capital of Burgundy. Dutch officials
arrived to run the three government
councils that were now based here.

For the first time the city had a court.
Both aristocratic families and immigrants, eager to cash in on the city's
expansion, were drawn to the heady
mix of tolerance, intellectual sophistication and business. Brussels quickly
emerged as the most powerful city in
Flanders, overtaking its long-standing
rivals Bruges and Antwerp.

However, the Reformation, begun
in Germany by Martin Luther,
was to usher in a period of
religious conflict. When
Charles V abdicated in
1555, he fractured the
empire's unity by leaving
the Holy Roman Empire to
his brother Ferdinand and
all other dominions to his
devoutly Catholic son, Philip
II of Spain. His persecution of
the Protestant movement finally sparked the Revolt of the
Netherlands led by the House
of Orange. Brussels' Protestant rulers
surrendered to Philip in 1585. His power
ended when the English defeated the
Spanish Armada in 1588, by which time
8,000 Protestants had been put to death.

1400	1450	1500	1550	
	1419 Philip the Good succeeds as Count of Burgundy	**1506** Margaret of Austria moves the Burgundian capital from Brussels to Mechelen	**1515** Charles Hapsburg becomes Sovereign of Burgundy	**1555** Catholic Philip II succeeds Charles V as religious reformation comes to Brussels
	1430 Under Burgundian control, Brussels becomes the major administrative centre of the region	**1490** Plague decimates the city **1488** Civil war – Brussels joins Flanders against Maximillian of Austria	*Count Egmont*	**1566** Conseil des Troubles set up by Duke d'Alba. Prominent Counts Egmont and Hornes executed

The armies of Louis XIV, the Sun King, bombard Brussels' city walls

THE COUNTER-REFORMATION

From 1598 Archduchess Isabella and Archduke Albert were the Catholic rulers of the Spanish Netherlands, installing a Hapsburg governor in Brussels. They continued to persecute Protestants: all non-Catholics were barred from working. Thousands of skilled workers moved to the Netherlands. But such new trades as lacemaking, diamond-cutting and silk-weaving flourished. Isabella and Albert were great patrons of the arts, and supported Rubens in Antwerp (*see pp96–7*).

Protestant prisoners paraded in Brussels during the Counter-Reformation under Albert and Isabella

INVASION OF THE SUN KING

The 17th century was a time of of religious and political struggle all over Europe. The Thirty Years War (1618–48) divided western Europe along Catholic and Protestant lines. After 1648, France's Sun King, Louis XIV, was determined to add Flanders to his territory.

By 1633 both Albert and Isabella were dead and Philip IV of Spain, passed control of the Spanish Netherlands to his weak brother, the Cardinal-Infant Ferdinand. Keen to pursue his ambitions, Louis XIV besieged Maastricht in the 1670s and took Luxembourg. Having failed to win the nearby enclave of Namur, the piqued Sun King moved his army to Brussels, whose defences were weaker.

On August 13, 1695, the French bombarded Brussels from a hill outside the city walls, destroying the Grand Place (*see pp42–3*) and much of its environs. The French withdrew, but their desire to rule the region was to cause conflict over subsequent decades.

A PHOENIX FROM THE ASHES

Despite the destruction incurred by the bombardment, Brussels was quick to recover. The guilds ensured that the Grand Place was rebuilt in a matter of years, with new guildhouses as a testament to the on-going success of the city's economic life and craftsmanship.

The building of the Willebroek canal during the 17th century gave Brussels access to the Rupel and Scheldt rivers, and thus to Antwerp and the North Sea. Large industries began to replace local market trading. Factories and mills grew up around the city's harbour, and Brussels became an export centre.

TIMELINE

1599 Artist Antony van Dyck born in Antwerp	**1621** Archduke Albert dies amid new bout of Protestant/Catholic fighting	**1641** Van Dyck dies after glittering artistic career	
1600 Antwerp becomes the centre of Flemish art			*Louis XIV of France in costume*
1600	**1625**	**1650**	**1675**
1598 Isabella and Albert run strong Catholic, anti-Protestant regime	**1619** Manneken Pis installed in Brussels	**1640** Rubens dies after a 40-year career as painter of over 3,000 paintings	**1670** Louis XIV beseiges Maastricht and Luxembourg; William of Orange goes on defensive
Manneken Pis		**1633** Cardinal-Infant Ferdinand is new ruler	

AUSTRIAN SUCCESSION

Subsequent decades were dogged by war as Austria and England sought to stave off French ambitions. When Philip of Anjou succeeded to the Spanish throne, it looked as if the combined threat of Spain and France would overwhelm the rest of Europe. Emperor Leopold I of Austria, together with England and many German states, declared war on France. The resulting 14-year War of the Spanish Succession ended with the Treaty of Utrecht in 1713, which ceded the Netherlands, including Brussels, to Austria.

Governor of Brussels, Duke Charles of Lorraine

The treaty did not end the conflict. Emperor Charles VI of Austria ruled after Leopold, but failed to produce a male heir. His death in 1731 sparked another 17 years of war – The War of the Austrian Succession over whether

his daughter Maria Theresa should be allowed to inherit the crown. It was not until 1748, with the signing of the Treaty of Aix-la-Chapelle, that Maria Theresa gained control.

THE BOOM PERIOD

The endless fighting took its toll, and Brussels, along with the rest of Belgium, was impoverished. Despite the sophistication of the aristocratic elite, the majority of the population were still ruled by feudal laws: they could not change jobs or move home without permission; and only three per cent of the population was literate.

In the 1750s Empress Maria Theresa of Austria installed her brother, Charles of Lorraine, in Brussels. Under the influence of the Enlightenment, his court attracted European artists and intellectuals, and Brussels became the most glamorous city in Europe. Industry also boomed with the construction of new roads and waterways. Brussels was transformed as the Place Royale and Parc de Bruxelles were laid out.

THE WORKERS' REVOLT

While the aristocracy and new middle-classes flourished, Brussels' workers were suffering. As the city's population grew there were more workers than jobs: wages plummeted and factory conditions were harsh.

When Joseph II succeeded Maria Theresa in 1780, he enforced a series of reforms including freedom of religion. However, he also cancelled the 500-year-old Charter of Liberties.

Influenced by the ideas of the French Revolution of 1789, the Belgians now demanded reform. Their rebellion was to result in an independent state.

French prince Philip of Anjou became Philip V of Spain, sparking the War of the Spanish Succession

1695 French Bombardment of Brussels	1713–14 Treaties of Utrecht and Rastadt mark beginning of Austrian period		1760s Brussels is cultural and artistic centre of Europe	1788 Joseph II cancels Charter of Liberties in liberal opposition
1700	**1725**		**1750**	**1775**
1697 Willebroek Canal completed, links Brussels to the sea via Antwerp	1731 Beginning of the 17-year-long war against Austrian rule	1748 Treaty of Aix-la-Chapelle restores the Netherlands to Austrian rule	1753 New roads and canals constructed, which boosts industry in Brussels	1789 Belgian revolt for independence fired by French Revolution

Ceramic Delft plate

The Fight for Independence

BELGIUM WAS AGAIN occupied by foreign powers between 1794 and 1830. First, by the French Republican armies, then, after Napoleon's defeat at Waterloo in 1815, by the Dutch. French radical reforms included the abolition of the guild system and fairer taxation laws. Although French rule was unpopular, their liberal ideas were to influence the Belgian drive for independence. William I of Orange was appointed King of the Netherlands (which included Belgium) after 1815. His autocratic style, together with a series of anti-Catholic measures, bred discontent, especially in Brussels and among the French-speaking Walloons in the south. The south was also angered when William refused to introduce tariffs to protect their trade – it was the last straw. The uprising of 1830 began in Brussels and Léopold I became king of the newly independent nation.

King William I of Orange
William's rule as King of the Netherlands after 1815 was unpopular.

A Cultural Revolution in Brussels
French ideas not only influenced the revolution, but also Belgian culture. Under Napoleon the city walls were demolished and replaced by tree-lined boulevards.

Liberals joined workers already protesting in the square outside.

The Battle of Waterloo
Napoleon's influence came to an end after the battle of Waterloo on 18 June, 1815. A Prussian army came to Wellington's aid, and by 5:30pm Napoleon faced his final defeat. This led to Dutch rule over Belgium.

Agricultural workers
Harsh weather in the winter of 1829 caused hardship for both farmers and agricultural labourers, who also joined the protest.

The Revolution in Industry
Unemployment, low wages and factory closures during the early decades of the 19th century sparked unrest in 1830.

La Théâtre de la Monnaie
A patriotic song, L'Amour Sacré de la Patrie led the audience in the theatre on the night of 25 August, 1830, to join demonstrators outside.

BELGIAN REVOLUTION

High unemployment, poor wages and a bad winter in 1829 provoked protests about living and working conditions. The revolution was ignited by a patriotic and radical opera at the Brussels' opera house, and the largely liberal audience rushed out into the street, raising the Brabant flag. Ten thousand troops were sent by William to quash the rebels, but the Belgian soldiers deserted and the Dutch were finally driven out of Belgium.

The initial list of demands asked for administrative independence from the Dutch, and for freedom of press.

This symbolic illustration of the revolution shows both liberals and workers ready to die for their country.

King of Belgium, Léopold I
The crowning of German prince, Léopold of Saxe-Coburg, in Brussels in 1831 finally established Belgium's independence.

TIMELINE

1790 Republic of United Belgian States formed. Temporary end of Austrian rule	**1799** Emperor Napoleon rules France *Wellington*		**1815** Battle of Waterloo. Napoleon defeated by army led by the Duke of Wellington	**1830** Rebellion begins at the Théâtre de la Monnaie in Brussels
1790	**1800**	**1810**	**1820**	**1830**
1794 Brussels loses its importance to The Hague **1790** War between France and Austria		**1815** Belgium, allied with Holland under the United Kingdom of the Netherlands, is ruled by William I of Orange. Brussels becomes second capital	**1831** State of Belgium formed on 21 July. Treaty of London grants independence **1835** Continental railway built from Brussels to Mechelen	

THE FLEMISH AND THE WALLOONS: THE BELGIAN COMPROMISE

Linguistically and culturally, Belgium is divided. In the north, the Flemish have their roots in the Netherlands and Germany. In the south are the Walloons, the French-speaking Belgians, culturally connected to France. The "Linguistic Divide" of 1962 officially sanctioned this situation, dividing Belgium into Flemish- and French-speaking zones. The exception is Brussels, an officially bilingual city since the formation of Bruxelles-Capitale in 1963, and a national region by 1989 when it came to comprise 19 outlying districts. Conflicts still erupt over the issue, but the majority of Belgians seem to be in favour of a united country.

Bilingual road signs

CONSOLIDATING THE NEW STATE

During its early days as an independent nation, Brussels was a haven for free-thinkers, including the libertarian poet Baudelaire, and a refuge for exiles, such as Karl Marx and Victor Hugo. Belgium's industries also continued to expand throughout the 19th century.

King Léopold III visits a goldmine in the Congo in Africa

By 1870 there were no less than four main railway stations in Brussels able to export goods all over Europe. However, the population of Brussels had almost doubled, resulting in poor-quality housing and working conditions. Towards the end of the reign of Belgium's second monarch, Léopold II (r.1865–1909), industrial unrest led to new legislation which improved conditions, and all men over 25 gained the right to vote in 1893. But the king's principal concern was his colonialist policy in the Congo in Central Africa.

THE GERMAN OCCUPATIONS

Albert I succeeded Léopold II as Belgium's new king. He encouraged the nation's artists and architects, and was a keen supporter of Art Nouveau (see pp16–17). All of this ended as the country entered its bleakest period.

Despite its neutral status, Belgium was invaded by the German army in the summer of 1914. All of the country, except for the northern De Panne region, was occupied by the Germans. Some of the bloodiest battles of World War I were staged on Belgian soil. Flanders was the scene of brutal trench warfare, including the introduction of poison gas at Ypres (see p107). Today, Belgium contains several vast graveyards, which include the resting places of the tens of thousands of soldiers who died on the Western Front.

The Belgians conducted resistance from their stronghold in De Panne, cutting telephone wires and destroying train tracks. The Germans responded by confiscating property, deporting Belgians to German labour camps

TIMELINE

1840	1870	1900	1925
1847 Opening of Europe's first shopping mall, the Galéries St Hubert	**1871** Under Léopold II, the River Senne is reclaimed, and new districts built to cope with the growing city	**1898** Flemish language given equal status to French in law	**1914–18** World War I. Germany occupies Belgium
The Belgian Congo	**1884** Léopold II is granted sovereignty over the Congo	**1910** World Fair in Brussels promotes Belgium's industrial boom. Art Nouveau flourishes	**1929–31** Great Depression and reduction in foreign trade
1839 Treaty of London grants neutrality to Belgium			

German troops raising the German flag at the Royal Castle at Laeken, near Brussels

INTERNATIONAL STATUS

Belgium's history in the latter half of the 20th century has been dominated by the ongoing language debate between the Flemish and the French-speaking Walloons. From 1970 to 1994 the constitution was redrawn, creating a federal state with three separate regions; the Flemish north, the Walloon south and bilingual Brussels. While this smoothed over conflicts, cultural divisions run deep. Today, all parliamentary speeches have to be delivered in both French and Flemish.

Like most of Europe, Belgium went from economic boom in the 1960s to recession and retrenchment in the 1970s and 1980s. Throughout these decades Brussels' stature at the heart of Europe was consolidated. In 1958, the city became the headquarters for the European Economic Community (EEC), later the European Union. In 1967 NATO also moved to Brussels.

and murdering random hostages. Belgium remained under German occupation until the last day of the war, 11 November, 1918.

The 1919 Treaty of Versailles granted Belgium control of Eupen-Malmédy, the German-speaking area in the southeast. But by 1940 the country was again invaded by the Germans under Hitler. In May of that year, King Léopold III surrendered.

Despite national resistance to the Occupation, the King was interned at Laeken until 1944, after which he was moved to Germany until the end of the war. Rumours that Léopold had collaborated with the Nazis led to his abdication in 1951, in favour of his 20-year-old son, Baudouin.

THE EUROPEAN CAPITAL

Modern Brussels is a multilingual and cosmopolitan city at the forefront of Europe. This historically industrial city now prospers as a base for many large corporations such as ICI and Mitsubishi.

The European Parliament, Brussels

Despite its flourishing status, the city has had its fair share of disasters, including the deaths of 38 Italian football supporters at the Heysel stadium in 1985. Also, two tragic paedophile murder cases in the 1990s led many Belgians to protest against what they considered to be an incompetent police system. However, Brussels' future as a city of world importance seems certain as the centre of the EU's new European Monetary Union.

1939–45 World War II. Germany again occupies Belgium	1951 Abdication of Léopold III; Baudouin I succeeds	1962 The Belgian Congo is granted independence		1993 King Baudouin I dies; Albert II succeeds	2002 The euro becomes legal tender
		European flag			
	1950		**1975**	**2000**	
	1944 Benelux Unions with Holland and Luxembourg formed	1967 Brussels is new NATO HQ	1985 Heysel Stadium disaster	1989 Brussels is officially a bilingual city with 19 outlying districts	2001 Crown Prince Philippe and Princess Mathilde have a daughter, Elisabeth
	1934 Albert I is killed in a climbing accident				

Baudouin I

BRUSSELS
AREA BY AREA

THE LOWER TOWN

OST VISITS TO Brussels begin with a stroll around the Lower Town, the ancient heart of the city and home to its most famous area, the Grand Place. The original settlement of the city was here; most of the streets surrounding this huge market square date from as far back as the Middle Ages up to the 18th century. The architecture is an eclectic blend of Gothic, Baroque and Flemish Renaissance.

Maison du Cygne, Grand Place

In and around the Place de Brouckère and the busy Boulevard Anspach are the more recent additions to the city's history. These appeared in the 19th century when the slums around the River Senne were cleared to make way for ornate constructions such as the financial centre, La Bourse, and Europe's first shopping arcade, Galéries St-Hubert. With its many restaurants and cafés, the Lower Town is also popular at night.

SIGHTS AT A GLANCE

Historic Buildings and Monuments
Hôtel de Ville see pp44–45 **2**
Manneken Pis **3**
La Bourse **7**

Museums and Galleries
Musée du Costume et de la Dentelle **1**
Bruxella 1238 **8**
Centre Belge de la Bande Dessinée see pp50–51 **14**
Maison de la Bellone **21**

Churches
Notre-Dame de la Chapelle **4**
Eglise St-Nicolas **9**
Eglise St-Jean-Baptiste **19**
Eglise Ste-Catherine **22**

Shopping
Galeries St-Hubert **10**
Rue Neuve **16**

Streets and Squares
Rue des Bouchers **11**
Place de Brouckère **18**

Theatres
Théâtre Marionnettes de Toone **12**
Théâtre Royal de la Monnaie **13**
Théâtre Flamand **20**

Cultural Centres
Le Botanique **15**

Historic Districts
Quartier Marolles **5**
Halles St-Géry **6**

Hotels
Hôtel Métropole **17**

KEY

🚋	Tram stop
Ⓜ	Metro station
🚌	Bus terminus
ℹ	Tourist information
🅿	Parking

GETTING AROUND

The area is well served by trams which encircle the old town. However, the tiny streets are often pedestrianized, and usually the quickest and most enjoyable means of transport for short distances is on foot. Otherwise metro stations are well placed.

0 metres	500
0 yards	500

◁ **Detail of the façade of the Hôtel de Ville in the Grand Place – centre of the Lower Town**

The Grand Place

THE GEOGRAPHICAL, HISTORICAL and commercial heart of the city, the Grand Place is the first port of call for most visitors to Brussels. This bustling cobblestone square remains the civic centre, centuries after its creation, and offers the finest surviving example in one area of Belgium's ornate 17th-century architecture. Open-air markets took place on or near this site as early as the 11th century, but by the end of the 14th century Brussels' town hall, the Hôtel de Ville, was built, and city traders added individual guildhouses in a medley of styles. In 1695, however, two days of cannon fire by the French destroyed all but the town hall and two guild façades. Trade guilds were urged to rebuild their halls to styles approved by the Town Council, producing the harmonious unity of Flemish Renaissance buildings here today.

The morning flower market in bloom in the Grand Place

The Maison du Roi was first built in 1536 but redesigned in 1873. Once the residence of ruling Spanish monarchs, it is now home to the Musée de la Ville, which includes 16th-century paintings, tapestries, and the 400 tiny outfits of Manneken Pis.

① **NORTHEAST CORNER**

② **MAISON DU ROI**

The Hôtel de Ville occupies the entire southwest side of the square. Still a functioning civic building, Brussels' town hall is the architectural masterpiece of the Grand Place *(see pp44–5)*.

Ornate stone carvings

The spire was built by Jan van Ruysbroeck in 1449 and stands 96 m (315 ft) high; it is slightly crooked.

Everard 't Serclaes was murdered defending Brussels in the 14th century; touching the bronze arm of his statue is said to bring luck.

⑤ **EVERARD 'T SERCLAES**

⑥ **HÔTEL DE VILLE**

Le Pigeon was home to Victor Hugo, the exiled French novelist who chose the house as his Belgian residence in 1852. Some of the most complimentary comments about Brussels emerged later from his pen.

LOCATOR MAP
See Brussels street finder, map 2

La Maison des Ducs de Brabant is a group of six guildhouses. Designed by the Controller of Public Works, Guillaume de Bruyn, the group is Neo-Classical with Flemish additions.

Stone busts of the ducal line along the façade gave this group of houses their name.

③ LE PIGEON

④ LA MAISON DES DUCS DE BRARANT

Le Renard was built in the 1690s as the guild-house of the haber-dashers by the Flemish architects Marc de Vos and van Nerum. Façade details show St Nicolas, patron saint of mer-chants, and cherubs playing with haber-dashery ribbons.

Le Cornet displays Italianate Flemish style. This Boatmen's Guildhouse (1697) is most notable for its gable, which is constructed in the form of a 17th-century frigate's bow.

⑦ LE RENARD, LE CORNET AND LE ROI D'ESPAGNE

La Maison des Boulangers, also known as "Le Roi d'Esp-agne", was a showpiece built by the wealthy and powerful guild of bakers. The 1676 octag-onal copper dome is topped by a dancing golden figure.

Le Roi d'Espagne now houses the Grand Place's finest bar with a view of the bustling square and its splendours above ground level. *(see p154)*. The gilt bust over the front entrance represents Saint Aubert, patron saint of bakers. A vast bust of Charles II of Spain sits in stone drapery on the third floor.

Musée du Costume et de la Dentelle ❶

Rue de Violette 6, 1000 BRU.
Map 2 D3. 📞 (02) 512 7709.
Ⓜ Bourse, de Brouckère.
⭕ 10am–12:30pm, 1:30–5pm
Mon, Tue, Thu, Fri; 2–4:30pm
Sat, Sun. ⬤ Wed.
▨ ♿ 📷 on request.

FOUND WITHIN two 18th-century gabled houses is the museum dedicated to one of Brussels' most successful exports, Belgian lace (see pp20–21). The intricate skill employed by Belgian lace-makers has contributed a vital economic role in the city since the 12th century, and the

A wedding dress at the Musée du Costume et de la Dentelle

collection explains and displays the history of the craft. On the ground floor costumes from the 18th to the 20th centuries are displayed on mannequins, demon-strating how lace has adorned fashions of every era. The second floor houses a collec-tion of antique lace, carefully stored in drawers and demonstrating the various schools of lacemaking in France, Flanders and Italy.

Manneken Pis ❸

Rues de l'Etuve & du Chêne, 1000
BRU. **Map** 1 C3. 🚌 34, 48. 🚊 23,
52, 55, 56, 81. Ⓜ Bourse.

AN UNLIKELY ATTRACTION, this tiny statue of a young boy barely 30 cm (1 ft) high reliev-ing himself into a small pool is as much a part of Brussels as

Hôtel de Ville ❷

Stone gargoyle

THE IDEA OF having a town hall to reflect Brussels' growth as a major European trading centre had been under consideration since the end of the 13th century. It was not until 1401 that the first foundation stone was laid and the building was finally completed in 1459, emerging as the finest civic building in the country, a stature it still enjoys.

Jacques van Thienen was commissioned to design the left wing and belfry of the building, where he used orn-ate columns, sculptures, turrets and arcades. The tower and spire begun in 1449 by Jan van Ruysbroeck helped seal its reputation. In 1995, the 1455 statue of the city's patron saint, Michael, was restored and returned to its famous position on top of the tower in 1997, where it is used as a weather vane. Tours are available of the interior, which contains 15th-century tapestries and works of art.

A detail of the delicately carved façade with stone statues

137 statues adorn walls and many mullioned windows.

★ Aldermen's Room
Still in use today for the meetings of the aldermen and mayor of Brussels, this council chamber contains a series of 18th-century tapestries depicting the history of 6th-century King Clovis.

STAR SIGHTS

★ **Conference Room Council Chamber**

★ **Aldermen's Room**

the Trevi Fountain is part of Rome or Trafalgar Square's reclining lions are of London.

The original bronze statue by Jérôme Duquesnoy the Elder, was first placed on the site in 1619, the tongue-in-cheek design reflecting a genuine need for fresh drinking water in the area. Its popularity led, in 1770, to the addition of an ornate stone niche, giving more prominence to the small figure. Several attempts to steal the statue were made during the 18th century, notably by the French and then British armies in 1745, but it was the theft in 1817 by a former convict, Antoine Licas, which caused the most alarm – the robber smashed the bronze figure shortly after procuring it. A replica of the statue was cast the following year and returned to its revered site, and it is this copy that is seen today. In 1698 governor Maximilian-Emmanuel donated a suit of clothing with which to dress the statue. It was to be the beginning of a tradition that continues to this day. Visiting heads of state to Brussels donate miniature versions of their national costume for the boy, and now 400 outfits, including an Elvis suit, are housed in the Musée de la Ville (see p42).

THE LEGENDS OF MANNEKEN PIS

The inspiration for this famous statue remains unknown, but the mystery only lends itself to rumour and fable and increases the little boy's charm. One theory claims that in the 12th century the son of a duke was caught urinating against a tree in the midst of a battle and was thus commemorated in bronze as a symbol of the country's military courage.

The belfry was built by architect Jan van Ruysbroeck. A statue of St Michael tops the 96 m (315 ft) spire.

Aldermen's Room

The gabled roof, like much of the town hall, was fully restored in 1837, and cleaned in the 1990s.

Cabinets des Echevins

Ornamental stone balcony staircase

★ **Conference Room Council Chamber**
The most splendid of all the public rooms, ancient tapestries and gilt mirrors line the walls above an inlaid floor.

Wedding Room
A Neo-Gothic style dominates this civil marriage office, with its many ornate carved timbers, including ancient ebony and mahogany.

Notre-Dame de la Chapelle ❹

Place de la Chapelle 1, 1000 BRU.
Map 1 C4. ☎ *(02) 513 5348.*
🚌 *34, 95, 96.* 🚊 *91, 92, 93, 94.*
Ⓜ *Porte de Namur.* ⏱ *5:30pm
Mon – Sat; Mass 6:30pm daily.*

IN 1134 KING Godefroid I
decided to build a chapel
outside the city walls. It quickly
became a market church, serving the many craftsmen living
nearby. In 1210 its popularity
was such that it was made a
parish church, but it became
really famous in 1250, when a
royal donation of five pieces
of the True Cross turned the
church into a pilgrimage site.

Originally built in Romanesque style, the majority of the
church was destroyed by fire
in 1405. Rebuilding began in
1421 in a Gothic style typical
of 15th-century Brabant architecture, including gables decorated with finials and interior
capitals decorated with cabbage leaves at the base. The
Bishop of Cambrai consecrated
the new church in 1434.

One of the most striking
features of the exterior are the
monstrously lifelike gargoyles
which peer down on the community – a representation of
evil outside the sacred interior.
The Baroque belltower was
added after the 1695 bombardment by the French *(see p32)*.
Another moving feature is the
carved stone memorial to the
16th-century Belgian artist
Pieter Brueghel the Elder
(see p14), who is buried here.

**The cool, elegant interior of
Notre-Dame de la Chapelle**

Rue Haute in the Quartier Marolles, with old-style shops and cafés

Quartier Marolles ❺

Map 1 C5. 🚌 *20, 48.* 🚊 *91.*
Ⓜ *Louise, Porte de Hal.*

KNOWN COLLOQUIALLY as "Les
Marolles", this quarter of
Brussels is traditionally working
class. Situated between the two
city walls, the area was home
to weavers and craftsmen.
Street names of the district,
such as Rue des Brodeurs
(Embroiderers' St) and Rue des
Charpentiers (Carpenters' St),
reflect its artisanal history.

Today the area is best known
for its fine daily flea market,
held in the **Place du Jeu de
Balle**. The flea market has
been held on this site since
1640. Between 7am and 2pm,
with the biggest and best markets on Thursday and Sunday,
almost anything from junk to
pre-war collector's items can
be found among the stalls.

Shopping of a different kind
is on offer on nearby Rue
Haute, an ancient Roman road.
A shopping district since the
19th century, it is still popular
with arty types with its specialist stores, interior and
antique shops. The street has
a long artistic history, too –
the elegant red-brick house at
No. 132 was home to Pieter
Brueghel the Elder and the
sculptor Auguste Rodin had a
studio at No. 224. No. 132
now houses the small **Maison
de Brueghel**, dedicated to the
16th-century Flemish painter.

At the southern end of Rue
Haute is **Porte de Hal**, the
stone gateway of the now-
demolished outer city walls.
Looming over the Marolles is

the imposing Palais de Justice
(see p69), which has hilltop
views of the area west of the
city, including the 1958 Atomium *(see p83)* and the Basilique
Sacré-Coeur *(see p81)*.

🏛 **Maison de Brueghel**
Rue Haute 132, 1000 BRU.
⏱ *May – Sep: Wed & Sun pm*
(groups with written permission only).
● *Oct – Apr.* 📷

Halles St-Géry ❻

Place St-Géry, 1000 BRU. **Map** 1 C2.
🚌 *47.* 🚊 *23, 52, 55, 56, 81.*
Ⓜ *de Brouckère.*

IN MANY WAYS, St-Géry can be
considered the birthplace of
the city. A chapel to Saint Géry
was built in the 6th century,
then in AD 977 a fortress took
over the site. A 16th-century
church followed and occu-
pied the location until the
18th century. In 1881 a

**Busy restaurants and cafés
outside Halles St-Géry**

covered meat market was erected in Neo-Renaissance style. The glass and intricate ironwork was renovated in 1985, and the hall now serves as a cultural centre with an exhibition on local history.

La Bourse ❼

Palais de la Bourse, 1000 BRU.
Map 1 C2. 📞 *(02) 509 1211.*
🚊 *47.* 🚇 *23, 52, 55, 56, 81.*
Ⓜ *Bourse.* ⏰ *10am daily, by appointment.* ⬤ *Sat & Sun, public hols.* 🔲 *of the exchange market.*

BRUSSELS' Stock Exchange, La Bourse, is one of the city's most impressive buildings, dominating the square of the same name. Designed in Palladian style by architect Léon Suys, it was constructed from 1867 to 1873. Among the building's most notable features are the façade's ornate carvings. The great French sculptor, Auguste Rodin, is thought to have crafted the groups representing Africa and Asia, as well as four caryatids inside. Beneath the colonnade, two beautifully detailed winged figures representing Good and Evil were carved by sculptor Jacques de Haen. Some areas of the building are open to the public, but a screen divides visitors from the frantic bidding and trading that takes place on weekdays on the trading floor.

Detail of a Rodin statue, La Bourse

Bruxella 1238 ❽

Rue de la Bourse, 1000 BRU. **Map** 1 C3. 📞 *(02) 279 4350.* 🚊 *34, 48, 95, 96.* 🚇 *23, 52, 55, 56, 81.*
Ⓜ *Bourse, de Brouckère.* ⏰ *10:15am, 11:15am, 1:45pm, 2:30pm, 3:15pm, Wed.* 📷 🔲 *obligatory, starts from Maison du Roi, Grand Place.*

ONCE HOME to a church and 13th-century Franciscan convent, in the early 19th century this site became a Butter Market until the building of the Bourse commenced in 1867. In 1988 municipal roadworks began alongside the

Place de la Bourse. Medieval history must have been far from the minds of the city authorities but, in the course of working on the foundations for the Bourse, important relics were found, including 13th-century bones, pottery and the 1294 grave of Duke John I of Brabant. Visitors can now see these and other pieces of Burgundian history in a small museum built on the site.

Eglise St-Nicolas ❾

Rue au Beurre 1, 1000 BRU. **Map** 1 C2. 📞 *(02) 513 8022.* 🚊 *34, 48, 95, 96.* 🚇 *23, 52, 55, 56, 81.*
Ⓜ *Bourse, de Brouckère.* ⏰ *10am–4pm daily, except during services.*

AT THE END of the 12th century a market church was constructed on this site, but, like much of the Lower Town, it was damaged in the 1695 French Bombardment. A cannon ball lodged itself directly into an interior pillar and the belltower finally collapsed in 1714. Many restoration projects were planned but none came to fruition until as late as 1956, when the west side of the building was given a new, Gothic-style façade. Named after St Nicolas, the patron saint of merchants, the church contains choir stalls dating from 1381 which display detailed medallions telling St Nicolas' story. Another interesting feature is the chapel, constructed at an angle, reputedly to avoid the flow of an old stream. Inside the church, works of art by Bernard van Orley and Peter Paul Rubens are well worth seeing.

The 19th-century domed glass roof of Galéries St-Hubert

Galeries St-Hubert ❿

Rue des Bouchers, 1000 BRU. **Map** 2 D2. 🚊 *29, 38, 60, 63, 65, 66, 71.*
Ⓜ *Gare Centrale.* ♿

SIXTEEN YEARS after ascending the throne as the first king of Belgium, Léopold I inaugurated the opening of these grand arcades in 1847.

St-Hubert has the distinction of being the first shopping arcade in Europe, and one of the most elegant. Designed in Neo-Renaissance style by Jean-Pierre Cluysenaar, the vaulted glass roof covers its three sections, Galerie du Roi, Galerie de la Reine and Galerie des Princes, which house a range of luxury shops and cafés. The ornate interior and expensive goods on sale soon turned the galleries into a fashionable meeting place for 19th-century society, including resident literati – Victor Hugo and Alexandre Dumas attended lectures here. The arcades remain a popular venue, with shops, a cinema, theatre, cafés and restaurants.

Gothic-style façade of Eglise St-Nicolas

Pavement displays of restaurants along Rue des Bouchers

Rue des Bouchers ⑪

Map 2 D2. 🚌 29, 60, 63, 65, 66, 71. 🚇 23, 52, 55, 56, 81, 90. Ⓜ *Gare Centrale, Bourse.*

L IKE MANY streets in this area of the city, Rue des Bouchers retains its medieval name, reminiscent of the time when this meandering, cobble-stoned street was home to the butchers' trade. Aware of its historic importance and heeding the concerns of the public, the city council declared this area the Ilot Sacré (sacred islet) in 1960, forbidding any of the architectural façades to be altered or destroyed, and commanding those surviving to be restored. Hence Rue des Bouchers abounds with 17th-century stepped gables and decorated doorways.

Today, this pedestrianized thoroughfare is best known as the "belly of Brussels", a reference to its plethora of cafés and restaurants. Many cuisines are on offer here, including Chinese, Greek, Italian and Indian. But the most impressive sights during an evening stroll along the street are the lavish pavement displays of seafood, piled high on mounds of ice, all romantically lit by an amber glow from the streetlamps.

At the end of the street, at the Impasse de la Fidélité, is a recent acknowledgement of sexual equality. Erected in 1987, Jeanneke Pis is a coy, cheeky female version of her "brother", the more famous Manneken Pis *(see p45).*

Théâtre Marionettes de Toone ⑫

Impasse Schuddeveld 6, off the Petite Rue des Bouchers, 1000 BRU. **Map** 2 D2. 📞 (02) 511 7137. 🚌 29, 34, 48, 60, 63, 65, 66, 71, 95, 96. 🚇 23, 52, 55, 56, 81. Ⓜ *Bourse, Gare Centrale.* ◯ *bar: noon–midnight daily; theatre: performance times (8:30pm Tue–Sat).* ● *Sun, pub hols.* 📷 📹 *on request, for tour reservations* 📞 (02) 217 2753. **Museum** ◯ *intervals.*

A POPULAR pub by day, at night the top floor of this tavern is home to a puppet theatre. During the time of the Spanish Netherlands *(see p32),* all theatres were closed because of the satirical performances by actors aimed at their Latin rulers. This began a fashion for puppet shows, the vicious dialogue more easily forgiveable from inanimate dolls. In 1830, Antoine Toone opened his own theatre and it has been run by

Harlequin puppet

the Toone family ever since; the owner is the seventh generation, Toone VII. The classics are enacted by these wooden marionettes in the local Bruxellois dialect, and occasionally in French, English, German or Dutch.

Théâtre Royal de la Monnaie ⑬

Place de la Monnaie, 1000 BRU. **Map** 2 D2. 📞 (02) 229 1211. 🚌 29, 60, 65, 66. 🚇 23, 52, 55, 56, 81. Ⓜ *de Brouckère, Bourse.* ◯ *performance times, Mon–Sat; box office: 11am–6pm Tue–Sat.* ● *Sun, public hols.* 📷 📹 *noon Sat only.*

T HIS THEATRE was first built in 1817 on the site of a 15th-century mint (Hôtel des Monnaies) but, following a fire in 1855, only the front and pediment of the original Neo-Classical building remain. After the fire, the theatre was redesigned by the architect, Joseph Poelaert, also responsible for the imposing Palais de Justice *(see p69).*

The original theatre was to make its historical mark before its destruction, however, when on 25 August, 1830, a performance of *La Muette de Portici* (*The Mute Girl*) began a national rebellion. As the tenor began to sing the nationalist *Amour Sacré de la Patrie* (*Sacred love of the homeland*), his words incited an already discontented city, fired by the libertarianism of the revolutions taking place in France, into revolt. Members of the audience ran out into the street in a rampage that developed into the

The original Neo-Classical façade of Théâtre Royal de la Monnaie

The 19th-century glasshouse of Le Botanique in summer

Similar to London's Oxford Street, but now pedestrianized, this is the heart of commercial shopping. It houses well-known international chainstores and shopping malls, such as **City 2**, which has shops, cafés and the media store Fnac all under one roof. Inno department store was designed by Horta *(see p78)*, but after a fire in 1967 was entirely rebuilt.

To the east of Rue Neuve is Place des Martyrs, a peaceful square where a monument pays tribute to the 450 citizens killed during the 1830 uprising.

🏠 **City 2**
Rue Neuve 123, 1000 BRU. 📞 *(02) 211 4060.* 🕐 *10am–7pm Mon–Thu & Sat, 10am–8pm Fri.* ● *Sun, public hols.*

September Uprising *(see p34–5)*. The theatre today remains the centre of Belgian performing arts; major renovations took place during the 1980s. The auditorium was raised 4 m (13 ft) to accommodate the elaborate stage designs, but the luxurious Louis XIV-style decor was carefully retained and blended with the new additions. The central dome is decorated with an allegory of Belgian arts.

Centre Belge de la Bande Dessinée ⑭

See pp50–51.

Le Botanique ⑮

Rue Royale 236, 1210 BRU. **Map** 2 E1. 📞 *(02) 226 1211.* 🚌 *38, 58, 61.* 🚋 *92, 93, 94.* Ⓜ *Botanique.* 🕐 *10am–8pm daily.* ♿

IN 1797, THE CITY of Brussels created a botanical garden in the grounds of the Palais de Lorraine as a source of reference for botany students. The garden closed in 1826, and new gardens were relocated in Meise, 13 km (9 miles) from Brussels.

A grand glass-and-iron rotunda was designed at the centre of the gardens by the French architect Gineste. This

iron glasshouse still stands, as does much of the 19th-century statuary by Constantin Meunier *(see p15)*, including depictions of the Four Seasons. The glasshouse is now home to the French Community Cultural Centre and offers plays, concerts and exhibitions.

Rue Neuve ⑯

Map 2 D2. 🚌 *29, 60, 63, 65, 66, 71.* 🚋 *23, 52, 55, 56, 81, 90.* Ⓜ *Bourse, de Brouckère, Rogier.*

BRUSSELS shoppers have been flocking to the busy Rue Neuve since the 19th century for its reasonably priced goods and well-located stores.

Rue Neuve, the longest pedestrian shopping street in the city

Hôtel Métropole ⑰

Place de Brouckère 31, 1000 BRU. **Map** 2 D2. 📞 *(02) 217 2300.* 🚌 *29, 60, 65, 66.* 🚋 *23, 52, 55, 56, 81.* Ⓜ *de Brouckère.*

THE AREA lying between Place Rogier and Place de Brouckère is known as the hotel district of Brussels, and one of the oldest and grandest hotels in the area is the Métropole.

In 1891 the Wielemans Brewery bought the building and commissioned the architect Alban Chambon to redesign the interior, with money no object. The result was a fine Art Nouveau hotel which opened for business in 1894 and has since accommodated numerous acclaimed visitors to the city, including actress Sarah Bernhardt. In 1911 the hotel was the location of the science conference Conseil Physique Solvay, attended by the great scientists Marie Curie and Albert Einstein.

The Hôtel Métropole continues to welcome guests from all walks of life, at surprisingly reasonable cost given its beauty, history and location. It is particularly popular for drinks in its café and heated pavement terrace, which are both open to non-residents to enjoy cocktails and cappuccinos in elegant surroundings.

Centre Belge de la Bande Dessinée ⓪

AFFECTIONATELY KNOWN as *cébébédé*, the Museum of Comic Strip Art pays tribute to the Belgian passion for comic strips or *bandes dessinées* and to many world-famous comic strip artists from Belgium and abroad.

Arranged over three levels, the collection is housed in a Horta-designed Art Nouveau building. One of the most popular permanent exhibitions is a tour of the great comic strip heroes, from *Tintin* to *The Smurfs*, both of whose creators were Belgian. Other displays detail the stages of putting together a comic strip, from examples of initial ideas and pencil sketches through to final publication. The museum regularly holds major exhibitions featuring the work of famous cartoonists and studios, and also houses some 6,000 original plates, displayed in rotation, as well as a valuable archive of photographs and artifacts.

Three Comic Figures
Tintin, Professor Calculus and Captain Haddock greet visitors on the 1st floor.

The Smurfs
These tiny blue characters first appeared in the Spirou *journal in 1958. By the 1980s they had their own TV show and hit records.*

A Suivre
Founded in 1978, A Suivre *expanded the comic strip genre, and led to the new form of graphic novels: adult stories in cartoon form.*

★ **Life-size Cartoon Sets**
A series of authentic comic scenes encourages children to enter the world of their favourite comic strip characters.

STAR SIGHTS

★ **Entrance Hall**

★ **Life-size Cartoon sets**

The famous Tintin rocket

VISITORS' CHECKLIST

20 rue des Sables, 1000 BRU.
Map 2 E2. *(02) 219 1980.*
38, 58, 61. 56, 81, 90. M
Botanique, Rogier, Centrale.
10am–6pm Tue–Sun. Mon,
1 Jan, 25 Dec.

★ **Entrance Hall**
*This airy space designed by
Victor Horta features stained
glass and wrought-ironwork.*

Comic Library
*The museum library
doubles as a study
centre for both art
students and enthu-
siasts of all ages. This
unique collection
includes a catalogue
of hundreds of old
comic strips, artists'
equipment, biogra-
phies, comic novels
and photographs.*

A HORTA-DESIGNED BUILDING

This beautiful building was constructed
between 1903 and 1906 to the design
of the Belgian Art-Nouveau architect
Victor Horta. Originally built as a fabric
warehouse, and known as the Waucquez
Building, it was one in a series of department stores and warehouses in the city
designed by him. Saved from demolition by
the French Cultural Commission of Brussels,
in 1989 the building re-opened as a museum
dedicated to the comic strip, Belgium's so-
called Ninth Art *(see pp18–19)*. Carefully
restored, the building has many classic
features of Art Nouveau design, including
the use of curves on structural iron pillars.
In the impressive entrance hall is a display of Horta's architectural drawings
for the building, and on the right the
Brasserie Horta serves traditional Belgian dishes in a
charming glass and marble Art Nouveau setting.

**Cast-iron
pillar**

THE CHANGING FACE
OF HERGÉ'S TINTIN
Perhaps the best-known Belgian
comic character, *Tintin* made his
debut in a children's paper in 1929.
He began life as a simple black line
drawing, featuring the famous quiff,
but no mouth. By 1930 Hergé began
to produce *Tintin* in book-form and
gave him both a mouth and a more
complex character suggested by a
greater range of facial expressions.
By the 1940s *Tintin* was appearing
in colour, alongside such new
characters as Captain Haddock, the
Thompsons and Professor Calculus.

Horta's drawing of the CBBD building in the museum

Nineteenth-century building in Place de Brouckère

Place de Brouckère ⓲

Map 2 D2. 🚌 *29, 60, 63, 65, 66, 71.* 🚋 *23, 52, 55, 56, 81, 90.* Ⓜ *de Brouckère, Bourse.*

IN 1872 A DESIGN competition was held to encourage the construction of buildings of architectural interest in de Brouckère. Twenty winning applicants were selected and commissioned to give prominence to this Brussels junction. The Parisian contractor Jean-Baptiste Mosnier was responsible for taking the original plans through to completion.

The French influence of Mosnier and his workers is still evident on the square. Many of the buildings were erected in stone, common in France at the end of the 19th century, whereas brickwork was more usual in Brussels. Several original façades survive today, including the 1874 Hôtel Continental by Eugene Carpentier.

One of the great hotels of Brussels, the Hôtel Métropole (*see p49*) is situated on the south side of the square. The 1900–10 interior is splendidly gilded and can be seen either through the doorway or by pretending to be a guest. Café Métropole next door is, however, open to the public; here the lavishly ornate surroundings date from around 1890.

In the 20th century, architectural style was still at a premium in the district. In 1933 a

Neo-Classical cinema was erected with an impressive Art Deco interior. During the 1960s, two imposing glass buildings blended the contemporary with the classical. Today, the varied historic architecture of Place de Brouckère enhances one of the city's busiest squares, despite recent additions of advertising hoardings.

Eglise St-Jean-Baptiste-au-Béguinage ⓳

Place du Béguinage, 1000 BRU. **Map** 1 C1. 📞 *(02) 217 8742.* 🚌 *47.* Ⓜ *Ste-Cathérine.* 🕘 *9am–5pm Tue–Sat, 9:30am–noon Sun.* ● *Mon.* ♿

THIS STONE-CLAD church was consecrated in 1676 around the long-standing and largest béguine community in the country, established in 1250. Fields and orchards around the site contained cottages and houses for up to 1,200 béguine women, members of a lay religious order who took up charitable work and enclosed living after widowhood or failed marriages. In medieval times the béguines ran a laundry, hospital and windmill for the people of the city. Still a popular place of worship, the church is also notable for its Flemish Baroque details from the 17th century, especially the onion-shaped turrets and ornamental walls. The nave is also Baroque, decorated with ornate winged cherubs, angels and scrolls. The confessionals are carved with allegorical figures and saints. A more unusual feature are the aisles, which have been widened to allow more light in. In the apse is a statue of St John the Baptist. The 1757 pulpit is a fine example of Baroque woodcarving, showing St Dominic and a heretic.

Théâtre Flamand ⓴

Rue de Laeken 146, 1000 BRU. **Map** 1 C1. 🚌 *47.* 🚋 *18.* Ⓜ *Yser.* ● *for renovations.* 🌐 *www.kvs.be*

THE FORMER QUAY area of Brussels, on the banks of the old River Senne, still survives as a reminder that the city was once a thriving port. In 1882, architect Jean Baes was commissioned to enlarge one of the former waterfront warehouses and then turn it into a theatre but was instructed to retain the original 1780 façade. Baes solved this problem ingeniously by placing the façade directly behind the frontage of the new building. The

The ornate façade of Eglise St-Jean-Baptiste-au-Béguinage

Théâtre Flamand has other interesting design features peculiar to the late 19th century. The four exterior metal terraces and a staircase leading to the ground were built for audience evacuation in the event of fire. The theatre is now undergoing restoration, due to finish in 2004. For the duration, the resident Flemish theatre company are staging productions nearby in rue de Launoy (call 02 412 7040).

The 19th-century interior staircase of Théâtre Flamand

Maison de la Bellone ㉑

Rue de Flandre 46, 1000 BRU.
Map 1 C2. *(02) 513 3333.* 63.
Ste-Catherine. 10am–6pm
Tue–Fri (exhibition centre open
noon–6pm). Sat–Mon, Jul.

THIS 17TH-CENTURY aristocratic residence, now shielded under a glass roof and no longer visible from the street, was once the headquarters of the Ommegang procession (see p25). The original façade is notable for its decoration. There is a statue of Bellona (goddess of war), after whom the house is named, above the central arch, and the window ledges have medallions of Roman emperors.

Today the house, its exhibition centre and once-private theatre are open for dance and cinema shows, and temporary exhibitions of art and furniture.

Stonework on the Maison de la Bellone

THE BÉGUINE MOVEMENT

The béguine lifestyle swept across Western Europe from the 12th century, and Brussels once had a community of over 1,200 béguine women. The religious order is believed to have begun among widows of the Crusaders, who resorted to a pious life of sisterhood on the death of their husbands. The women were lay nuns, who opted for a secluded existence devoted to charitable deeds, but not bound by strict religious vows. Most béguine convents disappeared during the Protestant Reformation in

Béguine lay nun at prayer in a Brussels béguinage

much of Europe during the 16th century, but begijnhofs (béguinages) continued to thrive in Flanders. The grounds generally consisted of a church, a courtyard, communal rooms, homes for the women and extra rooms for work. The movement dissolved as female emancipation spread during the early 1800s, although 20 convents remain, including those in Bruges (see p117) and Ghent.

Eglise Ste-Catherine ㉒

Place Ste-Catherine 50, 1000 BRU.
Map 1 C2. *(02) 513 3481.*
47. 23, 52, 55, 56, 81, 90.
Ste-Catherine, De Brouckère.
8:30am–5:30pm daily. on request.

SADLY, THE ONLY remnant of the first church here, built in the 15th century, is its Baroque tower, added in 1629. Inspired by the Eglise St-Eustache in Paris, the present church was redesigned in 1854–59 by Joseph Poelaert in a variety of styles. Notable features of the interior include a 14th-century statue of the Black Madonna and a portrait of St Catherine herself. A typically Flemish pulpit was installed at some stage; it may have come from the parish of Mechelen. Two impressive tombs were carved by Gilles-Lambert Godecharle. To the east of the church is the Tour Noire (Black Tower), a surviving remnant of the 12th-century stone city walls.

Although this area has been dedicated to the saint since the 13th century, the square

of Place Ste-Catherine was only laid in front of this large church after the basin once here was filled in. Paved in 1870, the square contrasts the peacefulness of the religious building with today's vigorous trade in good fish restaurants.

The central square was once the city's main fish market, and this is still the best place to indulge in a dish or two of Brussels' famous seafood, but prices are generally high. Flanking the square, Quai aux Briques and Quai au Bois à Brûler (Brick Quay and Timber Quay, named after their industrial past), contain lively parades of fish restaurants.

Eglise Ste-Catherine showing the spacious Victorian interior

THE UPPER TOWN

BRUSSELS' UPPER TOWN is separated from the lower part of the city by an escarpment that runs roughly north-south from the far end of Rue Royale to the Palais de Justice. Modern developments are now scattered across the whole city, and the difference between the two areas is less distinct than in the past; traditionally the Lower Town was mainly Flemish-speaking and a bustling centre

Peter Pan statue in
Palais d'Egmont

for trade, while the Upper Town was home to French-speaking aristocrats and royalty. Today the Upper Town is known for its beautiful Gothic churches, modern architecture and fine museums. The late 18th-century elegance of the Parc de Bruxelles and Place Royale is complemented by Emperor Leopold II's sweeping 19th-century boulevards that connect the Parc du Cinquantenaire to the city centre.

SIGHTS AT A GLANCE

0 metres		500
0 yards		500

KEY

Street-by-Street map
see pp56-57

Tram stop

M Metro station

Bus terminus

P Parking

GETTING AROUND

The main metro stations for exploring the Upper Town are Parc and Porte de Namur in the west and Schuman and Maelbeek in the east. Most trams circle this area, so the best option is to take one of the many buses that run through the Upper Town.

◁ **Detail of a façade in a terrace of Art Nouveau houses in Square Ambiorix**

Street-by-Street: Quartier Royal

THE QUARTIER ROYAL has traditionally been home to Brussels' nobility and rulers. Chosen because the air was purer on the hill than it was in the Lower Town, the area once known as Coudenberg Hill was occupied by the 15th-century Coudenberg Palace, home to the Dukes of Brabant and Renaissance rulers. In 1731, the palace was destroyed in just six hours by a fire. Slowly rebuilt during the 18th and 19th centuries, four new palaces and much of the park were designed in Neo-Classical style chosen by Charles de Lorraine (*see p33*). Today the Royal Quarter presents a peaceful elegance, with some of Europe's finest 18th-century buildings framing the tree-lined paths and fountains of Parc de Bruxelles.

Fountain in park

Rue Royale runs for 2 km (1 mile) from the Quartier Royal to Jardin Botanique. In contrast to the 18th-century Neo-Classicism of its beginnings, along its route many fine examples of Victorian and Art Nouveau architecture stand out.

RUE ROYALE

Eglise St-Jacques-sur-Coudenberg
One of Brussels' prettiest churches, St-Jacques' 18th-century façade was modelled exactly on a classical temple. The barrel-vaulted nave and half-domed apse are sprinkled with floral plasterwork and contain several fine Neo-Classical paintings ❸

★ Place Royale
In the centre of this attractive, symmetrical square is a statue of Godefroi of Bouillon, a Brabant soldier who fought the first Catholic Crusades and died in Palestine ❹

PLACE ROYALE

KEY

– – – Suggested route

STAR SIGHTS

★ Palais Royal

★ Parc de Bruxelles

★ Place Royale

Place des Palais divides Palais Royal and the park. In French, "Palais" refers to any large stately building, and does not have royal connotations.

0 metres   100

0 yards   100

★ **Parc de Bruxelles**
On the site of medieval hunting grounds once used by the dukes of Brabant, the park was redesigned in the 1770s with fountains, statues and tree-lined walks.

LOCATOR MAP
See Streetfinder Map 2

RUE DE LA LOI

RUE DUCALE

LACE DES PALAIS

Palais de la Nation
Designed by French architect Barnabé Guimard, the Palais de la Nation was built in 1783 and restored in 1883 after a fire. Since 1831, it has been the home of both chambers of the Belgian Parliament.

★ **Palais Royal**
The largest of the palaces, the low-rise Palais Royal is the official home of the Belgian monarch and family. A flag flies to indicate when the king is in the country ❷

Palais des Académies
Built in 1823 as the residence of the Crown Prince, this has been the private premises of the Académie Royale de Belgique since 1876.

Musée de la Dynastie ❶

Place des Palais 7, 1000 BRU.
Map 2 E4. ☎ (02) 511 5578.
🚌 20, 34, 38, 54, 60, 71, 95, 96.
🚃 92, 93, 94. Ⓜ Trone, Parc.
◷ 10am–5pm Tue–Sun. ⬤ Mon,
1 Jan, 21 Jul, 25 Dec.

THE MUSÉE de la Dynastie
contains a broad collection
of paintings, documents and
other royal memorabilia chart-
ing the history of the Belgian
monarchy from independence
in 1830 to the present day.
Since 1992 it has been housed
in the former Hôtel Bellevue,
an 18th-century Neo-Classical
building lying adjacent to the
Palais Royal, which was
annexed to the palace in 1902.
A permanent exhibition in
honour of the late, immensely
popular, King Baudouin
(r.1951–1993) was added in

**The Neo-Classical façade of the
Musée de la Dynastie**

1998. As well as official
portraits, informal photographs
are on display which give a
fascinating insight into the
private lives of the Belgian
royal family. The collection
is displayed in chronological
order in a series of rooms
with a bust of the sovereign
to which it is devoted at the
entrance to each one.

Eglise St-Jacques-sur-Coudenberg ❸

Place Royale, 1000 BRU. **Map** 2 E4. ☎
(02) 511 7836. 🚌 95, 96. 🚃 92, 93,
94. Ⓜ Trone, Parc. ◷ 3–5pm Mon,
10am–6pm Tue–Sat, 9am–noon Sun.

THE PRETTIEST building in the
Place Royale, St-Jacques-
sur-Coudenberg is the latest
in a series of churches to
have occupied this site. There
has been a chapel here since
the 12th century, when one
was built to serve the dukes
of Brabant. On construction
of the Coudenberg Palace in
the 13th century, it became
the ducal chapel. The chapel
suffered over the years: it was
ransacked in 1579 during
conflict between Catholics
and Protestants, and was so
badly damaged in the fire
of 1731 that destroyed the
Coudenberg Palace that it

Palais Royal ❷

THE PALAIS ROYAL is the most important of the palaces
around the Parc de Bruxelles. An official residence of
the Belgian monarchy, construction of the modern palace
began in the 1820s on the site of the old Coudenberg
Palace. Work continued under Léopold II (r.1865–1909),
when much of the exterior was completed. Throughout
the 20th century the palace underwent interior improvements and restoration of its older sections. It is open
only from July to September, but this is a
fine opportunity to tour Belgium's
lavish state reception rooms.

**The Field Marshal's
Room** contains a portrait
of the first Belgian king,
Léopold I, after Winter-
halter's 1843 original.

STAR SIGHTS

★ **Throne Room**

★ **Hall of Mirrors**

★ **Throne Room**
*One of Brussels' original state-
rooms, the huge throne room is
decorated in grand style, with
huge pilastered columns, 11
large candelabras and 28
wall-mounted chandeliers.*

The 19th-century cupola of Eglise St-Jacques-sur-Coudenberg

was demolished soon after. The present church was built on the same site in the Neo-Classical style of the rest of the area and was consecrated in 1787, although it served several years as a Temple of Reason and Law during the French Revolution, returning to the Catholic Church in 1802. The cupola was completed in 1849. The interior is simple and elegant, with two large paintings by Jan Portaels on either side of the transept, and a royal pew.

Place Royale ❹

Map 2 E4. 🚌 38, 60, 71, 95, 96. 🚊 92, 93, 94. Ⓜ Trone, Parc.

THE INFLUENCE of Charles de Lorraine is still keenly felt in the Place Royale. As Governor of Brussels from 1749 to 1780 he redeveloped the site once occupied by the Coudenberg Palace along Neo-Classical lines reminiscent of Vienna, a city he greatly admired.

When the area was being worked on, the ruins of the burnt-down palace were demolished and the entire site was rebuilt as two squares.

However, in 1995, excavation work uncovered ruins of the 15th-century Aula Magna, the Great Hall of the former palace. This was part of the extension of the palace started under the dukes of Brabant in the early 13th century and then developed under the rule of the dukes of Burgundy, in particular Philip the Good. It was in this room that the Hapsburg emperor Charles V abdicated in favour of his son, Philip II. The ruins can now be seen in a corner of the Place Royale.

Although criss-crossed by tramlines and traffic, the Place Royale maintains a feeling of dignity with its tall, elegant, cream buildings symmetrically set around a cobbled square. Visitors can tour the area on foot, admiring the stateliness of Brussels' parade of exceptional Neo-Classical buildings.

The Long Gallery features exquisite late 19th-century ceiling paintings representing Dawn, Day and Dusk.

The Empire Room

Small White Room
Rows of 19th-century royal portraits dominate this gilt chamber with its large candle-lit chandeliers and late 18th-century rococo furnishings.

★ **Hall of Mirrors**
This large room is famous for its grandiose effect similar to the mirrored chamber at Versailles. Ceremonial occasions are often held here, where invited guests are presented to the king and queen.

The Victor Horta-designed façade of the Palais des Beaux-Arts

Palais des Beaux-Arts **5**

Rue Ravenstein 23, 1000 BRU.
Map 2 E3. **(** (02) 507 8200,
511 3433. 20, 71, 60, 95, 96.
92, 93, 94. **M** Centrale.
11am–7pm daily. public hols.

THE PALAIS des Beaux-Arts owes its existence to Henri Le Boeuf, a music-loving financier who gave his name to the main auditorium. In 1922 he commissioned the architect Victor Horta (*see p78*) to design a cultural centre which would house concert halls and exhibition areas open to all visitors and embracing the artistic fields of music, theatre, cinema and art. The construction took seven years as the building was on a slope but could not be so tall as to block the view of the town from the Palais Royal: Horta had to revise his plans six times. The centre was the first of its kind in Europe.

The complex has a fine reputation and has played a key role in the cultural life of Brussels for over 70 years. It is the focus for the city's music and dance, and is home to the Belgian National Orchestra.

The complex also houses the **Musée du Cinema**, set up in 1962, with its fine archive and exhibition of old cameras and lenses. Its main activity is the daily screening of classic films.

Ⅲ Musée du Cinema
Rue Baron Horta 9, 1000 BRU.
((02) 507 8370. 5:30–10:30pm
daily.

Hôtel Ravenstein **6**

Rue Ravenstein 3, 1000 BRU.
Map 2 E3. 20, 95, 96. 92,
93, 94. **M** Parc. restaurant only.

OVER THE centuries the Hôtel Ravenstein has been the home of patrician families, soldiers and court officials, and, for the past 100 years, the Royal Society of Engineers. The building was designed at the end of the 15th century for Adolphe and Philip Cleves-Ravenstein; in 1515 it became the birthplace of Anne of Cleves. Consisting of two parts, joined by gardens and stables, it is the last remaining example of a Burgundian-style manor house. The Hôtel Ravenstein was acquired by the town in 1896 and used to store artworks. Sadly, it fell into disrepair and renovation

The pretty open courtyard of the Hôtel Ravenstein

took place in 1934. One half is now a Belgian restaurant, the other the Royal Society of Engineers' private HQ. However, the pretty, original inner courtyard which links the two elegant gabled red-brick buildings can still be seen.

Musée Instrumental **7**

Rue Montagne de la Cour 2, 1000
BRU. **Map** 2 E4. **(** (02) 545 0130.
9:30am–5pm Tue–Fri (to 8pm
Thu), 10am–5pm Sat & Sun. 20,
95, 96. 92, 93, 94. **M** Parc.

ONCE A department store, the building known as Old England is a striking showpiece of Art Nouveau architecture located by the Place Royale.

Architect Paul Saintenoy gave full rein to his imagination when he designed these shop premises for the Old England company in 1899. The façade is made entirely of glass and elaborate wrought iron. There is a domed gazebo on the roof, and a turret to one side. Surprisingly, it was only in the 1990s that a listed buildings policy was adopted in Brussels, which has secured treasures such as this.

Old England, home to the Musée Instrumental

Much preservation work is now taking place. Old England is one of the buildings that has undergone extensive renovation work, having been used until recently as a temporary exhibition space. The building is now home to the Musée Instrumental, moved from the Sablon. Meanwhile, the Old England company is still flourishing, with its premises now at No. 419 in the fashionable Avenue Louise.

The collection of the Musée Instrumental began in the 19th century when the state bought 80 ancient and exotic instruments. It was doubled in 1876 when King Léopold II donated a gift of 97 Indian musical instruments presented to him by a maharajah. A museum displaying all of these artifacts opened in 1877, and by 1924 the museum boasted 3,300 pieces and was recognized as a leader in its field. Today the collection contains more than 6,000 items and includes many fine examples of wind, string and keyboard instruments from medieval times to the present. Chief attractions include a collection of prototype instruments by Adolphe Sax, the Belgian inventor of the saxophone, mini violins favoured by street musicians and a faithful reproduction of a violin maker's studio. In June 2000 the museum moved to its specially designed home in the newly renovated Old England building, where there is much more room in which to display this world-class collection.

Antique violin

Palais de Charles de Lorraine ❽

Place du Musée 1, 1000 BRU. **Map** 2 D4. █ (02) 519 5371. ▉ 20, 95, 96. ▉ 92, 93, 94. Ⓜ Parc. ○ 1–5pm Mon–Tue, Thu–Fri. ● pub hols, last two weeks in Aug, 25 Dec–1 Jan. ▉ for details █ (02) 519 5786.

HIDDEN BEHIND this Neo-Classical façade are the few rooms that remain of the palace of Charles de Lorraine,

The state room with marble floor at the Palais de Charles de Lorraine

Governor of Brussels during the mid-18th century. He was a keen patron of the arts, and the young Mozart is believed to have performed here. Few original features remain, as the palace was ransacked by marauding French troops in 1794. Extensive renovations were recently completed. The bas-reliefs at the top of the stairway, representing air, earth, fire and water, reflect Charles de Lorraine's keen interest in alchemy. Most spectacular of all the original features is the 28-point star set in the floor of the circular drawing room. Each of the points is made of a different Belgian marble, a much sought-after material which was used in the construction of Versailles, and St Peter's Basilica in Rome.

Musée Charlier ❾

Avenue des Arts 16, 1210 BRU. **Map** 2 F2. █ (02) 218 5382, 220 2690. ▉ 23, 63, 65, 66. Ⓜ Madou, Arts-Loi. ○ 1:30–5pm Mon–Fri (by appointment). ● Sat–Sun. ▉ ▉

THIS QUIET MUSEUM was once the home of Henri van Cutsem, a wealthy collector and patron of the arts. In 1890 he asked the young architect Victor Horta to re-design his house as an exhibition space for his extensive collections. Van Cutsem died, and his friend, the sculptor Charlier, installed his own art collection in the house. Charlier commissioned Horta to build another museum, at Tournai in southern Belgium, to house van Cutsem's collection. On Charlier's death in 1925 the house and contents were left to the city as a museum.

The Musée Charlier opened in 1928. It contains paintings by a number of different artists, including portraits by Antoine Wiertz (see p72) and early landscapes by James Ensor. The collection also includes sculptures by Charlier, and the ground floor contains collections of glassware, porcelain, chinoiserie and silverware. Of special note are the tapestries, some from the Paris studios of Aubusson, on the staircases and the first floor, and the displays of Louis XV- and Louis XVI-style furniture on the first and second floors.

Musée Charlier, home to one of Belgium's finest individual collections of art and furnishings

Musées Royaux des Beaux-Arts: Musée d'art ancien ⑩

Façade of museum
Corinthian columns and busts of Flemish painters adorn the entrance.

JOINTLY KNOWN AS the Musées Royaux des Beaux-Arts, The Musée d'art ancien and Musée d'art moderne are Brussels' premier art museums. The museums' buildings, adjacent to the Place Royale, are home to exhibits from two eras, *ancien* (15th–18th century) and *moderne* (19th century–present day). Housed in a Neo-Classical building designed by Alphonse Balat between 1874 and 1880, the Musée d'art ancien is the larger of the two sections.

Hercules Sculpture

The art collection dates back to the 18th century when it consisted of the few valuable works left behind by the French Republican army, which had stolen many of Brussels' treasures and taken them back to Paris. This small collection was initially exhibited in the Palais de Charles de Lorraine (*see p61*), but donations, patronage and the recovery of some pieces from the French, enlarged the collection. The present gallery opened in 1887. The Musée d'art ancien is best known for the finest collection of Flemish art in the world, and many Old Masters, including van Dyck and Rubens, are also well represented.

★ The Assumption of the Virgin (*c.1610*)
Pieter Paul Rubens (1577–1640) was the leading exponent of Baroque art in Europe, combining Flemish precision with Italian flair. Here, Rubens suppresses background colours to emphasize the Virgin's blue robes.

Ground level

Interior of the Main Hall
Founded by Napoleon in 1801 to relieve the packed Louvre in Paris, these are the oldest museums in Belgium. More than 2,500 works are exhibited in the museums' buildings.

Entrance

Entrance to Musée d'art moderne

Lower level

STAR EXHIBITS

- ★ The Assumption of the Virgin by Rubens

- ★ The Annunciation by the Master of Flémalle

Upper level

VISITORS' CHECKLIST

Rue de la Régence 3, 1000 BRU.
Map 2 D4. **☎** *(02) 508 3211.* 🚌
25, 95, 96. 🚋 *91, 92, 93, 94.*
Ⓜ *Gare Centrale.* ◯ *10am–
noon, 1–5pm Tue–Sun.* ● *Mon,
public hols.* ♿🎫📷🏛📚🍴
Ⓦ *www.fine-arts-museum.be*

The Census at Bethlehem *(1610)*
*Pieter Brueghel the Younger (c.1564–1638) produced
a version of this subject some 40 years after the original
by his father. Shown together, the two works illustrate
the development of Flemish painting in its peak period.*

**Madonna with Saint Anne
and a Franciscan donor** *(1470)*
*Hugo van der Goes (c.1440–82) was
commissioned to paint this symbolic
work for the monk shown on the
right for his personal devotional use.*

★ The Annunciation *(c.1406–7)*
*The Master of Flémalle (c.1378–1444) sets the
holy scene of the Archangel Gabriel announc-
ing the impending birth of the Messiah in a
homely, contemporary setting, with daily objects
an apparent contrast to the momentous event.*

KEY

☐	15th–16th century (blue route)
☐	17th–18th century (brown route)
☐	Sculpture gallery
☐	Temporary exhibitions
☐	Non-exhibition space

GALLERY GUIDE
*In the gallery different coloured signs are
used to lead the visitor through different
eras of art (see pp66–7). On the first floor,
in rooms 10 to 34, the blue route covers the
15th and 16th centuries. The brown route is
in rooms 50 to 62 and covers the 17th and
18th centuries. The sculpture gallery is
housed on the lower ground floor.*

Musées Royaux des Beaux-Arts: Musée d'art moderne

O PENED IN 1984, the Musée d'art moderne is situated in a unique setting: eight levels of the building are underground, but a lightwell allows many of the works to be seen by natural daylight filtering in from the Place du Musée. The top three levels above ground are temporary exhibition space. As is the case for the Musee d'art ancien, the collection of works is wide and varied, displayed in chronological order. Many well-known 20th-century artists from 1900 to the present day are included, but the most popular paintings are those of the Belgian Surrealists.

level 4

level 3

Skeletons Fighting over a Pickled Herring (1891)
Moving from a naturalistic style, James Ensor became the leading light of the Belgian Surrealist artists. His uneasy preoccupation with death and the macabre is shown in this witty, disturbing oil.

level 2

View of London (1917)
Heavily influenced by Monet's work, Emile Claus developed a variant of Impressionism with fellow artists called "Luminism". The Belgian Claus was a refugee to London, and his Luminist interest in light effects is shown through the damp fog of this London twilight. The painting shows a clarity of definition that is almost realist in technique.

level 1

Ground level

The Orange Market at Blidah (1898)
Henri Evenepoel is known for his use of raw colour and tone; here, the market bustle is secondary to the arrangement of the shades in the traders' bright robes.

level -1

To Musée d'art ancien

level -2

STAR EXHIBITS

- ★ **Woman in a Blue Dress** by Rik Wouters

- ★ **The Domain of Arnheim** by René Magritte

GALLERY GUIDE
The yellow route, in rooms 69–91, is dedicated to the 19th century. Level -4 covers work from the first quarter of the 20th century and its various art movements, such as Fauvism and Cubism. Level -5 contains the Surrealist collection. Level -6 includes the Magritte exhibition, the Jeune Peinture Belge and COBRA schools. Levels -7 and -8 exhibit works from the 1960s to the present day. Levels 2, 3 and 4 contain temporary exhibitions that are changed regularly.

Composition *(1921)
(detail shown)*
*Two stylized human
figures form the centre
of this work by Belgian
painter Pierre-Louis
Flouquet, combining
Futurism and Cubism
in a "plastic" style.*

★ **Woman in a Blue
Dress in front of a
Mirror** *(1914)*
*Rik Wouters was a
Fauvist painter
whose fascination
with colour led him
to innovative spatula
painting techniques,
as seen here.*

**Draped Woman on
Steps** *(1957–8)*
*The prolific British
artist Henry Moore
is the world's most
exhibited sculptor.
This piece reveals
his characteristic
fluidity of line,
together with
tension in
the waiting
figure.*

level -4

level -3

★ **The Domain of
Arnheim** *(1962)*
*The museum contains
the world's largest col-
lection of work by sur-
realist René Magritte
(see p15). Here, an
eagle-mountain rears
over a small bird's
nest. The inexplicable
nature of the eerie
composition draws its
elements into question,
but answers are made
deliberately difficult.*

level -6

level -5

level -8

level -7

KEY

☐ 19th century (yellow route)

☐ 20th century (green route)

☐ Non-exhibition space

Exploring the Musées Royaux des Beaux-Arts

SIX CENTURIES OF ART, both Belgian and international, are displayed in the two museums that make up the Musées Royaux des Beaux-Arts. The combination of the two museums contains works from many artistic styles, from the religious paintings of the 15th-century Flemish Primitives to the graphic art of the 1960s and 1970s. The Musée d'art moderne also stages regular temporary exhibitions. The museums are very well set out, guiding the visitor easily through the full collection or, if time is short, directly to the art era of special interest. Each section is highly accessible, as both museums are divided into different coloured routes which relate to the art of each century, taking the visitor through galleries representing the varied schools of art by period.

Flemish still life, *Vase of Flowers* (1704) by Rachel Ruysch

THE BLUE ROUTE

THIS ROUTE leads visitors through a large display of works dating mostly from the 15th and 16th centuries. In the first few rooms are works by the renowned Flemish Primitive School (*see p14*). As is the case with much painting of the Middle Ages, the pictures are chiefly religious in nature and depict a variety of biblical scenes and details from the lives of saints. A work of particular note is *The Annunciation* by the Master of Flémalle, which shows the Archangel Gabriel appearing to the Virgin Mary as she sits at her fireside in a typically Flemish parlour. Also on display are a number of pictures by Rogier van der Weyden, the most famous of all the Flemish Primitive artists and city painter to Brussels during the mid-15th century; of note is his version of the

Lamentation. The work of Bruges artist Hans Memling is mostly shown in his native city, but his *The Martyrdom of Saint Sebastian* is found here.

The most important works in this collection are the paintings by the Brueghels, father and son. Both were renowned for their scenes of peasant life, and on display are *The Bird Trap* (1565) by Pieter Brueghel the Elder, and *The Village Wedding* (1607) by his son, Pieter.

Also on view are beautiful tapestries and the Delporte Collection, which groups sculpture, paintings and *objets d'art* from around the world.

THE BROWN ROUTE

THE SECOND route wends its way through the works of the 17th and 18th centuries. The rooms are wider and taller here in order to house the larger canvases of that time.

A highlight of the route is the world-famous collection of works by Pieter Paul Rubens (1557–1640), which affords a fine overview of the artist's work. As well as key examples of his religious works, there are some excellent portraits, such as *Hélène Fourment*, a portrait of his young wife. Of special interest are the sketches and paintings made in preparation for Rubens' larger works, such as *Four Negro Heads*, a work made in preparation of the 1620 *Adoration of the Magi.*

Other works of note in this section are the paintings by Old Masters such as van Dyck's *Portrait of a Genoese Lady with her Daughter* of the 1620s and Frans Hals' *Three Children with Goatcart*, as well as several paintings by representatives of later Flemish schools, including Jacob Jordaens and his depiction of myths, such as *Pan and Syrinx* (c.1645) and *Satyr and Peasant.* Baroque and Flemish art are all well represented on the tour, a journey through the best painting of the time.

Also on display are some small sculptures which were studies of larger works by Laurent Delvaux, a leading sculptor of the 18th century, particularly *Hercules and Erymanthian Boar*, a study for the sculpture by the staircase in the Palais de Charles de Lorraine (*see p61*).

Works of the Italian, Spanish and French schools of this era are also represented, notably a depiction by Claude Le Lorrain in 1672 of the classical poetic scene *Aeneas hunting the Stag on the Coast of Libya.*

Lamentation (c. 1420–50) by Rogier van der Weyden

THE YELLOW ROUTE

THIS SECTION covers the 19th century and is closer to the contemporary collection both in position and period. It is an informed introduction to the cutting-edge displays nearby.

The works along the yellow route vary greatly in style and subject matter, from Romanticism, exemplified by David, and Neo-Classicism, to Realism and Symbolism. There are, as in the other sections, examples of work by artists from outside Belgium, including Pierre Bonnard's *Nude against the Light* (1907), Edouard Vuillard's *Two Schoolchildren* (1894) and Monet's *Sunset at Etretat* (1885), but once again most emphasis is on Belgian artists.

Social realist artist Constantin Meunier (1831–1905) is represented by many of his sculptures, including *Firedamp* (1888). Much of the work of James Ensor (1890–1949) remains in his native city Ostend, but many of his macabre works are displayed here, such as *Scandalized Masks* (1883) and *Two Skeletons Fighting over a Pickled Herring* (1891). This section also offers the chance to see pictures by artists who are less well known outside Belgium, such as Henri Evenepoel (1872–99) whose lively Arab scene *Orange Market at Blidah* (1898) provides a contrast to the stark works of painters such as Ensor. The work of Impressionist Emile Claus is of value to followers of the movement. Of local interest is the landscape of Brussels by van Moer, painted in 1868,

Le Joueur Secret (1927) by Magritte

which clearly shows the River Senne before it was covered over for hygiene reasons. Moving from the passion of Romanticism to grim industrial realism and gentle Impressionism, this survey is definitive.

The underground Sculpture Gallery, with carvings and bronzes

THE ORANGE ROUTE

ANYONE WITH an interest in sculpture should follow this route down to the lower ground level in the Musée d'art ancien. Here, 18th- and 19th-century stone, marble and bronze Belgian sculpture is displayed alongside an exhibition explaining various methods behind many of the works on show, from carving to casting and burnishing in the materials of past centuries. There is also access to a sculpture terrace from outside the entrance of the Musée d'art ancien.

Death of Marat (1793) by David, **a leading work on the yellow route**

THE GREEN ROUTE

THE COLLECTION of modern art is wide and varied and includes works by well-known 20th-century painters from Belgium and around the world. There is no clearly defined route to follow within this section, nor are the exhibits strictly grouped by period or movement, so it is best to wander through the collection, stopping at areas of interest.

There are a number of works by the leading Belgian artists of the 20th century, such as Fauvist painter Rik Wouters' (1882–1916) *The Flautist* (1914). International artists include Matisse, Paul Klee and Chagall. But the real draw for most people is the collection of pictures by the Belgian Surrealists, in particular René Magritte (1898–1967). His best-known paintings, including *The Domain of Arnheim* (1962), are on display here. Another noted Surrealist, Paul Delvaux, is also well represented with works such as *Evening Train* (1957) and *Pygmalion* (1939).

Belgian art of the 20th century tends to be severe and stark, but the postwar *Jeune Peinture Belge* school reintroduced colour in an abstract way and is represented in works such as Marc Mendelson's 1950s *Toccata et fugue*.

Sculpture highlights in this section include Ossip Zadkine's totem pole-like *Diana* (1937) and Henry Moore's *Draped Woman on Steps* (1957–8).

Busy café scene at Place du Grand Sablon

Place du Grand Sablon ⓫

Map 2 D4. 🚌 *34, 48, 96.* 🚊 *92, 93, 94.* Ⓜ *Gare Centrale, Louise.*

Sᴵᴛᴜᴀᴛᴇᴅ ᴏɴ the slope of the escarpment that divides Brussels in two, the Place du Grand Sablon is like a stepping stone between the upper and lower halves of the city. The name "sablon" derives from the French "*sable*" (sand) and the square is so-called because this old route down to the city centre once passed through sandy marshes.

Today the picture is very different. The square, more of a triangle in shape, stretches from a 1751 fountain by Jacques Berge at its base uphill to the Gothic church of Notre-Dame du Sablon. This is a chic, wealthy and busy part of Brussels, an area of up-market antiques dealers, fashionable restaurants and trendy bars, which come into their own in warm weather when people stay drinking outside until the early hours. Wittamer, at No. 12, is a justifiably well-known *patisserie* and chocolate shop which also has a tea room on the first floor.

Every weekend the area near the church plays host to a lively and thriving, if rather expensive, antiques market. At No. 40 the old **Musée des postes et des telécommunications** houses a vast collection of letterboxes, uniforms and antique telephones. Set up in 1516 by the Tour et Taxis family, the postal service was useful for its political power, and later became Europe's first international postal service.

🏛 **Musée des postes et des telécommunications**
Place du Grand Sablon 40, 1000 BRU. 📞 *(02) 511 7740.* 🕐 *10am–4:30pm Tue–Sat, 11am–4pm Sun.* ⬤ *Mon, public hols.* 🖼

Notre-Dame au Sablon ⓬

Rue Bodenbroeck 6, 1000 BRU.
Map 2 D4. 📞 *(02) 511 5741.* 🚊 *92, 93, 94.* Ⓜ *Gare Centrale, Louise.* 🕐 *8am–6pm Mon–Fri, 10am–7pm Sat & Sun.* ♿ 📷 *on request.*

Aʟᴏɴɢ ᴡɪᴛʜ ᴛʜᴇ Cathédrale Sts Michel et Gudule (*see p70–71*), this lovely church is one of the finest remaining examples of Brabant Gothic architecture in Belgium.

A church was first erected here when the guild of cross-bowmen was granted permission to build a chapel to Our Lady on this sandy hill. Legend has it that a young girl in Antwerp had a vision of the Virgin Mary who instructed her to take her statue to Brussels. The girl carried the statue of the Virgin to Brussels down the Senne river by boat and gave it to the crossbowmen's chapel, which rapidly became a place of pilgrimage. Work to enlarge the church began

Notre-Dame du Sablon window

around 1400 but, due to lack of funds, was not actually completed until 1550.

The interior of the church is simple but beautifully proportioned, with inter-connecting side chapels and an impressive pulpit dating from 1697. Of particular interest, however, are the 11 magnificent stained-glass windows, 14 m (45 ft) high, which dominate the inside of the church. As the church is lit from the inside, they shine out at night across the Rue de la Régence like welcoming beacons. Also worth a visit is the chapel of the Tour et Taxis family, whose mansion once stood near the Place du Petit Sablon. In 1517 the family had tapestries commissioned to commemorate the legend that led to the chapel becoming a place of pilgrimage. Some now hang in the Musées Royaux d'art et d'histoire in Parc du Cinquantenaire (*see p75*), but others were stolen by the French Revolutionary army in the 1790s.

The magnificent interior of the church of Notre-Dame du Sablon

Place du Petit Sablon ⓭

Map 2 D4. 🚌 *20, 34, 48, 96.* 🚊 *92, 93, 94.* Ⓜ *Gare Centrale, Louise.*

Tʜᴇsᴇ ᴘʀᴇᴛᴛʏ, formal gardens were laid out in 1890 and are a charming spot to stop for a rest. On top of the railings that enclose the gardens are 48 bronze statuettes by Art Nouveau artist Paul Hankar, each one representing a different medieval guild of the city.

One of the lavish fountains in the gardens of Petit Sablon

At the back of the gardens is a fountain built to commemorate Counts Egmont and Hornes, the martyrs who led a Dutch uprising against the tyrannical rule of the Spanish under Philip II, and were beheaded in the Grand Place in 1568 (*see p31*). On either side of the fountain are 12 further statues of 15th- and 16th-century figures, including Bernard van Orley, whose stained-glass windows grace the city's cathedral. Gerhard Mercator, the Flemish geographer and mapmaker, whose 16th-century projection of the world forms the basis of most modern maps, is also featured.

Statue of Peter Pan in Palais d'Egmont gardens

has twice been rebuilt, in 1750 and again in 1891, following a fire. Today it belongs to the Belgian Foreign Ministry. It was here that Great Britain, Denmark and Ireland signed as members of the EEC in 1972.

Though the palace itself is closed to the public, the gardens, whose entrances are on the Rue du Grand Cerf and the Boulevard de Waterloo, are open. There is a statue of Peter Pan, a copy of one found in Kensington Gardens, in London. Many of the gardens' buildings are now run down, and plans have started to restore the ancient orangery and the disused ice house.

Palais d'Egmont **⑭**

Rue aux Laines, 1000 BRU.
Map 2 E4. 🚌 *34.* 🚋 *91, 92, 93, 94.* Ⓜ *Louise.* ♿

THE PALAIS d'Egmont (also known as the Palais d'Arenberg) was originally built in the mid-16th century for Françoise of Luxembourg, mother of the 16th-century leader of the city's rebels, Count Egmont. This palace

Palais de Justice **⑮**

Place Poelaert 1, 1000 BRU. **Map** 1 C5.
📞 *(02) 508 6111.* 🚌 *34.* 🚋 *91, 92, 93, 94.* Ⓜ *Louise.* ⏰ *9am–noon, 1:30–4pm Mon–Fri.* ⬛ *Sat & Sun, public hols.* ♿ ✉ *on request.*

THE PALAIS DE JUSTICE rules the Brussels skyline and can be seen from almost any vantage point in the city. Of all the ambitious projects of King Léopold II, this was perhaps the grandest. It occupies an area larger than St Peter's Basilica in Rome, and was one of the world's most impressive 19th-century buildings. It was built between 1866 and 1883 by architect Joseph Poelaert who looked for inspiration in classical temples, but sadly died mid-construction in 1879. The Palais de Justice is still home to the city's law courts.

Detail of a cornice at the Palais de Justice

Galerie Bortier **⑯**

Rue de la Madeleine 55, 1000 BRU.
Map 2 D3. 🚋 20, 38. 🚌 92, 93,
94. Ⓜ *Gare Centrale.* ◯ *9am–6pm
Mon–Sat.* ◯ *Sun, public hols.* ♿

G ALERIE BORTIER is the only
shopping arcade in the
city dedicated solely to book
and map shops, and it has
become the haunt of students,
enthusiasts and researchers
looking for secondhand French
books and antiquarian finds.

The land on which the
gallery stands was originally
owned by a Monsieur Bortier,
whose idea it was to have a
covered arcade lined with
shops on either side. He put

160,000 francs of his own
money into the project, quite
a considerable sum in the
1840s. The 65-m (210-ft) long
Galérie Bortier was built in
1848 and was designed by
Jean-Pierre Cluysenaar, the
architect of the Galéries St-
Hubert nearby (*see p47*). The
Galérie Bortier opened along
with the then-adjacent Marché
de la Madeleine, but the latter
was unfortunately destroyed
by developers in 1958.

A complete restoration of
Galérie Bortier was ordered by
the Ville de Bruxelles in 1974.
The new architects kept strictly
to Cluysenaar's plans and
installed a replacement glass
and wrought-iron roof made

to the original 19th-century
Parisian style. The Rue de la
Madeleine itself also offers
plenty of browsing material
for bibliophiles and art lovers.

**Crammed interior of a bookshop
at the Galérie Bortier**

Cathédrale Sts Michel et Gudule **⑰**

T HE CATHEDRALE Sts Michel et Gudule is the national
church of Belgium, although it was only granted
cathedral status in 1962. It is the finest surviving example
of Brabant Gothic architecture. There has been a church
on the site of the cathedral since at least the 11th
century. Work began on the Gothic cathedral in 1226
under Henry I, Duke of Brabant, and continued over a
period of 300 years. It was finally completed with the
construction of two front towers at the beginning of
the 16th century under Charles V. The cathedral is
made of a sandy limestone, brought from local
quarries. The interior is very bare;
this is due to Protestant iconoclast
ransacking in 1579–80 and thefts
by French revolutionists in
1783. It was fully restored and
cleaned in the 1990s and
now reveals its splendour.

The twin towers rise above
the city. Unusually, they were
designed as a pair in the
1400s; Brabant architecture
typically has only one.

★ **Last Judgement window**
*At the front of the cathedral,
facing the altar, is a magnificent stained-glass window of
1528 depicting Christ awaiting
saved souls. Its vivid reds, blues
and yellows place it in the 16th-
century style. The Renaissance
panes are surrounded by later
Baroque garlands of flowers.*

STAR SIGHTS

★ **Last Judgement
window**

★ **Baroque pulpit**

Romanesque remains of
the first church here, dating
from 1047, were discovered
during renovation work.
They can be seen and
toured in the crypt.

Chapelle de la Madeleine ⑱

Rue de la Madeleine, 1000 BRU.
Map 2 D3. 🄲 *(02) 511 2845.*
🚌 *20, 38.* 🚋 *92, 93, 94.* Ⓜ *Gare Centrale.* ⭘ *7am–7pm Mon–Sat; 7am–noon, 5pm–8pm Sun.* ♿

THIS LITTLE church once stood on the site now occupied by the Gare Centrale, but it was moved, stone by stone, further down the hill to make way for the construction of the Art Deco-style station and its car park during the early 1950s.

The 17th-century façade of the church has been restored. The original 15th-century interior has been replaced by

A view of the Chapelle de la Madeleine with restored brickwork

a plain, modest decor, with simple stone pillars and modern stained-glass windows. Off the regular tourist track, the

chapel is used by people as a quiet place for worship. The Baroque chapel which was once attached has now gone.

The transept windows represent the rulers of Belgium in 1538. Jan Haeck made the designs after Bernard van Orley's sketches.

Sainte Gudule
This 7th-century saint is very dear to the people of Brussels. Her relics were scattered to the winds by ransacking Protestants in 1579, but this only served to reinforce her cult.

VISITORS' CHECKLIST

Parvis Ste-Gudule, 1000 BRU.
Map 2 E2. 🄲 *(02) 217 8345, 219 1170.* 🚌 *65, 66.* 🚋 *92, 93, 94.* Ⓜ *Gare Centrale.* ⭘ *8am–6pm daily.* ♿ *to crypt.* ✝ *regular services throughout the day.* ♿ *on request.*

The Statue of St Michael is the cathedral's symbol of its links with the city. While the gilded plaster statue is not itself historically exceptional, its long heritage is; the patron saint of Brussels, the Archangel St Michael is shown killing the dragon, symbolic of his protection of the city.

The Lectern

★ **Baroque pulpit**
The flamboyantly carved pulpit in the central aisle is the work of an Antwerp-born sculptor, Henri-François Verbruggen. Designed in 1699, it was finally installed in 1776.

The Art Nouveau façade of No. 11 Square Ambiorix

Square Ambiorix ⑲

Map 3 B2. 🚌 54, 63. Ⓜ *Schuman.*

Close to the EU district, but totally different in style and spirit, lies the beautiful Square Ambiorix. Together with the Avenue Palmerston and the Square Marie-Louise below that, this marshland was transformed in the 1870s into one of the loveliest residential parts of Brussels, with a large central area of gardens, ponds and fountains.

The elegant houses, some Art Nouveau, some older, have made this one of the truly sought-after suburbs in the city. The most spectacular Art Nouveau example is at No. 11. Known as the Maison St Cyr after the painter

The Justus Lipsius, the pink granite EU Council building

whose home it once was, this wonderfully ornate house, with its curved wrought-iron balustrades and balconies, is a fine architectural feat considering that the man who designed it, Gustave Strauven, was only 22 years old when it was built at the turn of the 20th century.

Quartier Européen ⑳

Map 3 B3. 🚌 20, 54. Ⓜ *Maelbeek.*

The area at the top of the Rue de la Loi and around the Schuman roundabout is where the main buildings of the European Union's administration are found.

The most recognizable of all the EU seats is the star-shaped Berlaymont building, now nearing completion following the removal of large quantities of poisonous asbestos discovered in its structure. The Berlaymont, formerly the headquarters of the European Commission, will continue to be modernized and refurbished until further notice. The commission workers (the civil servants of the EU) are at present dotted around the area. The Council of Ministers, which comprises representatives of member-states' governments, now meets in the sprawling pink granite block across the road from the Berlaymont, known as Justus Lipsius, after a Flemish philosopher. Further down the road from the Justus Lipsius building is the Résidence Palace, a luxury 1920s housing complex that boasts a theatre, a pool and a roof garden as well as several floors of private flats. It

now houses the International Press Centre. Only the theatre is now open to the public, but EU officials are allowed into the Art Deco swimming pool.

This area is naturally full of life and bustle during the day, but much quieter in the evenings and can feel almost deserted at weekends. What is pleasant for both workers and visitors, though, is the close proximity of the city's green spaces including Parc Léopold, Parc du Cinquantenaire (*see pp 74–5*) and the verdant Square Ambiorix.

Paintings and sculpture on show in the Musée Wiertz gallery

Musée Wiertz ㉑

Rue Vautier 62, 1000 BRU. **Map** 3 A4. 🎧 *(02) 648 1718.* 🚌 *34, 80.* Ⓜ *Maelbeek, Schuman, Trone.* ⏰ *10am– noon, 1–5pm Tue –Fri; every 2nd weekend.* ⬤ *Mon, weekends Jul–Aug, public hols.* 📷

Musée Wiertz houses some 160 works, including oil paintings, drawings and sculptures, that form the main body of Antoine Wiertz's (1806–65) artistic output. The collection fills the studio built for Wiertz by the Belgian state, where he lived and worked from 1850 until his death in 1865, when the studio became a museum.

The huge main room contains Wiertz's largest paintings, many depicting biblical and Homeric scenes, some in the style of Rubens. Also on display are sculptures and his death mask. The last of the six rooms contains two of his more gruesome efforts, one a scene of poverty entitled *Madness, Hunger and Crime.*

A tall European parliament building rising up behind the trees of Parc Léopold in the Parliament Quarter

Parliament Quarter 22

Map 3 A4. 🚌 20, 54, 80.
Ⓜ Maelbeek, Schuman.

THE VAST, MODERN, steel-and-glass complex, situated just behind Quartier Léopold train station, is one of three homes of the European Parliament, the elected body of the EU. Its permanent seat is in Strasbourg, France, where the plenary sessions are held once a month. The administrative centre is in Luxembourg and the committee meetings are held in Brussels.

This gleaming state-of-the-art building has many admirers, not least the parliamentary workers and MEPs themselves, who were proud of what was at one point the largest building site in Europe. But it also has its critics: the huge domed structure housing the hemicycle that seats the 600-plus MEPs has been dubbed the "*caprices des dieux*" ("whims of the gods"), which refers both to the shape of the building which is similar to a French cheese of the same name, and to its lofty aspirations. Many people also regret that, to make room for the new complex, a large part of Quartier Léopold has been lost. Though there are still plenty of restaurants and bars, a lot of the charm has gone. When the MEPs are absent, the building is often used for meetings of European Union committees.

Institut Royal des Sciences Naturelles 23

Rue Vautier 29, 1000 BRU. **Map** 3 A4.
☎ (02) 627 4238. 🚌 34, 80.
Ⓜ Maelbeek, Schuman. ⏱ 9:30am–4:45pm Tue–Fri, 10am–6pm Sat & Sun. ● Mon, 1 Jan, 1 May, 25 Dec.
◪ ◪ ⚹ ▭ ▯

THE INSTITUT Royal des Sciences Naturelles is best known for its fine collection of iguanadon skeletons dating back 250 million years. The museum also contains interactive and educational displays covering all aspects and evolutionary eras of natural history.

Parc Léopold 24

Rue Belliard. **Map** 3 B4. 🚌 20, 59.
Ⓜ Maelbeek.

PARC LEOPOLD occupies part of the grounds of an old estate and a walk around its lake follows the old path of the Maelbeek river which was covered over in the 19th-century for reasons of hygiene.

At the end of the 19th century, scientist and industrialist Ernest Solvay put forward the idea of a science park development. Solvay was given the Parc Léopold, the site of a zoo since 1847, and set up five university centres here. Leading figures including Marie Curie and Albert Einstein met here to discuss new scientific issues. The park is still home to many scientific institutes, as well as a haven of peace in the heart of this busy political area.

Whale skeleton inside the Institut Royal des Sciences Naturelles

Parc du Cinquantenaire 🄬

★ **Musée de l'Armée**
Opened in 1923, the museum covers all aspects of Belgium's military history, and exhibits over 200 years of militaria. Historic aircraft are on display in the hall next door.

Musée de l'Armée gun

THE FINEST OF LEOPOLD II's grand projects, the Parc and Palais du Cinquantenaire were built for the Golden Jubilee celebrations of Belgian independence in 1880. The park was laid out on unused town marshes. The palace, at its entrance, was to comprise a triumphal arch and two large exhibition areas, but by the time of the 1880 Art and Industry Expo, only the two side exhibition areas had been completed. Further funds were eventually found, and work continued for 50 years. Before being converted into museums, the large halls on either side of the central archway were used to hold trade fairs, the last of which was in 1935. They have also been used for horse races and to store homing pigeons. During World War II, the grounds of the park were used to grow vegetables to feed the Brussels people.

View of Park with Arch
Based on the Arc de Triomphe in Paris, the arch was not completed in time for the 50th Anniversary celebrations but was finished in 1905.

The Grand Mosque was built in Arabic style as a folly in 1880. It became a mosque in 1978.

Tree-lined Avenue
In part formal garden, part forested walks, many of the plantations of elms and plane trees date from 1880.

Pavillon Horta

Underpass

STAR SIGHTS

★ **Musées Royaux d'Art et d'Histoire**

★ **Musée de l'Armée**

0 metres   100

0 yards   100

The Central Archway
Conceived as a gateway into the city, the arch is crowned by the symbolic bronze sculpture Brabant Raising the National Flag.

VISITORS' CHECKLIST

Ave de Tervuren, 1040 BRU. **Map**
3 C3. 🚌 *28, 36, 67.* 🚊 *81, 82.*
Ⓜ *Schuman, Mérode.* ♿ 🚻
Autoworld: *(02) 736 4165.*
🕐 *10am–5pm daily (Apr–Sep:
to 6pm).* ● *1 Jan, 25 Dec.* 💳
♿ 🚻 **The Grand Mosque:**
(02) 735 2173. 🕐 *10am–6pm
daily. Please dress with respect.*

Autoworld
Housed in the south wing of the Cinquantenaire Palace, Autoworld is one of the best collections of automobiles in the world. There are some 300 cars, including an 1886 motor, and a 1924 Model-T Ford that still runs.

The park is popular with Brussels' Eurocrats and families at lunchtimes and weekends.

★ **Musées Royaux d'Art et d'Histoire**
Belgian architect Bordiau's plans for the two exhibition halls, later permanent showcases, were partly modelled on London's Victorian museums. The use of iron and glass in their construction was inspired by the Crystal Palace.

Musées Royaux d'Art et d'Histoire
Parc du Cinquantenaire 10. 📞 *(02)
741 7211.* 🕐 *9:30am–5pm Tue–Sun
(from 10am Sun and pub hols).* ● *1
Jan, 1 May, 1 & 11 Nov, 25 Dec.* 💳

Also known as the Musée du Cinquantenaire, this excellent museum has occupied its present site since the early 1900s, but the history of the collections goes back as far as the 15th century, and the quantity of exhibits is vast. Sections on ancient civilizations include Egypt and Greece, and also Persia and the Near East. Other displays feature Byzantium and Islam, China and the Indian Subcontinent, and the Pre-Columbian civilizations of the Americas. There are decorative arts from all ages, with glassware, silverware and porcelain as well as a fine collection of lace and tapestries. Religious sculptures and stained glass are displayed around a courtyard in the style of church cloisters.

**The aircraft display at the Musée
Royal de l'Armée**

Musée Royal de l'Armée et d'Histoire Militaire
Parc du Cinquantenaire 3.
📞 *(02) 737 7811.* 🕐 *9am–noon,
1–4:30pm Tue–Sun.* ● *Mon, 1 Jan,
1 May, 1 Nov, 25 Dec.*

Together with the section on aviation, displays cover the Belgian Army and its history from the late 1700s to today, including weapons, uniforms, decorations and paintings. There is a section covering the 1830 struggle for independence *(see p34–5)*. Two new sections show both World Wars, including the activities of the Resistance.

GREATER BRUSSELS

PAST THE heart-shaped ring-road of Brussels city centre lie 19 suburbs (*communes*) which form the Bruxelles-Capitale region. While many are residential, a handful are definitely worth the short ride to sample outlying treasures of Brussels' fascinating history. For fans of early 20th-century architecture, the suburb of St-Gilles offers numerous original examples of striking Art Nouveau buildings including Musée Horta. In Koekelberg and visible from the Upper Town is the huge Sacré-Coeur basilica, started

Detail from annexe of Chinese Pavilion, Laeken

in 1904. To the north, Heysel offers attractions whose modernity contrasts with the historical city centre. The 1958 Atomium, now restored, stands next to the Bruparck theme park. To the east, the Central Africa Museum reflects Belgium's colonial past in the Congo, and the tram museum takes a journey through Brussels' urban past. Peace and tranquillity can be found close to the metropolis, in the orderly landscape of Royal Laeken and the lush open spaces of the Bois de la Cambre and the Fôret de Soignes.

SIGHTS AT A GLANCE

Churches and Cathedrals
Basilique Nationale du
  Sacré-Coeur ❽

Historic Monuments, Buildings and Districts
Anderlecht ❼
Avenue Louise ❷
Ixelles ❹
St-Gilles ❸
Uccle ❻

Parks and Gardens
Bruparck ⓭
*Domaine de Laeken
  see pp82–3* ⓫
Fôret de Soignes ❺

Museums and Exhibition Areas
The Atomium ⓬
Musée Horta see p78 ❶
Musée du Tram ❾

Musée Royal de
  l'Afrique Centrale ❿

KEY
▦	Central Brussels
▢	Greater Brussels
✈	Airport
▬	Major Road
▭	Minor Road

Musée Horta ●

VISITORS' CHECKLIST

Rue Américaine 23–25, 1060
BRU. ☎ (02) 543 0490. ▣ 54.
▣ 81, 82, 91, 92. Ⓜ Albert,
Louise. ◯ 2–5:30pm Tue–Sun.
● Mon, public hols.

ARCHITECT VICTOR HORTA (1861–1947) is considered by many to be the father of Art Nouveau, and his impact on Brussels architecture is unrivalled by any other designer of his time. A museum dedicated to his unique style is today housed in his restored family home, which he designed from 1898 to 1901. His skill lay not only in his grand, overall vision but in his equal talent as an interior designer, blending themes and materials into each detail. The airy interior of the building displays trademarks of the architect's style – iron, glass and curves – in every detail, while retaining a functional approach.

Art Nouveau candelabra

★ Central Staircase
Decorated with curved wrought iron, the stairs are enhanced further by mirrors and glass, bringing natural light into the house.

The bedroom
features Art Nouveau furniture, including a wardrobe inlaid with pale and dark wood.

★ Dining Room
White enamel tiles line the walls, rising to an ornate ceiling, decorated with the scrolled metalwork used in other rooms.

Madame Horta's sitting-room features blue-and-cream wool rugs woven to Horta's design, and a marble fireplace.

Front Entrance

Living Room
The detail of Horta's work can be best seen here, from sculpted bannister ends to finely wrought door handles that echo larger forms.

STAR FEATURES

★ Central Staircase

★ Dining Room

Exclusive boutique in the chic Avenue Louise

Avenue Louise ❷

Map 2 D5. 🚋 34, 54. 🚎 93, 94.
Ⓜ Louise.

MOST VISITORS to Brussels travelling by car will come across this busy thoroughfare, its various underpasses constructed in the 1950s and 1960s to link up the city centre with its suburbs. In fact, the avenue was constructed in 1864 to join the centre with the suburb of Ixelles. However, the north end of the avenue retains a chic atmosphere; by the Porte de Namur, fans of designer labels can indulge themselves in Gucci and Versace, as well as investigating the less expensive but no less chic boutiques.

The avenue also has its architectural treasures. The **Hôtel Solvay** at No. 224 was built by Victor Horta in 1894 for the industrialist Solvay family. Its ornate doorway, columns and balconies are a fine example of Art Nouveau style *(see p16–17)*. The house is still a private home. At No. 346, **Hôtel Max Hallet** is one of Horta's masterpieces, built in 1903. Continuing south leads to the peaceful atmosphere of Ixelles and its parkland.

St-Gilles ❸

🚋 20, 48. 🚎 23, 55, 90.
Ⓜ Porte de Hal, Parvis St-Gilles.

NAMED AFTER THE patron saint of this district's main church, St-Gilles is traditionally one of Brussels' poorer areas. However, amid the low-quality functional housing are architectural survivors which make the suburb well worth a visit. Art Nouveau and *sgraffiti* gems *(see p17)* can be found in streets such as Avenue Jean Volders and Rue Vanderschrick. The **Hôtel Hannon** (1902), now a photography gallery, remains one of the city's most spectacular Art Nouveau structures. Restored in 1985, it has a stained-glass window and ornate statuary that take this architectural style to its peak *(see p16)*.
Art Nouveau details can be seen in the nearby streets, particularly in Rue Felix Delhasse and Rue Africaine.

One of the most striking features of St-Gilles is the **Porte de Hal**. Brussels' second set of town walls, built in the 14th century, originally included seven gateways, of which Porte de Hal is the only survivor *(see p12)*. Used as a prison from the 16th to 18th centuries, it escaped the modernizing influence of the Austrian Emperor Joseph. Restored in 1870, it is now a small museum of folk art, including a collection of 19th-century toys.

🏛 Hôtel Hannon
Ave de la Jonction 1, BRU 1060.
🅲 (02) 538 4220. Ⓜ Albert.
🏛 Porte de Hal
Blvds de Midi & de Waterloo, BRU 1000. 🅲 (02) 534 1518.
⬤ for renovation until further notice.

Art Nouveau detail on façade in Rue Africaine

Ixelles ❹

🚋 54, 71, 95, 96. 🚎 81, 82, 93, 94.
Ⓜ Porte de Namur.

ALTHOUGH ONE of Brussels' largest suburbs and a busy transport junction, the heart of Ixelles remains a peaceful oasis of lakes and woodland.

The idyllic **Abbaye de la Cambre** was founded in 1201, achieving fame and a degree of fortune in 1242, when Saint Boniface chose the site for his retirement. The abbey then endured a troubled history in the wars of religion during the 16th and 17th centuries. It finally closed as an operational abbey in 1796 and now houses a school of architecture. The abbey's pretty Gothic church can be toured and its grassy grounds and courtyards offer a peaceful walk.

South of the abbey, the Bois de la Cambre remains one of the city's most popular public parks. Created in 1860, it achieved popularity almost immediately when royalty promenaded its main route. Lakes, bridges and lush grass make it a favoured picnic site.
The **Musée Communal d'Ixelles** nearby has a fine collection of posters by 19th- and 20th-century greats, such as Toulouse Lautrec and Magritte, as well as sculptures by Rodin. The former home of one of Belgium's finest sculptors is now **Musée Constantin Meunier**, with 170 sculptures and 120 paintings by the artist, and his studio preserved in its turn-of-the-century style.

🏛 Abbaye de la Cambre
Ave de Général de Gaulle, BRU 1050.
🅲 (02) 648 1121. ⬤ 9am–noon, 3–6:30pm daily. ⬤ public hols.
🏛 Musée Communal d'Ixelles
Rue J Van Volsem 71, BRU 1050.
🅲 (02) 511 0984. ⬤ 1–6:30pm Tue–Fri, 10am–5pm Sat–Sun.
⬤ Mon, public hols.
🏛 Musée Constantin Meunier
Rue de l'Abbaye 59, BRU 1050.
🅲 (02) 648 4449. ⬤ 10am–noon, 1–5pm Tue–Sun. ⬤ Mon, public hols.

The Forêt de Soignes, once a royal hunting ground and now a park

Forêt de Soignes ❺

🚌 71, 72. 🚋 23, 90. Ⓜ Demey, Hermann Debroux. ✔ Thu, Sun. 🎫 (02) 215 1740.

THE LARGE FORESTED area to the southeast of Brussels' city centre has a long history: thought to have had prehistoric beginnings, it was also here that the Gallic citizens suffered their defeat by the Romans (see p29). However, the forest really gained renown in the 12th century when wild boar roamed the landscape, and local dukes enjoyed hunting trips in the woodland.

The density of the landscape has provided tranquillity over the ages. In the 14th and 15th centuries it became a favoured location for monasteries and abbeys. Few have survived, but Abbaye de Rouge-Cloître is a rare example from this era.

In a former 18th-century priory is the **Groenendaal Arboretum**, in which more than 400 forest plants are housed, many of which are extinct elsewhere. The most common sight, however, is the locals enjoying a stroll.

🌿 **Groenendaal Arboretum**
Duboislaan 14, 1560 BRU.
🎫 (02) 657 0386.
🕐 8:30am–5pm, Mon–Fri.

Uccle ❻

🚌 49, 50. 🚋 18, 52.

UCCLE IS A smart residential district, nestling in its tree-lined avenues. Not immediately a tourist destination, it is worthwhile taking a trip to the

Musée David et Alice Buuren. The 1920s residence of this Dutch couple is now a small private museum, displaying their eclectic acquisitions. Amid the Dutch Delft-ware and French Lalique lamps are great finds, such as original sketches by Van Gogh. Visitors will also enjoy the modern landscaped gardens at the rear.

🏛 **Musée David et Alice Buuren**
Ave Léo Errera 41, 1180 BRU. 🎫 (02) 343 4851. 🕐 1–5:45pm Sun, 2–5:45pm Mon. Group visits by appointment. ● 24–31 Dec. ✔

Anderlecht ❼

🚌 63, 89. 🚋 82. Ⓜ Bizet, Clemenceau.

CONSIDERED to be Brussels' first genuine suburb (archaeological digs have uncovered remnants of Roman housing), Anderlecht is now best known

Mirò-style drawings, Anderlecht

as an industrial area, for its meat market, and its successful football club of the same name. Despite this, the Modernist Spanish painter Joan Mirò added a unique artistic contribution inspiring bright cartoon-like murals on Rue Porcelaine.

Although only a few pockets of the suburb are now residential, during the 15th century this was a popular place of abode and some houses remain from that era. **Maison Erasme**, built in 1468, is now named after the great scholar and religious reformer, Erasmus (1466–1536), who lived here for five months in 1521. The house was restored in the 1930s. Now a museum dedicated to the most respected thinker of his generation, it displays a collection of 16th-century furniture and portraits of the great humanist by Holbein and van der Weyden.

Nearby is the huge edifice of **Eglise Sts-Pierre-et-Guidon**. This 14th-century Gothic church, completed with the addition of a tower in 1517, is notable for its sheer size and exterior gables, typical of Brabant architecture. The life of St Guidon, patron saint of peasants, is depicted on interior wall murals.

Illustrating a more recent history, the **Musée Gueuze** is an operational family brewery that has opened its doors to the public to witness the production of classic Belgian beers such as lambic, gueuze and kriek (see pp142–3).

Maison Erasme in Anderlecht, with its courtyard and fountain

The Basilique Nationale du Sacré-Coeur rising over the city

🏛 **Maison Erasme**

Rue du Chapitre 31, 1070 BRU.
🔲 *(02) 521 1383.* ◯ *10am–5pm
Tue–Sun.* ⬤ *Mon, 1 Jan, 25 Dec.* 🖼

⛪ **Eglise Sts-Pierre-et-Guidon**

Place de la Vaillance, 1070 BRU.
◯ *9am–noon, 2:30–6pm Mon–Fri.*
⬤ *Sat & Sun.*

🏛 **Musée Gueuze**

Rue Gheude 56, 1070 BRU.
🔲 *(02) 521 4928.* ◯ *8:30am–5pm
Mon–Fri, 10am–5pm Sat.*
⬤ *Sun, public hols.* 🖼 *including 1
free beer.*

Basilique Nationale du Sacré-Coeur ❽

Parvis de la Basilique 1, Koekelberg,
1083 BRU. 🔲 *(02) 425 8822.*
Ⓜ *Simonis.* ▦ *87.* 🚆 *19.* ◯ *9am–
4pm (5pm summer), daily.*
🖼 *by appointment.*

Aᴌᴛʜᴏᴜɢʜ ᴀ small and
popular suburb among
Brussels' residents, there is
little for the visitor to see in
Koekelberg other than the
striking Basilique Nationale
du Sacré-Coeur, but this does
make the journey worthwhile
for those interested in the
best of Art Deco.

King Léopold II was keen
to build a church in the city
which could accommodate
vast congregations to reflect
the burgeoning population of
early 20th-century Brussels.

He commissioned the church
in 1904, although the building
was not finished until 1970.
Originally designed by Pierre
Langerock, the final construction, which uses sandstone
and terracotta, was the less
expensive adaptation by
Albert van Huffel. Very much
a 20th-century church, in
contrast to the many medieval
religious buildings in the city
centre, it is dedicated to those
who died for Belgium, in
particular the thousands of
Belgian soldiers who were
never to return from the two
world wars, killed in battles
fought on their own terrain.

The most dominating fea-
ture of the church is the vast
green copper dome, rising 90
m (295 ft) above ground. For
those who do not manage to
visit the church itself, it is this
central dome that is visible
from many points in the city,
including the Palais de Justice.

Musée du Tram ❾

Ave de Tervuren 364b, BRU 1150. 🔲
(02) 515 3108. 🚆 *39, 44.* ◯ *Apr–
Sep: 1:30pm–7pm Sat & Sun, pub hols.
Group tours possible. Every Sun and
pub hol, the museum organizes a tour
to Heysel (9:45am).* ⬤ *Oct–Mar.* 🖼

Tʜɪs ᴍᴜsᴇᴜᴍ traces the
history of public transport
in Belgium, with marvellous
displays of heritage machinery.
Horse-drawn trams are
available to transport visitors
round the site, which features
fully-working early versions of
the electric tram, buses and
plenty of interactive exhibits.

Musée Royal de l'Afrique Centrale ❿

Leuvensesteenweg 13, Tervuren 3080.
🔲 *(02) 769 5211.* ◯ *10am–
5pm Tue–Fri, 10am–6pm, Sat & Sun.*
⬤ *Mon, public hols.* 🖼

Iɴ ᴛʜᴇ 19th century, the
colony of the Belgian Congo
was Belgium's only territorial
possession. It was handed back
to self-government in 1960 and
eventually renamed Zaire (now
the Democratic Republic of
Congo). This museum, opened
in 1899, is a collection gleaned
from over 100 years of colonial
rule. Galleries show ceremonial African dress and masks,
and displays on colonial life.

Dugout canoes, pagan idols,
weapons and stuffed wildlife,
feature heavily. There is a
horrifying collection of conserved giant African insects,
much beloved by children.
The museum has been adding
constantly to its collection
and is now a memento to a
past way of life in the Congo.

The Musée Royal de l'Afrique Centrale façade in Tervuren

Domaine de Laeken ⓫

I**N THE 11TH CENTURY** Laeken became popular among
pilgrims after reported sightings of the Virgin Mary.
Since the 19th century, however, it has been firmly
etched in the minds of all Belgians as the residence of
the nation's monarchy. A walk around the sedate and
peaceful area reveals impressive buildings constructed
in honour of the royal location, not least the sovereign's
official residence and its beautifully landscaped parkland.
More surprising is the sudden Oriental influence. The
great builder, King Léopold II, wanted to create an architectural world tour; the Chinese and Japanese towers are
the only two buildings that came to fruition, but
show the scope of one monarch's vision.

★ **Pavillon Chinois**
*Architect Alexandre Marcel
designed this elaborate building in 1909; inside are examples of Oriental porcelain.*

**Tour
Japonais**

Parc de Laeken

Villa Belvedere
was once the resi-
dence of the Royal
Family, and is
now home to
the heir to
the throne.

**Monument
Léopold**
stands as the
focus of the
park complex
and layout. It
honours Léopold I,
first king of the
Belgians. Built in Neo-
Gothic style, it has
a filigree cast-iron
canopy and tracery
around the base.

Place de la Dynastie
is part of the attractive
park that was once the
Royal Family's private
hunting ground.

★ **Serres Royales**
*These late 19th-century glasshouses are home to
exotic trees, palms and camellias. Open to the public
annually in April, they are the King's private property.*

Château Royal
*The Belgian royal residence, in the
heart of the 160-ha (395-acre)
estate, was heavily restored in 1890,
with a façade by architect Poelaert
covering the 18th-century original.*

Domaine Royale de Laeken is the royal estate, adjacent to the Parc de Laeken in the city district of Laeken; the woodland features old magnolias and blooming hawthorns.

The Atomium rising 100 m (325 ft) over the Bruparck at dusk

The Atomium ⑫

Boulevard du Centenaire, 1020 BRU. 📞 (02) 474 8977. Ⓜ Heysel. 🕐 Apr–Aug: 9am–7:30pm; Sep–Mar: 10am–5:30pm. 📷

Bᵁᴵᴸᵀ ꜰᴏʀ ᴛʜᴇ 1958 World Fair (see p37), the Atomium is probably the most identifiable symbol of Brussels, as recognizable as the Eiffel Tower of Paris or the Coliseum in Rome. As the world moved into a new age of science and space travel at the end of the 1950s, so the design by André Waterkeyn reflected this with a structure of an iron atom, magnified 165 billion times. Now a small museum, each of the nine spheres that make up the "atom" are 18 m (60 ft) in diameter, and linked by escalators.

Bruparck ⑬

Boulevard du Centenaire, 1020 BRU. 📞 (02) 474 8377. 🚌 84, 89. 🚃 23, 81. Ⓜ Heysel. **Mini-Europe & Océade** 📞 (02) 478 0550 (Mini-Europe); (02) 478 4220 (Océade). 🕐 Apr–Sep: 9:30am–6pm daily (Jul–Aug: to midnight); Oct–mid-Jan: 10am–5pm daily. 🔒 end Jan–Mar. 📷 **Kinepolis** 📞 (02) 474 2600. 🕐 performances. 📷 for film screenings.

Aᴸᴛʜᴏᵁɢʜ ɴᴏᴡʜᴇʀᴇ near as large or as grand as many of the world's theme parks, Bruparck's sights and range of fast-food restaurants are always a popular family destination.
The first and favourite port of call for most visitors is Mini-Europe, where more than 300 miniature reconstructions take you around the landscapes of the European Union. Built at a scale of 1:25, the collection displays buildings of social or cultural importance, such as the Acropolis in Athens, the Brandenburg Gate of Berlin and the Houses of Parliament from London. Even at this scale the detail is such that it can be second only to visiting the sights themselves.

For film fans, Kinepolis cannot be beaten. Large auditoriums show a range of popular films from different countries on 29 screens. The IMAX cinema features surround sound and a semi-circular 600 sq m (6,456 sq ft) widescreen.

If warmth and relaxation are what you are looking for, Océade is a tropically heated water park, complete with giant slides, wave machines, bars, cafés and even realistic re-created sandy beaches.

London's Houses of Parliament in small scale at Mini-Europe

0 metres   250

0 yards   250

BEYOND BRUSSELS

Exploring Beyond Brussels

BELGIUM OCCUPIES one of the most densely populated parts of Europe, with a concentration of towns and villages across the flat landscapes of the Flemish plain. Along the North Sea coast there are fewer settlements, set among fertile farmland. To the north and west of Brussels are the three easy-to-reach towns of Antwerp, Ghent and Bruges which, with their ancient buildings and vibrant cultural life, are attractive destinations. East of Brussels is the charming university town of Leuven, and further on is the open-air museum of Bokrijk, whose restored buildings focus on the the history of the Flemish people.

Bronze statue of Silvius Brabo in Antwerp's Grote Markt

BRUGES 20

OOSTENDE
N34 N376 N49
N61
E40
E40 E17
GHENT 19 4 DENDERMOND
A25 A17
E17 OUDENAARDE
IEPER 17 KORTRIJK 18 PAJOTTENLAND 5
N60 N42
HALLE 6
RONSE E429
E429 16 ATH 15
TOURNAI N56
E19
MONS 14 N40

KEY

▨ Motorway

▨ Major road

▨ Minor road

▨ River

0 km   20

0 miles   20

View over Bruges from the Belfort

SIGHTS AT A GLANCE

GETTING AROUND

In Belgium distances are short, with a wide choice
of routes – even the tiniest village is easily reached.
Brussels sits at the hub of several major highways
such as the E19 and the E40 (which link the capital
to the country's principal towns). The fully integ-
rated public transport system has frequent train
services and a comprehensive bus network.

Namur's Citadel from the River Meuse

Street-by-Street: Antwerp **❶**

FANNING OUT FROM the east bank of the River Scheldt, Antwerp is Belgium's second-largest city. It is also the centre of the international diamond trade, which is run from the unassuming buildings that line the streets near Centraal Station. Today, the city's industries lie away from its medieval core whose narrow streets and fine buildings cluster around the cathedral and the Grote Markt. Most sites of interest are within easy walking distance of the Grote Markt whose surrounding streets house museums, shops and exuberant cafés and bars.

Gilt statue on guildhouse

Nationaal Scheepvaart-museum
This model of an 18th-century armed merchant ship is in Antwerp's Maritime Museum.

To Koninklijk Museum voor Schone Kunsten

The Vleeshuis
Occupied by the Butcher's Guild for three centuries, this beautiful 1504 building has striking layers of brick and stone that look like alternating strips of fat and lean meat.

The Ethnografisch Museum has artifacts from around the world.

Stadhuis

The Brabo Fountain
This statue, in the centre of the Grote Markt, depicts the fearless soldier, Silvius Brabo. Said to be the nephew of Julius Caesar, Brabo is shown throwing the hand of the mythical giant, Antigonius, into the River Scheldt.

KEY

- - - Suggested route

STAR SIGHTS

★ Grote Markt

★ Kathedraal

VISITORS' CHECKLIST

500,000. ✕ 6 km (3 miles) E of the city. ▣ Centraal, Pelikaanstraat. Franklin Rooseveltplaats. Steenplein. ℹ Grote Markt 15, (03) 232 0103.

Sint Pauluskerk

This imposing church was built in 1517, but has a magnificent Baroque gate and spire dating from the late 17th century. Inside, there is a noted collection of paintings, including one especially fine work by Rubens.

↓ To Centraal Station

★ Grote Markt

Antwerp's golden age of trade in the 16th century is reflected in the square's cosmopolitan 1565 town hall, built by architects from all over Europe.

★ Onze Lieve Vrouwe Kathedraal

The largest Gothic cathedral in Belgium, this building occupies a 1-ha (2.5-acre) site in Antwerp's centre. Work began on this elegant church, noted for its spire, in 1352 and took two centuries to complete.

↘ To Rubenshuis

Groenplaats

The Groenplaats or Green Square is a pleasant open space with trees and flower beds. Lined with cafés, bars and restaurants, the square is a popular spot with both locals and visitors for a peaceful stroll or meal.

0 metres	50
0 yards	50

Exploring Antwerp

THERE HAS BEEN a settlement here, on the banks of the River Scheldt, since the 2nd century. The city of Antwerp grew up and became part of the Duchy of Brabant in 1106. Within 200 years it was a thriving hub of the European cloth industry and Brabant's main port. Today, Antwerp is the principal city of Flemish-speaking Belgium. It is a large metropolis whose port and older residential areas surround a compact centre packed with evidence of its rich history. There are exquisite guild-houses, where the medieval merchants once traded, and imposing churches and several museums, where collections of paintings by the city's most famous son, Pieter Paul Rubens (1577–1640), are also to be found. Antwerp also has many contemporary attractions, such as excellent restaurants, busy nightclubs and bars. Thanks to the Antwerp Six, a group of adventurous designers, the city also has a reputation for cutting-edge fashion.

Carvings above the cathedral door depict the Last Judgement

Visitors tour Antwerp on an historic horse-drawn bus

Getting Around
The best way to get around Antwerp is by using the public transport system. The excellent bus and tram network is focused on Centraal Station, where most visitors arrive. Fast and frequent trams and buses travel from here to the centre. Most of the city's main sights are within walking distance of the Grote Markt.

Grote Markt
Grote Markt. **[** (03) 232 0103. **[&]**
Antwerp's central square, or Grote Markt, is flanked by the ornately gabled Stadhuis (town hall), which was built in 1565 by the architect and sculptor Cornelis Floris. Its interior was restored in the 19th century and houses a series of paintings which celebrate the city's history. The north side of the square has a series of guild-houses, each of which is decorated with gilded figures. The tallest of these is the House of the Crossbowmen at number seven, on top of which is a statue of St George and the dragon. The Brabo fountain in the middle of the square is one of Antwerp's noted landmarks.

Onze Lieve Vrouwe Kathedraal
Groenplaats 21 or Handschoenmarkt. **[** (03) 213 9940. **◯** 10am–5pm Mon–Fri, 10am–3pm Sat, 1–4pm Sun.
The building of Antwerp's Onze Lieve Vrouwe Kathedraal (Cathedral of Our Lady) took almost two centuries, from 1352 to 1521. This magnificent structure has a graceful tiered spire that rises 123 m (404 ft) above the winding streets of the medieval city centre. Inside, the impression of light and space owes much to its seven-aisled nave and vaulted ceiling. The collection of paintings and sculpture includes three works by Rubens, of which two are triptychs – the *Raising of the Cross* (1610) and the *Descent from the Cross* (1612).

Sint Pauluskerk
St-Paulusstraat 22 or Veemarkt 14. **[** (03) 231 3321. **◯** Easter Sat–Sep: 2–5pm daily. **☑** 3pm Sun & pub hols.
Completed in the early 17th century, this splendid church is distinguished by its combination of both Gothic and Baroque features. The exterior dates from about 1517, and has an added elaborate Baroque gateway. The interior is noted for its intricately carved wooden choir stalls. St Paulus also possesses an outstanding series of paintings illustrating the Fifteen Mysteries of the Rosary, one of which, *The Scourging of the Pillar*, is an exquisite canvas by Rubens. There are also paintings by van Dyck and Jordaens.

Fresco paintings of the dukes of Brabant adorn the Stadhuis walls

⊞ Vleeshuis
Vleeshouwersstraat 38–40. ☏ (03) 233 6404. ⏱ 10am–4:45pm Tue – Sun, Easter Mon. ● 1 & 2 Jan, 1 May, Ascension, 1 & 2 Nov, 25 & 26 Dec. ♿

The Vleeshuis (Meat Hall) was completed in 1504 to a design by Herman de Waghemakere. The structure features slender towers with five hexagonal turrets and rising gables, all built in alternate strips of stone and brick – giving it a streaky bacon-like appearance.

Inside, there is an impressive collection of medieval wood-carvings and old musical instruments. In the 17th century, Antwerp was renowned for its manufacture of instruments, including the eccentrically shaped harpsichords and clavichords on display here. There are also paintings, but the highlight is the retable (altarpiece), depicting Christ's Entombment, Crucifixion and Ascent to Heaven, which was carved in wood by Jacob van Cothem in 1514.

⏛ Nationaal Scheepvaartmuseum
Steenplein 1. ☏ (03) 232 0850. ⏱ 10am–5pm Tue–Sun. ● Mon. ♿

The Maritime Museum is located in the gatehouse of Antwerp's original fortress, or

Statue of an ogre outside the Maritime Museum

Steen, the oldest building in the city. Built from the 10th to 16th centuries, it was used in medieval times as a prison. Today, this restored building has 12 rooms devoted to the history of all things nautical, from fearsome Viking ships' heads to the small but elegant gondola built for the visit of Napoleon to the city in 1808. Outside, moored along the riverside, is a selection of old canal tugs and barges.

⊞ Rubenshuis
See pp96–7.

⛪ Sint Jacobskerk
Lange Nieuwstraat 73–75, Eikenstraat. ☏ (03) 225 0414. ⏱ Apr–Oct: 2–5pm Mon–Sat; Nov–Mar: 9am–noon, Mon–Sat; Sun services only. ♿

Noted as Rubens' burial place, this sandstone chuch, built over three centuries from 1491 to 1656, occupies the site of a chapel which lay along the pilgrimage route of St James of Compostella. The rich interior contains the tombs of several other notable Antwerp families, as well as much 17th-century art, including sculptures by Hendrik Verbruggen, and paintings by van Dyck, Otto Venius (Rubens' first master) and Jacob Jordaens. When Rubens died, in 1640, he was buried in his family chapel, located in the ambulatory directly behind the high altar. The chapel altar is where one of Rubens' last paintings, *Our Lady Surrounded by Saints* (1634), is displayed.

⏛ Koninklijk Museum voor Schone Kunsten
See pp94–5.

⏛ Modenatie
Nationalestraat 28. ☏ (03) 226 1447. ⏱ call for details.

The Fashion Museum houses the Flanders Fashion Institute, the Fashion Department of Antwerp's Royal Academy and a museum of fashion (MOMU).

⏛ Provincial Diamond Museum
Koningin Astridplein 19–24. ☏ (03) 202 4890. ⏱ call for details.

This museum is a celebration of diamonds, one of Antwerp's best-known attributes.

Late 16th-century printing press in the Museum Plantin-Moretus

⏛ Museum Plantin-Moretus
Vrijdagmarkt 22–23. ☏ (03) 221 1450. ⏱ 10am–5pm Tue –Sun, Easter Mon. ● Mon, 1 & 2 Jan, 1 May, Ascension, 1 & 2 Nov, 25 & 26 Dec. ♿

This fascinating museum occupies a large 16th-century house that belonged to the printer Christopher Plantin, who moved here in 1576. The house is built around a court-yard, and its ancient rooms and narrow corridors resemble the types of interiors painted by Flemish and Dutch masters. The museum is devoted to the early years of printing, when Plantin and others began to produce books that bore no resemblance to earlier, illuminated medieval manuscripts.

Antwerp was a centre for printing in the 15th and 16th centuries, and Plantin was its most successful printer. Today, his workshop displays several historic printing presses, as well as woodcuts and copper plates. Plantin's library is also on show and includes an array of beautifully made volumes, ranging from medical books to French literature. One of the gems here is a Gutenberg Bible – the first book to be printed using moveable type, a new technique invented by Johannes Gutenberg in 1455.

View of the Vleeshuis' striking façade

Koninklijk Museum voor Schone Kunsten

A NTWERP'S LARGEST and most impressive fine art collection is exhibited in the Museum voor Schone Kunsten, which occupies a massive late 19th-century Neo-Classical building almost 2 km (1 mile) to the south of the Grote Markt. The permanent collection contains both ancient and modern works. The earlier collection on the upper floor begins with medieval Flemish painting and continues through the 17th century, with the 'Antwerp Trio' of Rubens, van Dyck and Jordaens well represented. At ground level, modern exhibits include the work of Belgian artists such as René Magritte, James Ensor and Paul Delvaux, as well as an important collection of work by Rik Wouters, a Fauvist influenced by Matisse. Tissot and van Gogh are among the foreign artists on show.

First Floor

Façade of Gallery
Building began on this imposing structure in 1884. The Neo-Classical façade with its vast pillars has carved women charioteers atop each side. It was opened in 1890.

★ **Saint Barbara** *(1437)*
Jan van Eyck's painting of Saint Barbara in several tones of grey shows the saint sitting in front of a huge Gothic cathedral tower still under construction, while a prayer book lies open on her lap.

Main Entrance

★ **Woman Ironing** *(1912)*
This peaceful domestic scene by Rik Wouters employs the muted colours of Impressionism. This was a productive period for Wouters who painted 60 canvases in 1912.

STAR PAINTINGS

★ **Saint Barbara**
   by Jan van Eyck

★ **Adoration of**
   the Magi by Pieter
   Paul Rubens

★ **Woman Ironing**
   by Rik Wouters

GALLERY GUIDE

The gallery is divided into two floors. Flemish Old Masters are housed on the first floor of the museum, and the ground floor focuses on the 19th and 20th centuries. Each room is lettered and visitors may view exhibits chronologically, starting with the de Keyser series in the entrance hall.

★ **Adoration of the Magi** (1624)
One of Rubens' masterpieces, this painting displays a remarkable freedom of composition.

VISITORS' CHECKLIST

Leopold de Waelplaats 1–9. ▮
(03) 238 7809. ▦ 1, 23, 290. ▤
4, 8. ◻ 10am–5pm Tue–Sun.
◼ 1 & 2 Jan, 1 May, Ascension,
25 Dec. ▨ ▧ ▮ ▯ ▯ ▮

As the Old Sang, the Young Play Pipes (1638)
Jacob Jordaens' (1593–1678) joyous celebration of life in this painting of a family enjoying a musical evening contrasts with his religious paintings.

Pink Bows (1936)
Paul Delvaux's dream-like style clearly shows the influence of Sigmund Freud's psycho-analytic theories on Surrealist painting.

Madame Récamier (1967)
René Magritte's macabre version of the original painting by David is a classic Surrealist work.

Ground Floor

KEY

◻	15th-century paintings
◻	16th-century paintings
◻	17th-century paintings
◻	17th century in Holland
◼	Re-creation of a 17th-century Art Gallery
◻	19th century
◻	19th-century salon
◻	20th century
◻	Temporary exhibitions
▨	Non-exhibition space

Rubenshuis

Statue of Neptune

R UBENSHUIS, ON Wapper Square, was Pieter
Paul Rubens' home and studio for the last
thirty years of his life, from 1610 to 1640. The
city bought the premises just before World
War II, but by then the house was little more
than a ruin, and what can be seen today is
the result of careful restoration. It is divided
into two sections. To the left of the entrance
are the narrow rooms of the artist's living
quarters, equipped with period furniture.
Behind this part of the house is the kunstkamer, or art gallery, where Rubens exhibited
both his own and other artists' work, and entertained
his friends and wealthy patrons, such as the Archduke
Albert and the Infanta Isabella. To the right of the
entrance lies the main studio, a spacious salon where
Rubens worked on – and showed – his works. A
signposted route guides visitors through the house.

Façade of Rubenshuis
*The older Flemish part of the
house sits next to the later house,
whose elegant early Baroque
façade was designed by Rubens.*

Formal Gardens
*The small garden is laid out formally
and its charming pavilion dates
from Rubens' time. He was influenced by such architects of the
Italian Renaissance as Vitruvius
when he built the Italian Baroque
addition to his house in the 1620s.*

★ Rubens' Studio
*It is estimated that Rubens produced some 2,500
paintings in this large, high-ceilinged room. In
the Renaissance manner, Rubens designed the
work which was usually completed by a team of
other artists employed in his studio.*

STAR SIGHTS

★ **Kunstkamer**

★ **Rubens' Studio**

Bedroom
The Rubens family lived in the Flemish section of the house, with its small rooms and narrow passages. The portrait by the bed is said to be of Rubens' second wife, Helena Fourment.

The Familia Kamer, or family sitting room, is cosy and has a pretty tiled floor. It overlooks Wapper Square.

VISITORS' CHECKLIST

Wapper 9–11. ☎ (03) 201 1555.
🚋 1, 9, 19. 🚌 2, 15. ◯ 10am–
5pm Tue–Sun, Easter Mon. ● 1 &
2 Jan, 1 & 2 Nov, 25 & 26 Dec. ♿

Dining Room
Intricately fashioned leather panels line the walls of this room, which also displays a noted work by Frans Snyders.

Chequered mosaic tiled floor

★ Kunstkamer
This art gallery contains a series of painted sketches by Rubens. At the far end is a semi-circular dome, modelled on Rome's Pantheon, displaying a number of marble busts.

Baroque Portico
One of the few remaining original features, this portico was designed by Rubens, and links the older house with the Baroque section. It is adorned with a frieze showing scenes from Greek mythology.

The Centenary Clock on Lier's Zimmertoren or watchtower

Lier ❷

🚶 30,000. 🚉 🚌 ℹ️ *Grote Markt 57, (03) 491 1393.* 🌐 *www.lier.be*

LIER IS AN attractive small town, just 20 km (12 miles) southeast of Antwerp. The Grote Markt is a spacious cobbled square framed by handsome historic buildings. The Stadhuis (town hall) was built in 1740, and its elegant dimensions contrast strongly with the square, turreted 14th-century Belfort (belfry) adjoining. Nearby is the **Stedelijk Museum Wuyts**, with its collection of paintings by Flemish masters including Jan Steen, Brueghel and Rubens. East of here the church of St Gummaruserk, with its soaring stone pillars and vaulted roof, evokes medieval times, and the carved altarpiece is notable for the intricate detail of its biblical scenes. The stained-glass windows are among the finest in Belgium and were a gift from Emperor Maximillian I in 1516.

One of Lier's highlights is the **Zimmertoren**, a 14th-century watchtower that now houses the clocks of Lodewijk Zimmer (1888–1970). This Lier merchant wanted to share his knowledge of timepieces.

🏛 **Stedelijk Museum Wuyts**
Florent van Cauwen straat 14. 🅲 *(03) 491 1396.* 🅾 *Apr–Oct: Wed–Sun.* 🈲
🎡 **Zimmertoren**
Zimmerplein18. 🅲 *(03) 491 1395.* 🅾 *daily.* 🈲

Mechelen ❸

🚶 75,000. 🚉 🚌 ℹ️ *Stadhuis 21, Grote Markt, (015) 29 7655.*

THE SEAT of the Catholic Archbishop of Belgium, Mechelen was the administrative capital of the country under the Burgundian prince, Charles the Bold, in 1473. Today, it is an appealing town whose expansive main square is flanked by pleasant cafés and bars. To the west of the square is the main attraction, **St Romboutskathedraal**, a huge cathedral that took some 300 years to complete. The building might never have been finished but for a deal with the Vatican: the cathedral was allowed to sell special indulgences (which absolved the purchaser of their sins) to raise funds, on condition that the pope received a percentage. Completed in 1546, the cathedral's tower has Belgium's finest carillion, a set of 49 bells, whose peals ring out at weekends and on public holidays. The church also contains *The Crucifixion* by Antony van Dyck (1599–1641).

Less well-known in Mechelen are three 16th-century houses by the River Dilje. They are not open to visitors, but their exteriors are delightful. The "House of the Little Devils" is adorned with carved demons.

Mechelen is famous for its local beers, and visitors should try the Gouden Carolus, a dark brew, which is said to have been the favourite tipple of the Emperor Charles V.

🏛 **St Romboutskathedraal**
St Romboutskerkhof. 🅲 *(015) 29 7655.* 📷 *obligatory. Easter–Sep: 2pm Sat, Sun & pub hols; Jun–Sep: 7pm Mon (Jul & Aug: also 2pm). Tours depart from the Tourist Office.*

Mechelen's main square, the Grote Markt, on market day

Dendermonde ❹

🚶 40,000. 🚉 🚌 ℹ️ *Stadhuis, Grote Markt, (052) 21 3956.*

A QUIET, INDUSTRIAL town, Dendermonde is about 20 km (12 miles) southeast of Ghent. Its strategic position, at the confluence of the Scheldt and Dender rivers, has attracted the attention of a string of invaders

Vleeshuis façade on the Grote Markt in Dendermonde

Wood panelled walls and paintings adorn the hall at Gaasbeek Castle

for its beers, especially lambic and gueuze. Lambic is one of the most popular types of beer in Belgium *(see pp142–3).*

♣ **Gaasbeek**
Kasteelstraat 40. 📞 *(02) 532 4372.*
🕐 *Apr–Nov: Tue–Thu, Sat & Sun (Jul & Aug: also on Mon).*
⬤ *Dec–Mar.* 📷

Halle ❻

🏠 *30,000.* 🚉 🚌 ℹ️ *Stadhuis, Grote Markt, (02) 356 4259.* 🌐 *www.halle.be*

LOCATED ON THE outskirts of Brussels, in the province of Brabant, Halle is a peaceful little town. It has been a major religious centre since the 13th century because of the cult of the Black Virgin, an effigy in the Onze Lieve Vrouwebasiliek, the town's main church. The holy statue's blackness is due to its stained colour, which is said to have occurred through contact with gunpowder during the religious wars of the 17th century.

The virgin has long been one of Belgium's most venerated icons and each year, on Whit Sunday, the statue is paraded through the town.

over the centuries, including the Germans who shelled Dendermonde in 1914. But the town is perhaps best-known as the site of the Steed Bayard, a carnival held every ten years at the end of August.

Today, the town's spacious main square is framed by the quaint turrets and towers of the the Vleeshuis or Meat Hall. The Town Hall is an elegant 14th-century building which was extensively restored in 1920. Dendermonde also possesses two exquisite early religious paintings by Anthony van Dyck which are on display in the Onze Lieve Vrouwekerk (Church of Our Lady).

Pajottenland ❺

🏠 *111,700.* ℹ️ *Toerisme Pajottenland en Zennevalaaei, (02) 356 4259.* 🌐 *www.toerismevlaanderen.be*

THE PAJOTTENLAND forms part of the Brabant province to the southwest of Brussels, and is bordered in the west by the Dender River. The gentle rolling hills of the landscape contain many farms, some of which date back to the 17th century. The village of Onze Lieve Vrouw Lombeek, just 12 km (7 miles) west of Brussels, is named after its church, an outstanding example of 14th-century Gothic architecture.

Just a few kilometres south of the village lies the area's main attraction, the castle and grounds of **Gaasbeek**. The

castle was remodelled in the 19th century, but actually dates from the 13th century, and boasts a moat and a thick curtain wall, strengthened by huge semi-circular towers. The castle's interior holds an excellent collection of fine and applied arts. Among the treasures are rich tapestries, 15th-century alabaster reliefs from England, silverware and a delightful ivory and copper hunting horn which belonged to the Protestant martyr Count Egmont in the 16th century. The Pajottenland is also known

THE STEED BAYARD

Dendermonde's famous carnival of the Steed Bayard occurs every ten years at the end of August. The focus of the festival is a horse, the Steed Bayard itself, represented in the carnival by a giant model. It takes 34 bearers to carry the horse which weighs 700 kg (1,540 lb) and is 5.8 m (19 ft) high. A procession of locals dressed in medieval costume re-enact the Steed Bayard legend – a complex tale of chivalry and treachery, family loyalty and betrayal. The four Aymon brothers (who were said to be the nephews of Emperor Charlemagne) ride the horse, and it is their behaviour towards the animal which serves to demonstrate their moral worth.

Waterloo ⓭

Death mask of Napoleon

THE BATTLE OF WATERLOO was fought on 18 June, 1815. It pitted Napoleon and his French army against the Duke of Wellington, who was in command of troops mostly drawn from Britain, Germany and the Netherlands. The two armies met outside the insignificant hamlet of Waterloo, to the south of Brussels. The result was decisive. The battle began at 11:30am and just nine hours later the French were in full retreat. Napoleon abdicated and was subsequently exiled to the island of St Helena, where he died in mysterious circumstances six years later.

Despite its importance, the battlefield has not been conserved, and part of it has been dug up for a highway. However, enough remains to give a general sense of the battle. The best place to start a visit here is at the Musée Wellington, some 3 km (2 miles) from the battlefield.

🏛 Musée Wellington

Chaussée de Bruxelles 147. 🕿 (02) 354 7806. ⬜ daily. ⬤ 1 Jan, 25 Dec. 🖼 🅦 www.waterloo.be

The Waterloo inn where Wellington spent the night before the battle has been turned into the Musée Wellington, its narrow rooms packed with curios alongside plans and models of the battle. One curiosity is the artificial leg of Lord Uxbridge, one of Wellington's commanders. His leg was blown off by a cannon ball during the battle and buried in Waterloo. After his death, the leg was sent to join the rest of him in England and, as recompense, his relatives sent his artificial one back to Waterloo.

🔒 Eglise St-Joseph

Chaussée de Bruxelles. 🕿 (02) 354 0011.

Across the road from the Musée Wellington is the tiny church of St-Joseph, which was built as a royal chapel at the end of the 17th century. Its dainty, elegant cupola predates the battle, after which it was extended, with the newer portions containing dozens of memorial plaques and flagstones dedicated to those British soldiers who died at Waterloo. Several of these plaques were paid for by voluntary contributions from ordinary soldiers in honour of their officers.

The Butte de Lion viewed from the Waterloo battlefield

🗼 Butte de Lion

149 Chaussée de Bruxelles, N5, 3km (2 miles) S of Waterloo. 🕿 (02) 354 9910. ⬜ daily. 🖼

Dating from 1826, the Butte de Lion is a 45-m (148-ft) high earthen mound built on the

WATERLOO TOWN CENTRE

Musée Wellington ①
Eglise St-Joseph ②

KEY

ℹ	Visitor information
🅿	Parking
🚌	Bus station
🚂	Train station

0 metres   300
0 yards   300

DREVE DES DIX METRES
AVENUE CLAIRE
DREVE DE L'INFANTE
AV DES BLES D'OR
DREVES DU MOULIN
CHAUSSEE DE BRUXELLES
DREVE DU MOULIN
AVENUE EMILE THEYS
DREVE DE L'INFANTE
RUE DE LA STATION
SENTIER DU BOIS
AVENUE DE L'ANGE
RUE DE LA STATION
CLOSE DE LA VIOLETTE
AVENUE DES SAULES
AVENUE DES SORBIERS
CHAUSSEE DE BRUXELLES
PLACE DE LA GARE
AVENUE ADOLPHE SCHATTENS
AVE DU CHAMPS DE MAI

Butte de Lion
Panorama de la Bataille
Musée de Cire
Le Caillou

spot where one of Wellington's Dutch generals, the Prince of Orange, was wounded during the battle. Steps lead to the top, which is guarded by a huge cast-iron lion, and from here there is a great view over the battlefield. The French army approached from the south and fought up the slope across farmland that became increasingly marshy as the day went on, while their opponents had the drier ridge at the foot of the mound. A plan of the battle is displayed at the top.

Panorama de la Bataille
252–254 Route du Lion, Braine-L'Alleud. N5, 3 km (2 miles) S of Waterloo. (02) 385 1912. daily.
This is perhaps the most fascinating of the several attractions located beneath the Butte de Lion. This circular painting of the battle by artist Louis Demoulin was erected in 1912. It is 110 m (360 ft) long and stretches right round a circular, purpose-built gallery. Panoramic, circular paintings came to be very popular in the late 19th century; this is one of the few works that remain intact.

Musée de Cire
315–317 Route du Lion, N5, 3 km (2 miles) S of Waterloo. (02) 384 6740. Apr–Oct: daily; Nov–Mar: pub hols, Sat & Sun.
The Musée de Cire is a wax museum where pride of place goes to the models of soldiers dressed in the military regalia of 1815. It seems strange today that the various armies dressed their men in such vivid colours, which made them easy targets. Indeed, many commanders paid for the uniforms of their men themselves, competing with each other for the most flamboyant design.

Napoleon's Last Headquarters
66 Chaussée de Waterloo, Vieux-Genappe, N5, 7 km (4.5 miles) S of Waterloo. (02) 384 2424. Tue–Sun. 1 Jan, 25 Dec.
Napoleon spent the eve of the battle in a farmhouse, Le Caillou. This is now a museum containing some artifacts from Napoleon's army, a bronze death mask of the Emperor and his army-issue bed.

Southeast side of Nivelles' imposing church, Collégiale Ste-Gertrude

Nivelles 8

20,000. Waux-Hall, Place Albert I, (067) 88 2275.

Tucked away among the rolling hills of the province of Brabant, the little town of Nivelles was, for centuries, the site of one of the wealthiest and most powerful abbeys in the region. Earlier it was the cradle of the Carolingian dynasty, whose most celebrated ruler was the Emperor Charlemagne (747–814). The main sight today is the vast church, the Collégiale Ste-Gertrude, that dominates the town centre. Something of an architectural hotchpotch, the church dates back to the 10th century and is remarkable in that it has two imposing chancels – one each for the pope and the king.

Leuven 9

See pp102–103.

Bokrijk Museum 10

See pp104–105.

Liège 11

400,000. En Féronstrée 92, (04) 221 9221.

Belgium's third-biggest city, Liège is a major river port and industrial conurbation at the confluence of the rivers Meuse and Ourthe. The city

has an unusual history in that it was an independent principality from the 10th to the 18th century, ruled by Prince Bishops. However, the church became widely despised and when the French Republican army arrived in 1794, they were welcomed by the local citizens with open arms.

Today, Liège possesses some notable attractions and highlights include the **Musée de la Vie Wallone** (Museum of Walloon Life), housed in an outstanding 17th-century mansion. The museum focuses on Walloon folklore and culture, which is depicted in a series of reconstructed interiors and craft workshops from the city's history.

Musée de la Vie Wallone
Cour des Mineurs. (04) 223 6094. Tue–Sat.

Namur 12

100,000. Square Léopold, (081) 24 64 49.

French-speaking Namur is a friendly, attractive town whose narrow central streets boast several elegant mansions and fine old churches, as well as lots of lively bars and outstanding restaurants. Until the Belgian army left in 1978, Namur was also a military town. The soldiers were stationed within the Citadel, located on top of the steep hill on the south side of the centre, which remains the town's main attraction. An exploration of its bastions and subterranean galleries takes several hours.

Namur's ancient walls or Citadel seen from the River Meuse

Leuven

WITHIN EASY STRIKING distance of Brussels, the historic Flemish town of Leuven traces its origins to a fortified camp constructed here by Julius Caesar. In medieval times, the town became an important centre of the cloth trade, but it was as a seat of learning that it achieved international prominence. In 1425, Pope Martin V and Count John of Brabant founded Leuven's university, and by the mid-1500s it was one of Europe's most prestigious academic institutions, the home of such famous scholars as Erasmus and Mercator.

Font Sapienza

Even today, the university exercises a dominant influence over the town, and its students give Leuven a vibrant atmosphere. The bars and cafés flanking the Oude Markt, a large square in the centre of town, are especially popular. Adjoining the square is the Grote Markt, a triangular open space which boasts two fine medieval buildings, the Stadhuis and St Pieterskerk.

Lively café society in the Oude Markt

🔲 Oude Markt

This handsome, cobble-stoned square is flanked by a tasteful ensemble of high-gabled brick buildings. Some of these date from the 18th century; others are comparatively new. At ground level these buildings house the largest concentration of bars and cafés in town, and as such attract the town's university students in their droves.

🔲 Stadhuis

Grote Markt. 📞 *(016) 21 1539.* ⭘ *daily.* 📷 📷 *obligatory. At 3pm daily (Apr–Sep: also at 11am Mon–Fri).*

Built between 1448 and 1463 from the profits of the cloth trade, Leuven's town hall, the Stadhuis, was designed to demonstrate the wealth of the city's merchants. This distinctive, tall building is renowned for its lavishly carved and decorated façade. A line of narrow windows rise up over three floors beneath a steeply pitched roof adorned with dormer windows and pencil-thin turrets. It is, however, in the fine quality of its stonework that the building excels, with delicately carved tracery and detailed medieval figures beneath 300 niche bases. There are grotesques of every description as well as representations of folktales and biblical stories, all carved in exuberant late-Gothic style. Within the niche alcoves is a series of 19th-century statues depicting local dignitaries and politicians. Guided tours of the interior are available, and include three lavishly decorated reception rooms.

Stone carvings of medieval figures decorate the Stadhuis façade

Huge buttresses support the tower of the Church of Saint Peter

🔒 St Pieterskerk and Museum voor Religieuze Kunst

Grote Markt. 📞 *(016) 29 5133.* ⭘ *Mar–Oct: daily, Nov–Feb: Tue–Sun.* 📷 *to museum.*

Across the square from the Stadhuis rises St Pieterskerk, a massive church built over a period of two hundred years from the 1420s. The nave and aisles were completed first, but when the twin towers of the western façade were finally added in 1507, the foundations proved inadequate and they soon began to sink. With money in short supply, it was decided to remove the top sections of the towers – hence the truncated versions of today.

Inside the church, the sweeping lines of the nave are intercepted by an impressive 1499 rood screen and a Baroque wooden pulpit, depicting the conversion of Saint Norbert. Norbert was a wealthy but irreligious German noble, who was hit by lightning while riding. He was unhurt but his horse died under him, and this led to his devoting himself to the church.

The church also houses the Religious Art Museum which has three exquisite paintings by Dieric Bouts (1415–75). Born in the Netherlands, Bouts spent most of his working life in Leuven, where he became the town's official artist. In his *Last Supper* (1468), displayed here, Bouts painted Judas's face in shadow, emphasizing the mystery of Holy Communion rather than the betrayal.

Fochplein

Adjacent to the Grote Markt is the Fochplein, a narrow triangular square containing some of Leuven's most popular shops, selling everything from fashion to food. In the middle is the Font Sapienza, a modern fountain that shows a student pouring water through his empty head – a pithy view of the town's student population.

Museum Vander Kelen-Mertens

Savoyestraat 6. *(016) 22 6906.*
Tue–Sun.
The Museum Vander Kelen-Mertens has fair claim to be Leuven's most enjoyable museum, with its well-presented collection arranged over two floors. Once the home of the Vander Kelen-Mertens family, the rooms are furnished in a variety of historical styles, ranging from a Renaissance salon to a rococo dining room.

Much of the art on display is by the early Flemish masters, including the work of Quentin Metsys (1466–1550), who was born in Leuven and is noted for introducing Italian style to north European art. The collection also includes a beautiful *Holy Trinity* by Rogier

van der Weyden (1400–1464). Fine art is located in the first-floor galleries where there is also an impressive display of 16th- and 17th-century embroidered vestments, stained glass and Oriental ceramics.

St Michielskerk

Naamsestraat.
Jun–Sep: Wed, Sat & Sun.
One of Leuven's most impressive churches, St Michielskerk was built for the Jesuits in the middle of the 17th century. The church was badly damaged during World War II, but has since been carefully restored. Its graceful façade with its flowing lines is an excellent illustration of the Baroque style. The interior is regularly open to visitors for three afternoons during the summer months. The stunning 1660 carved woodwork around the altar and choir are well worth seeing.

Groot Begijnhof

Schapenstraat. daily, for street access only.
Founded around 1230, the Groot Begijnhof was once one of the largest béguinages in Belgium, home to several hundred béguines *(see p53)*.

VISITORS' CHECKLIST

85,000. Bondgenotenlaan. Grote Markt 9.
Vanderkelenstraat 30, 3000 Leuven, (016) 21 1540.

The complex of 72 charming red-brick cottages (dating mostly from the 17th century) is set around the grassy squares and cobbled streets near the River Dijle. Leuven university bought the complex in 1961 and converted the cottages into student accommodation.

The red-brick houses of Leuven's Groot Begijnhof

LEUVEN TOWN CENTRE

Fochplein ④
Groot Begijnhof ⑦
Museum Vander
  Kelen-Mertens ⑤
Oude Markt ①
St Michielskerk ⑥
St Pieterskerk ③
Stadhuis ②

0 metres   300
0 yards   300

KEY

P Parking

i Visitor information

Train Station

Bokrijk Openluchtmuseum ❿

BOKRIJK VILLAGE CONTAINS an immensely popular open-air museum devoted to Flemish rural life before 1900. Set among the forest and rolling pasture of Limburg province, about 10 km (6 miles) northeast of the town of Hasselt, the open-air museum was established in 1953 by the provincial government. The land has been farmed since the Middle Ages, and in the early 20th century was used by the Belgian Farmer's Union for agricultural trials.

Bokrijk is made up several settlements which have been moved here and reconstructed, and has more than a hundred restored buildings. The collection is divided into three main sections, each representing a distinct geographical area. Manned by costumed guides, the farmhouses, barns and workshops offer various live demonstrations of an assortment of traditional crafts.

Costumed character
Characters such as this man, dressed in typical peasant's clothing of the 19th century, enhance the Bokrijk's authentic atmosphere.

Visitor riding historic bike
The museum offers the chance to participate in a range of activities from cycling and fishing to such traditional crafts as baking and even farming with antique tools.

The Old Town

Fertile Uplands: Brabant

Pigeon Tower
The pigeon nests in this 1634 tower were located in the upper part of the building, which was accessible only by ladder, to prevent the theft of the young birds.

Fertile Uplands: Limburg Haspengouw and the Maasland

★ Interior features
Most of the buildings here have original interior features. This 18th-century fireplace has Delft tiles that depict biblical scenes such as the birth of Christ.

VISITORS' CHECKLIST

Domain Bokrijk, 3600 Genk.
(011) 26 5300. FAX (011) 26 5310.
Bokrijk. Mar–Sep: 10am–6pm daily. Oct–Feb.
W www.limburg.be/bokrijk

The Fertile Lowlands: East and West Flanders

★ Agricultural architecture
This 16th-century farmhouse was built in Saxon style and has a fine thatched roof. The adjacent windmill dates from 1788 and was used to grind grain. It still contains the original millstones.

The Poor Heathlands, or the Kempen, is one of the principal geographical areas in the museum. It was an area of reclaimed land where villagers eked out a living from their farms.

Grain store
This elegant, timber-framed grain store, or spijker, *dates from the 16th century. This building comes from Limburg province, where it probably formed part of a brewery.*

Village priest
Many of the Bokrijk's costumed workers, such as this village priest, are on hand to explain what life was like in these pre-industrial rural areas.

STAR FEATURES

★ Agricultural architecture

★ Interior features

0 metres 50

0 yards 50

Charleroi

200,000. ⊠ 🚊 🚌 **i** *Square de la Gare du Sud, (071) 31 8218.*

WITH A POPULATION of more than 200,000, the industrial centre of Charleroi is one of the largest cities in French-speaking Belgium. Named after the Hapsburg king Charles II, who had the town fortified in 1666, it achieved prominence in the 1800s as the focus of a burgeoning coal-mining and steel area known as the Pays Noir (Black Country). Its busy centre fans out from the River Sambre, dividing into the Lower City, which is largely concerned with commerce and is of little interest to the casual visitor, and the Upper City, an older quarter around Place Charles II. The highlights are the **Photography Museum** and the **Musée du Verre** (Glass Museum), with its collection of glass ranging from Assyrian necklaces to contemporary glasswork. From Charleroi, it is around 20 km (12 miles) west to the little town of Binche, the site of one of Belgium's most famous carnivals. Every year in March, parties lead up to a Shrove Tuesday festival.

St Christophe's church in Charleroi's Upper City

🏛 **Photography Museum**
Avenue Paul Pastuur 11. **(** *(071) 43 5810.* ⊙ *Tue–Sun.* ● *Mon.* 🖉

🏛 **Musée du Verre**
Blvd Defontaine 10. **(** *(071) 31 0838.* ⊙ *Tue–Sun.* ● *Mon.* 🖉

Mons ⑭

90,000. 🚊 🚌 **i** *Grand Place 22, (065) 33 5580.*

PERHAPS BEST known for its association with both World Wars, Mons is actually an ancient town. The capital of the French-speaking province of Hainaut, Mons lies across the steep hill that first made it important. Natural strongpoints are rare in this part of the country and the Romans, observing the lay of the land, established a fortified camp here in the 1st century AD.

Today, Mons is a friendly town whose social life focuses around the Grand Place and its pavement cafés. Also overlooking the Grand Place is the 15th-century Hôtel de Ville, an imposing Gothic structure. A cast-iron monkey, known as the *Singe du Grand Garde*, sits on the outside wall near the main entrance, and is meant to bring good luck to those who stroke its head. Southwest of the Grand Place are the town's well-preserved medieval streets and the Collégiale Ste-Waudru, a late-Gothic church.

Mons' other important sights are the **Musée du Guerre**, which focuses on the role of Mons in both World Wars, and the **Musée du Vieux Namy**, with its collection of ceramics and Delftware.

🏛 **Musée du Guerre**
Rue Houdain 13.
(*(065) 33 5213.*
⊙ *Tue–Sun.*

🏛 **Musée du Vieux Namy**
Rue Mouzain 31, Namy.
(*(065) 36 0825.*
⊙ *May–Sep: Sat–Sun.*

The summer drawing room in the 18th-century Chateau d'Attre, near Ath

Ath ⑮

11,700. 🚊 🚌 **i** *Rue de Pintamont 54, (068) 26 9230, 26 5170.*

THIS QUIET TOWN grew up around the River Dendre. Ath is known for its festival – the Ducasse – which occurs every year on the fourth weekend in August. Held over two days, it features the "Parade of the Giants", a procession of gaily decorated giant figures representing characters from local folklore and the Bible, such as the Aymon brothers and the Steed Bayard (*see p99*), as well as David, Goliath and Samson.

The surrounding country of gently rolling hills is dotted with hamlets and farms, as well as historical sights. A few kilometres northeast of Ath is one of the most popular attractions

The Gothic church Collégiale Ste-Waudru, Mons

in the region, the **Château d'Attre**. This handsome 18th-century palace was built in 1752 by the Count of Gomegnies, chamberlain to the Hapsburg Emperor Joseph II, and was a favourite haunt of the Hapsburg aristocracy. Its interior is opulent, with ornate plasterwork, parquet floors and paintings. The River Dendre crosses the delightful grounds.

♣ Château d'Attre

Attre. ▐ (068) 45 4460. ▐ to Attre. �‌ Jul–Aug: Thu–Tue; Apr–Jun & Sep–Oct: Sat & Sun. ● Nov–Mar.

The southeast entrance of the chapel of St Hermes, Ronse

Ronse ⓰

🏠 25,000. ▐ 🚌 ℹ Stadhuis, Grote Markt, Oudenaarde, (05) 531 7251.

SET AMONG the pretty hills of the Flemish Ardennes, Ronse is famous for its *Zotte Maandag*, or Crazy Monday festivities. Every year, on the second weekend in January, a boisterous procession of masked medieval characters parades through the town.

In medieval times, Ronse was where thousands of the mentally ill were taken to seek a cure. The object of the pilgrimage was a visit to the chapel of Hermes, a Roman saint thought to be an expert in exorcism. Today, the chapel retains three rusty iron rings that recall the days when the insane were chained up awaiting a miracle. A painting here depicts St Hermes on a horse, dragging a devil behind him.

Ieper ⓱

🏠 35,000. ▐ 🏠 ℹ 34 Market Square, (057) 22 8584.

IEPER IS THE Flemish name of the town familiar to hundreds of thousands of British soldiers as Ypres – its French appellation. During World War I, this ancient town, which was once a centre of the medieval wool trade, was used as a supply depot for the British army fighting in the trenches just to the east.

The Germans shelled Ieper to pieces, but after the war the town was rebuilt to its earlier design, complete with an exact replica of its imposing, 13th-century Lakenhalle (cloth hall). The original building was located by the River Ieperlee (which now runs underground), and boats could unload their wares on site. Today, part of the interior has been turned into the excellent "In Flander's Fields" Museum, a thoughtfully laid-out series of displays that attempt to conjure the full horrors of World War I. There is a simulated gas attack, personal artifacts and an array of photographs.

Another reminder of war is the huge Menin Gate memorial (just east of the Grote Markt) inscribed with the names of over 50,000 British and Commonwealth troops who died in and around Ieper but have no known resting place. The last post is sounded here every evening at 8pm.

Weaving a tapestry at the Huis de Lalaing workshop, Oudenaarde

Oudenaarde ⓲

🏠 30,000. ▐ 🚌 ℹ Stadhuis, Grote Markt, (05) 531 7251.

STRATEGICALLY situated beside the River Scheldt, the little town of Oudenaarde has suffered at the hands of many invaders, and little remains of the old town. The 16th-century Stadhuis has survived, and is adorned with beautiful stonework. The interior is open to visitors and is famous for an exquisitely carved oak doorway and its outstanding collection of tapestries – one of the finest in the country.

Oudenaarde was once a centre of tapestry manufacture and its products were bought by monarchs across Europe. Today, visitors can see tapestries being made at the Huis de Lalaing, a workshop near the Grote Markt.

THE YPRES SALIENT

The Ypres Salient was the name given to a bulge in the line of trenches that both the German and British armies felt was a good place to break through each others' lines. This led to large concentrations of men and four major battles including Passchendaele in July 1917, in which hundreds of thousands of men died. Today, visitors can choose to view the site with its vast cemeteries and monuments by car or guided tour.

View of the battlefield at Passchendaele Ridge in 1917

Street-by-Street: Ghent ⑲

Bell on display in the Belfort

As a tourist destination, the Flemish city of Ghent has long been over-shadowed by its neighbour, Bruges. In part this reflects their divergent histories. The success of the cloth trade during the Middle Ages was followed by a period of stagnation for Bruges, while Ghent became a major industrial centre in the 18th and 19th centuries. The resulting pollution coated the city's antique buildings in layers of grime from its many factories. In the 1980s Ghent initiated a restoration programme. The city's medieval buildings were cleaned, industrial sites were tidied up and the canals were cleared. Today, it is the intricately carved stonework of its churches and antique buildings, as well as the city's excellent museums and stern, forbidding castle that give the centre its character.

★ Het Gravensteen
Ghent's centre is dominated by the thick stone walls and imposing gatehouse of its ancient Castle of the Counts.

★ Museum voor Sierkunst
This elegant 19th-century dining room is just one of many charming period rooms in the decorative arts museum. The collection is housed in an 18th-century mansion and covers art and design from the 1600s to the present.

Graslei
One of Ghent's most picturesque streets, the Graslei overlooks the River Leie on the site of the city's medieval harbour. It is lined with perfectly preserved guildhouses; some date from the 12th century.

STAR SIGHTS

★ St Baafskathedraal

★ Het Gravensteen

★ Museum voor Sierkunst

To Ghent St-Pieters

Korenmarkt
This busy square was once the corn market; the commercial centre of the city since the Middle Ages. Today, it is lined with popular cafés.

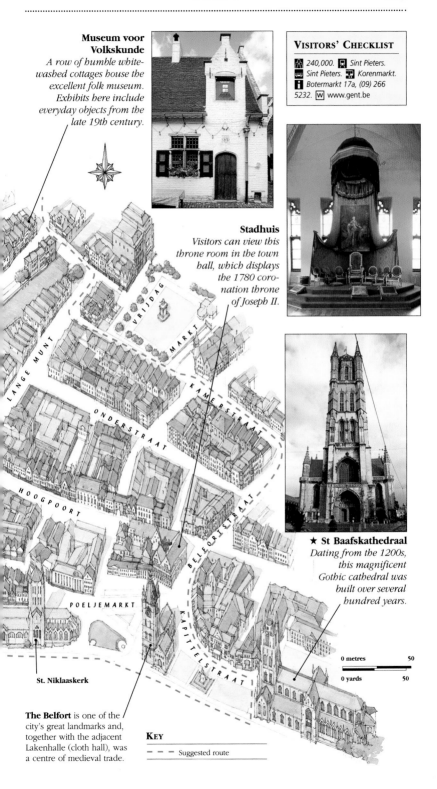

Museum voor Volkskunde
A row of humble white-washed cottages house the excellent folk museum. Exhibits here include everyday objects from the late 19th century.

VISITORS' CHECKLIST

240,000.   Sint Pieters.
Sint Pieters.   Korenmarkt.
Botermarkt 17a, (09) 266
5232.   W www.gent.be

Stadhuis
Visitors can view this throne room in the town hall, which displays the 1780 coronation throne of Joseph II.

★ St Baafskathedraal
Dating from the 1200s, this magnificent Gothic cathedral was built over several hundred years.

St. Niklaaskerk

The Belfort is one of the city's great landmarks and, together with the adjacent Lakenhalle (cloth hall), was a centre of medieval trade.

0 metres   50
0 yards   50

KEY

– – – Suggested route

Exploring Ghent

**Charles V's
coat of arms**

THE HEART OF Ghent's historic centre was originally built during the 13th and 14th centuries when the city prospered as a result of the cloth trade. Ghent was founded in the 9th century when Baldwin Iron-Arm, the first Count of Flanders, built a castle to protect two important abbeys from Viking raids. Despite constant religious and dynastic conflicts, Ghent continued to flourish throughout the 16th and early 17th centuries. After 1648, the Dutch sealed the Scheldt estuary near Antwerp, closing vital canal links, which led to a decline in the fortunes of both cities. By the 19th century there was a boom in cotton spinning, and the wide boulevards in the south of the city reflect the affluence of the factory owners. Today, textiles still form a big part of Ghent's industry.

The Gothic turrets of Sint-Niklaaskerk seen from St Michael's Bridge

Getting around

Ghent is a large city with an excellent bus and tram system. The main rail station, St Peters, adjoins the bus station from where several trams travel to the centre every few minutes. However, many of Ghent's main sights are within walking distance of each other. Canal boat trips are also available.

🔒 St Baafskathedraal

St Baafsplein. **C** (09) 225 1626.
🔾 daily. **Adoration of the Mystic Lamb** 🔾 Apr–Oct: daily; Nov–Mar: Sun–Fri. 📷
Built in several stages, St Baafskathedraal has features representing every phase of Gothic style, from the early chancel through to the later nave, which is the cathedral's architectural highlight. The cavernous nave is supported by slender columns and has a soft dappled light filtering through the windows. In a

small side chapel one of Europe's most remarkable paintings is on display, Jan van Eyck's polyptych *Adoration of the Mystic Lamb* (1432). Van Eyck is noted for his attention to detail, but is also universally respected as the first painter to master the art of working with oils. His use of colours and

tones is so realistic that even today, hundreds of years after the work was completed, the skin of his characters looks real enough to touch. The cover screens of this seminal work feature portraits of the donor – Joos Vijd – and his wife below an Annunciation scene. The inside is stunning. Here, God the Father, John the Baptist and the Virgin Mary are pictured on the upper level in radiant tones, while the Lamb, the symbol of Christ's sacrifice, is the centrepiece below.

🏛 Stadhuis

Botermarkt 1. **C** (09) 266 5211.
📷 🔾 May–Oct: 3pm Mon–Thu.
Tours depart from the Tourist Office.
The Stadhuis façade displays two different architectural styles. Overlooking Hoogstraat, the older half dates from the early 16th century, its tracery in the elaborate Flamboyant Gothic style. The plainer, newer part, which flanks the Botermarkt, is a characteristic example of post-Reformation architecture. The statues in the niches on the façade were added in the 1890s. Among this group of figures it is possible to spot the original architect, Rombout Keldermans, who is shown studying his plans.

The building still serves as the city's administrative centre. Guided tours allow a glimpse at a series of large rooms. Perhaps the most fascinating of these is the Pacification Hall, which was once the Court of Justice and the site of signing of the Pacification of Ghent (a treaty between Catholics and Protestants against Hapsburg rule) in 1576.

The tiled floor forms a maze in the Pacification Hall in Ghent's Stadhuis

Views of Graslei and 16th-century guildhouses along the River Leie

▓ Graslei

The Graslei runs along the River Leie and is the eastern side of the Tussen Bruggen, once Ghent's main medieval harbour. The quay possesses a fine set of guildhouses. Among them, at No. 14, the sandstone façade of the Guildhouse of the Free Boat-men is decorated with finely detailed nautical scenes, while the late 17th-century Corn Measurers' guildhouse next door is adorned by bunches of fruit and cartouches. The earliest building here is the 12th-century *Spijker* (Staple House) at No. 10. This simple Romanesque structure stored the city's grain supply for several hundred years until a fire destroyed the interior.

♣ Het Gravensteen

Sint-Veerleplein. ▐ (09) 225 9306, 269 3730. ◯ daily. ● 1 & 2 Jan, 25 & 26 Dec. ▓

Once the seat of the counts of Flanders, the imposing stone walls of Het Gravensteen (or the Castle of the Counts) over-look the city centre. Parts of the castle date back to the late 1100s, but most are later addi-tions. Up to the 14th century the castle was Ghent's main military stronghold, and from then until the late 1700s it was used as the city's jail. Later, it became a cotton mill.

From the gatehouse, a long and heavily fortified tunnel leads up to the courtyard, which is overseen by two large buildings, the count's medieval residence and the earlier keep. Arrows guide visitors round the interior of both buildings, and in the upper rooms there is a spine-chilling collection of medieval torture instruments.

▓ Museum voor Sierkunst

Jan Breydelstraat 5. ▐ (09) 267 9999. ◯ Tue–Sun. ▓

This decorative arts museum has a wide-ranging collection contained within an elegant 18th-century townhouse. The displays are arranged in two sections, beginning at the front with a series of lavishly furnished period rooms that feature textiles, furniture, and artifacts from the 17th to the 19th centuries. At the back, an extension completed in 1992 focuses on modern design from Art Nouveau to contemporary works, and includes furniture by Victor Horta (*see p78*), Marcel Breuer and Ludwig Mies van der Rohe. One highlight is an Art Nouveau room designed by noted Belgian artist Henry van der Velde.

Sofa at Sierkunst Museum

▓ The Patershol

North of the Kraanlei are the quaint little lanes and low brick houses of the Patershol, a district that developed in the 17th century to house the city's weavers. This once down-at-heel area underwent extensive refurbishment in the 1980s and is now one of the trendiest parts of town, with upmarket restaurants, cafés and shops.

▓ Museum voor Schone Kunsten

Citadelpark. ▐ (09) 222 1703. ◯ Tue–Sun. ▓

Ghent's largest collection of fine art is displayed in this Neo-Classical building dating from 1902. Inside, a rotunda divides the collection, with the older works in a series of rooms on the right and 19th- and 20th-century art to the left. The medieval paintings include the *Bearing of the Cross* by Hieronymus Bosch (1450–1516). There are also works by Rubens (*see pp14–15*), Anthony van Dyck (1599–1641) and Jacob Jordaens (1593–1678).

The museum will close for renovations at the end of 2003. Some pieces will temporarily be rehoused at the Archeo-logical Museum Van De Bijloke on Gods-huizenlaan (tel: 09 225 1106).

▓ Stedelijk Museum voor Actuele Kunst (SMAK)

Citadelpark. ▐ (09) 222 1703. ☒ www.smak.be.

This museum includes works by Belgian and international contemporary artists, such as Bacon, Beuys, Broodthaers, Long and Nauman.

The grand, Neo-Classical façade of the Museum voor Schone Kunsten

Street-by-Street: Bruges ⑳

Traditional organ grinder

WITH GOOD REASON, Bruges is one of the most popular tourist destinations in Belgium. An unspoilt medieval town, Bruges' winding streets pass by picturesque canals lined with fine buildings. The centre of Bruges is amazingly well preserved. The town's trade was badly affected when the River Zwin silted up at the end of the 15th century. It was never heavily industrialized and has retained most of its medieval buildings. As a further bonus Bruges also escaped major damage in both world wars.

Today, the streets are well maintained: there are no billboards or high rises, and traffic is heavily regulated. All the major attractions are located within the circle of boulevards that marks the line of the old medieval walls.

View of the River Dijver
A charming introduction to Bruges is provided by the boat trips along the city's canal network.

Onze Lieve Vrouwekerk
The massive Church of Our Lady employs many architectural styles. It took around 200 years to build, and its spire is Belgium's tallest.

Hans Memling Museum
Six of the artist's works are shown in the small chapel of the 12th-century St Janshospitaal, a city hospital that was still operating until 1976.

0 metres   100

0 yards   100

★ The Markt
Medieval gabled houses line this 13th-century market square at the heart of Bruges, which still holds a market each Saturday.

VISITORS' CHECKLIST

119,000. Stationsplein.
Stationsplein, Markt.
Burg 11, 8000 Bruges, (050) 44 8686. www.brugge.be

Oude Griffie, or Old Recorder's House

Blind Donkey Alley
This narrow, arched alley leads from the Burg to the 18th-century Vismarkt.

Heilig Bloed Basiliek

★ Stadhuis
One of the oldest and finest town halls in Belgium, this was built between 1376 and 1420. Inside, the beautifully restored Gothic hall is noted for its 1385 vaulted ceiling.

Groeninge Museum
(see pp118–19)

Arentshuis Museum

Gruuthuse Museum
(see pp116–17)

KEY

– – – Suggested route

The Belfort
Built in the 13th century, the Belfort or Belfry is a stunning octagonal tower where the city's medieval charter of rights is held.

STAR SIGHTS

★ The Markt

★ Stadhuis

Exploring Central Bruges

Bell maker in market

BRUGES DEVELOPED around a 9th-century fortress, built to defend the coast against the Vikings. Despite the vagaries of successive invasions by the French, between the 14th and 16th centuries Bruges became one of northern Europe's most sophisticated cities. Today, it owes its pre-eminent position to the beauty of its historic centre, whose narrow cobbled lanes and meandering canals are lined by an ensemble of medieval buildings. These are mostly the legacy of the town's heyday as a centre of the international cloth trade, which flourished for two hundred years from the 13th century. During this golden age, Bruges' merchants lavished their fortunes on fine mansions, churches and a set of civic buildings of such extravagance that they were the wonder of northern Europe.

Bruges' medieval buildings reflected in the River Dijver

Getting Around
The centre of Bruges is compact, and as most major sights are near each other, it is easiest to walk around. However, the bus service is useful for getting from the railway station to the centre. Half-hour boat trips along the canals leave from several jetties. From March to November, boats depart twice every hour.

The Vismarkt
Braambergstraat. ◯ daily.
From the Burg an attractive arched path called the Alley of the Blind Donkey (Blinde Ezelstraat) leads to the open-air fish market with its elegant 18th-century colonnades. Fish is still sold here early each morning and business is brisk.

♛ The Burg
The Burg, a pleasant cobbled square a few metres from the Markt, was once the political and religious focus of Bruges. It is also the site of the original fort around which the city grew. Some of the most imposing civic buildings are located here. The beautiful sandstone Stadhuis or town hall has a façade dating

from 1375, and is adorned with turrets and statues. In contrast, the Proostdij or Provost's House was built of grey stone in 1662 in the Baroque style and boasts an ornate entrance.

♛ Stadhuis
Burg 12. ☎ (050) 44 8111.
◯ daily. ⬛
The intricately carved façade of the Stadhuis was completed in 1375, but the niche statues are modern effigies of the counts and countesses of Flanders. These were added in the 1960s to replace those destroyed by the French army over a century before. The building is still used as a town hall. It is also a popular venue for Bruges weddings. Inside, a staircase leads up from the spacious foyer to the beautiful Gothic Hall, which is open to visitors year round. This magnificent parliamentary chamber was built around 1400. Immaculately restored, the ceiling boasts some lavish woodcarvings including 16 beautiful corbels (brackets) bearing representations of the seasons and the elements. A series of paintings around the hall was completed in 1895, each portraying a key event in the city's history.
In an adjacent building is the Renaissance Hall, which houses a massive wood, marble and alabaster chimney designed by Lanceloot Blondeel. The chimney is one of the best sculptural works of 16th-century Flanders.

⬟ Heilig Bloed Basiliek
Burg 10. ☎ (050) 44 8111, 33 3767.
◯ daily. ⬤ Mon (in winter).
The Basilica of the Holy Blood holds one of the most sacred reliquaries in Europe. The basilica divides into two distinct sections, the lower part being the evocative St Basil's chapel with its plain stone-pillared entrance and arches. The upper chapel was rebuilt in the 19th century after the French destroyed it in the 1790s. Here, brightly coloured decorations surround a silver tabernacle of 1611 which houses a sacred phial, supposed to contain a few drops of blood and water

washed from the body of Christ by Joseph of Arimathea. The phial was brought here from Jerusalem in 1150, and is still the object of great veneration. The church also has a museum that houses paintings, vestments and other artifacts.

♛ The Markt

The Markt is Bruges' main square and marketplace (a market has been held on this site since the 10th century). It is an impressive open space lined with 17th-century houses and overlooked by the Belfort on one side. The oldest façade on the square (dating from the 15th century) belongs to the Huis Bouchotte, which was the home of Charles II of England during part of his exile from 1656–7.

In the middle is a statue of Pieter de Coninck and Jan Breidel, two 14th-century guildsmen who led a rebellion against the French in 1302. Known as the *Bruges Matin*, they led Flemish soldiers to attack the French at dawn on May 18, 1302, killing almost all of them. This bloody uprising paved the way for a form of independence for the Low Countries' major towns. Rights such as the freedom to trade were subsequently enshrined in the towns' charters until the 15th century.

♛ The Belfort

Markt. ◯ *daily.* 🏛
The Markt is dominated by the belfry, whose octagonal belltower rises 83 m (272 ft) above the square. Built between the 13th and 15th centuries, the belfry is Bruges' most celebrated landmark as it was used to store the town's charter, and is therefore a constant reminder of the city's past as a centre of trade. Inside the tower a winding staircase leads up, past the chamber where the town's rights and privileges were stored, to the roof, where the views across Bruges are delightful.

Bruges' Belfort or belltower overlooking the Markt

Groeninge Museum

See pp118–19.

🏛 Arentshuis Museum

Dijver 16. 📞 *(050) 44 8763.* ◯ *Apr–Sep: daily; Oct–Mar: Wed–Mon.* 🏛
The Arentshuis Museum is housed in a genteel, 18th-century mansion overlooking the Dijver Canal. The interior is divided into two sections, with the ground floor devoted to a delightful selection of antique lace. Bruges was a centre of Belgian lace making and, although there were a few local factories, most of the work was done by women toiling in their own homes. The beautifully presented collection focuses on needlepoint and bobbin lace, with several fine examples of Bruges floral or Duchesse lace as well. Upstairs is the work of Frank Brangwyn (1867–1956), a painter and sculptor who was born in Bruges of Welsh parents. Most of Brangwyn's life was spent in Britain, but he bequeathed this collection to Bruges, as well as his drawings, furniture and carpets. Among his work, the dark and powerful canvases depicting industrial scenes are perhaps the most diverting.

Statue of Breidel and Pieter de Coninck

♛ Concertgebouw

't Zand. 📞 *(050) 47 6999.*
Built as part of the celebrations for Bruges' European City of Culture, this terracotta concert hall features a 28-m (92-ft) tower that offers great views.

Gruuthuse Museum

See pp116–17.

🏠 Onze Lieve Vrouwekerk

Mariastraat. ◯ *Apr–Sep: Sun–Fri; Oct–Mar: Mon–Sat.* 🏛 *mausoleum only.*
The Church of Our Lady took over two hundred years to build, starting in 1220, and incorporates a variety of styles. The interior, with its white walls, stark columns and black-and-white tiled floor has a medieval simplicity, while the side chapels and pulpit are lavishly decorated in the Baroque manner.

One of the church's artistic highlights is Michelangelo's sculpture *Madonna and Child* (1504–5), at the end of the southern aisle. This marble statue was imported by a Flemish merchant, and was the only one of the artist's works to leave Italy during his lifetime. In the choir there are fine paintings by Pieter Pourbus including a *Last Supper* (1562), and the carved mausoleums of the Burgundian prince Charles the Bold and his daughter Mary.

The soaring spire of the Church of Our Lady

Gruuthuse Museum

Facial fireguard

THE GRUUTHUSE MUSEUM occupies a large medieval mansion close to the Dijver Canal. In the 15th century, it was inhabited by the merchant (or Lord of the Gruuthuse) who had the exclusive right to levy a tax on the "Gruit", an imported mixture of herbs added to barley during the beer-brewing process. The mansion's labyrinthine rooms, with their ancient chimneypieces and wooden beams, have survived intact and nowadays hold a priceless collection of fine and applied arts. There are tapestries, wood carvings, furniture and even a medical section devoted to cures of everyday ailments such as haemorrhoids. The authentic kitchen and original 1472 chapel transport visitors back to medieval times.

2nd Floor

1st Floor

Ground Floor

Façade of the Gruuthuis
The museum's Gothic façade, with its elegant tower, stepped gables and fine stone windows, was built in the 15th century.

★ Charles V
This incredibly life-like terracotta and wood bust of Haps-burg king Charles V was carved in 1520 and is attributed to German sculptor Konrad Meit.

Entrance

STAR EXHIBITS

★ Charles V bust

★ Chapel

The Seven Free Arts
Dating from around 1675, this exquisite tapestry depicts the "free arts", which included music.

GALLERY GUIDE
*Laid out over three floors, the
collection is organized into
types of object from glassware,
porcelain and ceramics to
medical instruments in a
series of 22 numbered rooms.
Visitors may view the rooms
in sequence from 1–22 and
get a good sense of the
original uses and layout of
the house in doing so.*

★ Chapel
*Built in 1472, this oak-
panelled chapel on the
museum's second floor
overlooks the high altar
of the church next door.*

KEY

- ☐ Glassware, porcelain and ceramics
- ☐ Kitchen
- ☐ Chapel
- ☐ Musical instruments
- ☐ Coins
- ☐ Tapestries
- ☐ Tools, weights and measures
- ☐ Entrance hall
- ☐ Textiles and lace
- ☐ Household implements
- ☐ Renaissance works
- ☐ Baroque works
- ☐ Reliquary and furniture
- ☐ Medical instruments
- ☐ Great Hall
- ☐ Weaponry

House on the Southern Bridge at Minnewater

🏛 Hans Memling Museum
Mariastraat 38, 8000 Bruges.
☎ (050) 44 8771. ◯ Tue–Sun. ✍
This small museum (a former
13th-century hospital) contains
the works of Hans Memling
(1430–94), one of the most
talented painters of his era.
Among them, *The Mystical
Marriage of St. Catherine*
(1479), the central panel of a
triptych, is superb. The former
wards also house a collection
of paintings and furniture
related to the hospital's history.

⛪ Sint Salvator-Kathedraal
St Salvatorskof 1, 8000 Bruges.
☎ (050) 33 61 88. ◯ Apr–Sep:
daily. ● 1 Jan, 25 Dec. ✍
Built as a parish church from
the 12th and 15th centuries,
this large, yellow-brick building became Bruges' cathedral
in 1788 when the French army
destroyed the existing one. The
interior is enormous and quite
plain except for a handsome
set of Brussels' tapestries hang-
ing in the choir, and a 1682
organ adorned with angels.

**Pale brick tower of St Salvator-
Kathedraal in Bruges**

⚘ Minnewater
Just south of the Begijnhof,
Minnewater is a peaceful
park with a lake populated
by ducks and swans. Swans
have been here since 1448
when Maximilian of Austria
ordered they be kept in mem-
ory of his councillor, Pierre
Lanchais, who was beheaded
by the Bruges citizens.
   Once this was a bustling
harbour which connected to
the canal network and the sea.
Today, Minnewater can be
visited by one of the tourist
barges that take visitors on a
tour of Bruges by canal. It is
also a popular spot for walkers
and picnickers who may view
the pretty 15th-century lock
gate and house and the 1398
tower (Poedertoren).

⛪ Begijnhof
Wijngaardplein 1, 8000 Bruges.
☎ (050) 36 01 40. ◯ daily.
Béguines were members of
a lay sisterhood founded in
1245. They lived and dressed
as nuns but did not take vows
and were therefore able to
return to the secular world
at will. The begijnhof or
béguinage is the walled complex in a town that housed
the béguines. In Bruges, this
is an area of quiet tree-lined
canals faced by white, gabled
houses, with a pleasant green
at its centre. Visitors and locals
enjoy strolling here and may
visit the small, simple church
which was built in 1602. The
nuns who live in the houses
are no longer béguines, but
Benedictine sisters who moved
here in the 1930s. One of the
houses is open to visitors and
displays simple rustic furniture
and artifacts that illustrate the
women's contemplative lives.

Groeninge Museum

BRUGES' PREMIER FINE ARTS museum, the Groeninge, holds a fabulous collection of early Flemish and Dutch masters, featuring artists such as the influential Rogier van der Weyden (1399–1464), Jan van Eyck (d.1441), and Hans Memling (1430–94). Hieronymous Bosch (1450–94), famous for the strange freakish creatures of his moral allegories, is well represented too, as are Gerard David (d.1523) and Pieter Brueghel the Younger (1564–1638). These early works are displayed in the first ten rooms of the museum and beyond is a collection of later Belgian painters, most notably Paul Delvaux (1897–1994), and René Magritte (1898–1967). Originally built between 1929 and 1930, the museum is small and displays its collection in rotation.

Serenity *(1970)*
This unusually representative work by Paul Delvaux was commissioned by the museum, and retains elements of the artist's surrealist style.

Last Judgement
Painted on three oak panels in the early 16th century, this detail from Hieronymous Bosch's famous tryptich depicts scenes of cruelty and torture. The strong moral tone of the work suggests that man's sinful nature has created a hell on earth.

★ The Moreel Triptych *(1484)*
This panel of the triptych, by German-born artist Hans Memling, was designed to adorn the altar in a Bruges church. It is said to be the first ever group portrait.

STAR PAINTINGS

★ **Virgin and Child with Canon** by **Jan van Eyck**

★ **The Moreel Tryptich** by **Hans Memling**

★ Virgin and Child with Canon *(1436)*
Jan van Eyck's richly detailed painting is noted for its realism. It shows van Eyck's patron, the canon, being presented to St Donatian by St George.

1st Floor

Ground Floor

VISITORS' CHECKLIST

Dijver 12, 8000 Bruges. **(** *(050)
44 7841.* **▦** *Markt.* **○** *9:30am–
5pm Tue–Sun (tickets sold until
4:30pm).* **●** *1 Jan, 25 Dec.* **♿**

KEY

☐ 15th and 16th centuries

☐ 17th to 19th centuries

☐ 20th century

☐ Temporary exhibitions

▨ Non-exhibition space

GALLERY GUIDE
*The Groeninge is arranged
on one level with a two-
storey extension. The main
entrance leads to a series of
rooms displaying the early
Flemish masters and 20th-
century art. Works from the
17th to the turn of the 20th
century are exhibited in the
extension which is reached through
the back of the main gallery.*

Portrait of Bruges family *(1645)*
*Jacob van Oost the Elder's focus on the affluence of this
family overlooking their beloved city shows why he was
Bruges' most popular artist of the Baroque period.*

**Household
Cares** *(1913)*
*Rik Wouters used
his wife Nel as the
model for this
statue, cast in
bronze. The
work's Fauvist
style (see p15),
is reflected in the
bold planes that
enhance the
figure's anx-
ious stance.*

Museum Façade and Entrance
*Originally built in 1930, the gallery was
extended in 1994 to a design by architect Joseph Viérin. The entrance is based
on that of a Romanesque convent.*

Main
Entrance

Exploring Northeast Bruges

Statue of Jan van Eyck

IN THE HEIGHT OF THE summer and on holiday weekends, tourists pour into Bruges, and parts of the city centre often get too crowded for comfort. Fortunately, the narrow cobbled streets and picturesque canals to the north-east of the Markt never suffer from this, and this fascinating area remains one of the most delightful parts of Bruges. Streets of charming, medieval terraced houses are dotted with grand, yet elegant 18th-century mansions. The best approach is via Jan van Eyckplein, in medieval times the city's busiest harbour, from where it is a short stroll along Spinolarei and Potterierei streets to the many museums and churches that are found in this historic district.

Lace-making skills on show at the Kantcentrum lace centre

☗ Kantcentrum
Peperstraat 3. ▊ (050) 33 0072.
◻ Mon–Sat. 📷
The area from the white-washed cottages to the east of Potterierei Street is one of several old neighbourhoods where the city's lace workers plied their craft. Mostly, the women worked at home, receiving their raw materials from a supplier who also bought the finished product.

Lace-making skills are kept alive at the Kantcentrum, the Lace Centre at the foot of Balstraat, where local women (and a few men) fashion lace in a variety of styles, both modern and traditional. It is a busy place, and visitors can see the lace-making demonstrations held every afternoon during the summer. Some of the finished pieces are sold in the Kantcentrum shop at very reasonable prices.

🏛 Brugse Brouwerij-Mouterijmuseum
Verbrand Nieuwland 10. ▊ (050) 33 2697. ◻ daily. Call for details. 📷
Up to World War I there were 31 breweries operating in Bruges. This brewery museum,

housed in a malthouse built in 1902, lies south of the lace centre and the Jerzalemkerk. On display are artifacts and documents that tell the centuries-old story of beer and brewing in the city. Next door to the museum, De Gouden Boom is a working brewery founded in 1584 that produces the noted beer Brugse Tripel and the spicy wheat beer (known as *bière blanche*), Brugs Tarwebier.

⛪ Jeruzalemkerk
Peperstraat. ◻ Mon–Sat. 📷
Next door to the Kantcentrum, the Jeruzalemkerk is Bruges' most unusual church. The present building dates from the 15th century, and was built on the site of a 13th-century chapel commissioned by a family of wealthy Italian merchants, the Adornes family, whose black marble tomb can be seen inside. Based on the design of the church of the Holy Sepulchre in Jerusalem, the structure possesses a striking tower with two tiers of wooden, polygon-shaped lanterns topped by a tin orb. Inside, the lower level contains a macabre altarpiece, carved with skulls and assorted demons. Behind the altar is a smaller vaulted chapel; leading

The historic buildings and lovely canals of northeast Bruges

from this is a narrow tunnel guarded by an iron grate. Along the tunnel, a lifelike model of Christ in the Tomb can be seen at close quarters.

⛪ The Kruispoort and the windmills
Medieval Bruges was heavily fortified. It was encircled by a city wall which was itself protected by a moat and strengthened by a series of massive gates. Most of the wall was knocked down in the 19th century, but the moat

The Jeruzalemkerk was built in 1497

has survived and so has one of the gates, the Kruispoort, a monumental structure dating from 1402 that guards the eastern approach to the city. The earthen bank stretching north of the Kruispoort marks the line of the old city wall, which was once dotted with some 20 windmills. Today, only three remain overlooking the canal. The first windmill, the Bonne Chieremolen, was brought here from a village in Flanders in 1911, but the second – St Janshuismolen – is original to the city, an immaculately restored structure erected in 1770. The northernmost mill of the three is De Nieuwe Papegai, an old oil mill that was relocated here in 1970.

The massive Kruispoort is all that remains of Bruges' old city walls

🔒 English Convent

Carmersstraat 85. ☎ (050) 33 2424. 🕐 Mon–Sat. 📷 obligatory.

The English Convent was where dozens of English Catholics sought asylum following the execution of Charles I in 1642, and during Oliver Cromwell's subsequent rule as Lord Protector. The conventual buildings are not open to the public, but the nuns provide a well-informed tour of their beautiful church, which was built in the Baroque style in the 1620s. The interior has a delightful sense of space, its elegant proportions enhanced by its cupola, but the highlight is the altar, a grand affair made of around 20 types of marble.

🏛 Museum voor Volkskunde

Rolweg 40. ☎ (050) 33 0044. 🕐 Tue–Sun. 📷

The Museum voor Volkskunde is one of the best folk museums in Flanders. It occupies

These 17th-century almshouses house the Museum voor Volkskunde

an attractive terrace of low, brick almshouses located behind an old neighbourhood café called the "Zwarte Kat" (Black Cat), which serves as the entrance. Each of the almshouses is dedicated to a different aspect of traditional Flemish life, with workshops displaying old tools. Several different crafts are represented here, such as a cobbler's and a blacksmith's, through to a series of typical historical domestic interiors.

♟ Schuttersgilde St Sebastiaan

Carmersstraat 174. ☎ (050) 33 1626. 🕐 Tue–Thu & Sat (May–Sep: also open on Fri). 📷

The Archers' guild (the Schuttersgilde) was one of the most powerful of the militia guilds, and their 16th- and 17th-century red-brick guildhouse now houses a museum.

The commercial life of medieval Bruges was dominated by the guilds, each of which represented the interests

The St Sebastiaan guildhouse belonged to the archers

of a particular group of skilled workmen. The guilds guarded their privileges jealously and, among many rules and customs, marriage between children whose fathers were in different guilds was greatly frowned upon. The guild claimed the name St Sebastian after an early Christian martyr, who the Roman Emperor Diocletian had executed by his archers. The bowmen followed orders – and medieval painters often show Sebastian looking like a pincushion – but miraculously Sebastian's wounds healed and he had to be finished off by a band of club-wielding assassins. The guildhouse itself is notable for its collection of paintings of the guild's leading lights, gold and silver trinkets and guild emblems.

🏛 Museum Onze Lieve Vrouw van de Potterie

Potteriei 79. ☎ (050) 44 8777 🕐 Tue–Sun. 📷

Located by the canal in one of the quietest parts of Bruges, the Museum Onze Lieve Vrouw van de Potterie (Our Lady of Pottery) occupies part of an old hospital that was founded in 1276 to care for elderly women. There is a 14th- and 15th-century cloister, and several of the old sick rooms are now used to display a modest collection of paintings, the best of which are some realistic 17th- and 18th-century portraits of leading aristocrats. The hospital church is in excellent condition, too; it is a warm, intimate place with fine stained-glass windows and a set of impressive Baroque altarpieces.

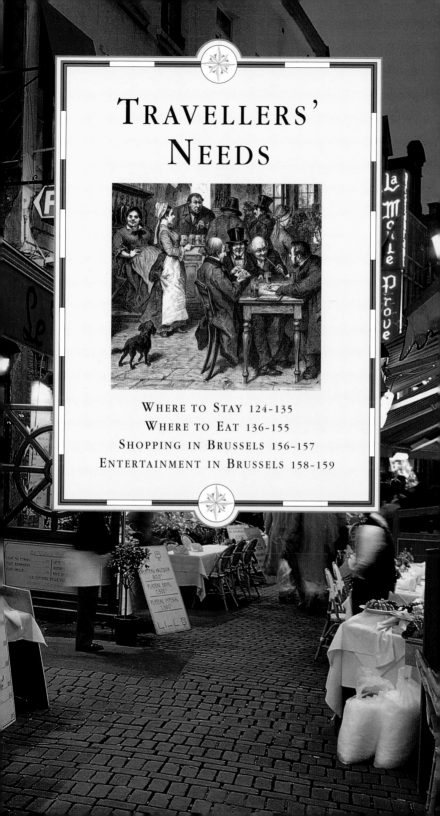

TRAVELLERS'
NEEDS

WHERE TO STAY

FOR MOST OF the year, Brussels is primarily a business or political destination, and accommodation is often priced accordingly. The wide range of top hotels has one fine advantage for the visitor; weekend and summer deals make it possible even on a modest budget to stay in some of Europe's most luxurious establishments. The mid-range of hotels is also well represented

Métropole bellboy

in the city, with period houses turned into stylish family-run hotels and chain hotels. To keep accommodation costs to a minimum, choose from Brussels' abundance of youth hostels and bed-and-breakfast options. *Choosing a Hotel* on pp128–9 will help you find at a glance the best hotels to suit your needs. A more detailed description of each hotel is listed on pp130–35.

Hallway in the Hôtel Métropole on Place de Brouckère (see p132)

HOTEL LOCATIONS

WHILE BRUSSELS does not have a specific hotel area, there are clusters of hotels in various parts of the city. Centrally, the most fertile ground is between Place Rogier and Place de Brouckère, which is within walking distance of both the Upper and Lower Town and a short bus ride from most major sights. The streets to the west of the Grand Place are also well supplied for those who want to be in the historic centre of town, but road noise can be a problem at night. To the north, Place Ste-Catherine and the streets behind Avenue de la Toison d'Or also have plenty of options. Following the pattern of cities worldwide, hotels generally reduce in price the further they are from the centre. Bed-and-breakfast rooms are dispersed across the capital and can often be found in residential

districts at very good rates. When arriving in the city from abroad by train or plane, it is worth knowing that the Gare du Midi and the airport both have nearby hotel colonies, although the station surroundings are run down in places. The airport has principally attracted chain hotels, which often offer good value package deals with the national airlines, although sightseeing from here is inconvenient.

ROOM RATES

HOTELS AT THE TOP end of the market offer exceptional standards of comfort and convenience to their largely corporate clients, and their prices reflect this. In general, prices are higher than in the rest of Belgium, but on a par with other European capitals. For a night in a luxury hotel, expect to pay €250 to €300 for a double room; the price for a room in the city averages in the €150 to €175 bracket.

Façade of the Crowne Plaza Hotel, one of the hotel chain (see p131)

However, there are numerous discounts available (*see Special Rates, p126*).

Single travellers can often find reasonable discounts on accommodation, although few places will offer rooms at half the price of a double. It is usual to be charged extra if you place additional guests in a double room. Travelling with children is not the financial burden it might be in this child-friendly society (*see p127*). Youth hostels cater very well to the budget student traveller and some also have family rooms.

TAXES AND CHARGES

ROOM TAXES and sales taxes should be included in the cost of your room, so the price quoted should be what appears as the total. The price of car parking may be added. Some hotels offer free parking, others charge up to €17 a night. In hotels with no private car park, it is worth checking discounts for public parking facilities if these are located nearby. While many hotels are happy to allow pets, many will add a small nightly charge to the bill.

Breakfast is not always included in the price of a room, even in very expensive establishments. However, many hotels do offer excellent free breakfasts, so ask when you book. The fare usually consists of continental breakfasts, including good coffee, warm croissants and brioche rolls, preserves and fruit juice. Bear in mind that if the expensive place where you are staying is charging €20 for a morning meal, there will be plenty of places nearby offering equal quality for much less money. The usual price for a hotel breakfast ranges upwards from €2.50, but coffee and rolls are usually priced at around €6.20. Unusually, youth hostels also offer lunches and dinners at around €9.90 each.

Phone calls from hotel rooms can be extremely expensive, with unit charges of €.60 for even a local call not uncommon. To make a long-distance call, buying a phonecard and using the efficient public payphone service is several times less expensive. Hotel faxes or modem charges, when available, can also mount up.

Minibar charges are usually very high, although no more so than in any other western European city. Watching satellite or pay-TV stations can also be expensive. However, Belgium's advanced cable network and proximity to other countries means that there are usually more than 20 free channels to choose from including the BBC as well as French and German television.

FACILITIES

I N A CITY with so many luxury hotels, fierce competition has led to ever more sophisticated gadgets and services for businesspeople. Several private phone lines, screened calls, free internet access, automatic check-out services, 24-hour news via Reuters, secretarial services, free mobile phones and even executive suites designed expressly for women

A business traveller's room at the Hotel Alfa Sablon *(see p132)*

are all on offer. Most of the top hotels also house extensive fitness facilities, including saunas and full gymnasiums, although there are few large swimming pools.

Brussels' reputation as a centre for fine dining is significantly enhanced by the hotel trade, with major hotels often offering several options, from expert gastronomy to excellent brasserie dining. For snacks and drinks, Brussels' hotels are known for their old-style, entertaining bars with piano music for those guests who prefer not to venture into the city at night. A handful have nightclub facilities where lively crowds meet for cocktails and dancing.

As one of Europe's major centres for the convention trade, Brussels is not short of meeting and function rooms, with the big hotels offering dozens of spaces for anything from conferences to society weddings and even relatively modest hotels offering good-sized rooms for business seminars and the like. Many

more expensive hotels have serviced apartments on offer; these can be useful for the greater freedom they provide.

19th-century courtyard of the Conrad International *(see p135)*

HOW TO BOOK

R OOMS ARE available in Brussels at most times of the year, but you should book several days in advance to ensure that you get the place you want. In mid- and top-range hotels, a credit card is the usual way to book, giving card details as a deposit; in smaller hotels, bookings can often be made simply by giving your name and details of the day and time of arrival.

The **Tourist Office** offers a free, same-day reservation service on-site. It also publishes a practical guide to Brussels hotels, updated annually, which is available on request. For booking by telephone, **Belgian Tourist Reservations** is a free service for visitors and very helpful.

Bar of the Hotel Arenberg, decorated with a cartoon mural *(see p131)*

View of the Grand Place from a room at Auberge Saint-Michel *(see p130)*

SPECIAL RATES

BRUSSELS IS AN exceptional destination, in that relatively few people come for the weekend or in July and August, meaning that often remarkable deals can be acquired at these times.

The cost of staying in one of the top hotels over the weekend or at off-peak times can plummet by as much as 65 per cent (for example, from €300 to €100 for a double room), so checking before booking about any special deals may save a large sum of money. A few hotels also offer discounts for guests who eat in their restaurants.

Some reservation services charge a small fee, but they can usually find competitively priced accommodation. Any deposit given is deducted from the final hotel bill.

Many travel agents also offer packages for visiting Brussels or Belgium, with accommodation working out less expensively than a custom-booked break.

Another option worth looking into is to check with your airline about possible discounts through its reservation services, and to find out about frequent-flyer bargains for affiliated hotels.

Bellboy at the Conrad International

DISABLED TRAVELLERS

HOTELS IN Brussels and the rest of Belgium take the needs of disabled travellers seriously. Many have one or more rooms designed with wheelchair-bound guests in mind. Bear in mind that many hotel buildings in Brussels are historic and therefore may not be suitable. Most staff, however, will be helpful. It is wise to ask in advance whether the hotel can cater to travellers with special needs. Most hotels will allow the visually handicapped to bring a guide dog onto the premises, although again it is best to make sure that this is the case before you arrive.

YOUTH ACCOMMODATION

BRUSSELS HAS several central, excellent youth hostels, with modern facilities, reasonably priced food and more privacy than is usually associated with hostel stays. Perhaps the best are the **Jacques Brel**, close to Place Madou, and the **Sleep Well**, which has disabled access. A bed in a four-person room should cost in the region of €11.70, rising to around €17.40 for a single room. Breakfast is sometimes included or costs from €2.50, with lunch and dinner for a charge of around €9.90. If you are not a member of the International Youth Hostel Foundation, rates will rise by €2.50 extra per night; membership cards, priced €12.40, are available at most hostels.

DIRECTORY

RESERVATION AGENCIES

Belgian Tourist Reservations
Boulevard Anspach 111, Brussels 1000. **Map** 1 C3.
[(02) 513 7484.

Tourist Information Board
Town Hall, Grand Place 1, Brussels 1000. **Map** 2 D3.
[(02) 513 8940.
[w] www.tib.be

AUBERGES DE JEUNESSE/YOUTH HOSTELS:

Jacques Brel
Rue de la Sablonnière 30, Brussels 1000. **Map** 2 F1.
[(02) 218 0187.

Jeugdherberg Bruegel
Rue du Saint-Esprit 2, Brussels 1000.
[(02) 511 0436.

Generation Europe
Rue de l'Eléphant 4, Brussels 1080. **Map** 1 A1.
[(02) 410 3858.

New Sleep Well
Auberge du Marais, Rue du Damier 23, Brussels 1000.
Map 2 D1. [(02) 218 50 50. [w] www.sleepwell.be

BED AND BREAKFAST

Bed and Breakfast Taxi Stop
Rue du Fossé-aux-Loups 28, Brussels 1000. **Map** 2 D2. [(02) 223 2310.

New Windrose
Avenue Brugmann, Brussels 1060.
[(02) 534 7191.

Bed & Brussels
Rue Kindermans 9, Brussels 1050. [(02) 646 0737.
[w] www.bnb-brussels.be

GAY AND LESBIAN ACCOMMODATION

Tels Quels
Rue du Marché au Charbon 81, Brussels 1000. **Map** 1 C3. [(02) 512 4587.

The Hilton Brussels, formerly the Albert Premier Rogier *(see p130)*

Joining is worthwhile when seeing the rest of Belgium, as there are over 30 hostels around the countryside.

GAY AND LESBIAN ACCOMMODATION

THERE ARE NO specifically gay or lesbian hotels in the city, but same-sex couples should have few problems finding welcoming accommodation. The **Tels Quels** association is the best source of information about suitable lodging, and also has a documentation centre covering most aspects of gay life in the city.

TRAVELLING WITH CHILDREN

CHILDREN ARE welcome at all hotels in Brussels. Most allow one or two under-12s to stay in their parents' room without extra charge; indeed, some hotels will extend this

principle to under-16s and under-18s. When travelling with children, it is worth reserving in advance as the hotel will find the room that best suits your needs. Families planning a long stay in Brussels should consider renting a suite or a self-catering apartment, which are economical.

SELF-CATERING APARTMENTS

THERE IS NO shortage of self-catering accommodation in Brussels, with many places available for a short stay as well as by the week or month. A few are attached to hotels as suites, with the rest run by private companies. Prices start at around €300 per week, for a fairly basic but furnished one- or two-bedroom apartment, to €990 or more for more luxurious lodgings. Contact the Belgian Tourist Reservations or visit the Tourist Office for a detailed list of suggestions.

BED-AND-BREAKFAST

BED-AND-BREAKFAST, also called *chambre d'hôte*, accommodation can be a very pleasant alternative to staying in a cheap hotel, and rooms can often be found even in the centre of town. You may come across a bargain by wandering the streets, but the easiest way to find bed-and-breakfast lodgings is through the Tourist Office or one of the capital's specialist agencies.

The interior of the George V hotel *(see p130)*

USING THE LISTINGS

Hotel listings are on pp128–35. Each hotel is listed according to area and price category. The symbols after each hotel summarize its facilities.

🛁 all rooms have bath and/or shower unless otherwise indicated
1 single-rate rooms available
🎏 rooms for more than two people available, or an extra bed can be put in a double room
24 24-hour room service
TV television in all rooms
🍸 mini-bar in all rooms
🚭 non-smoking rooms available
🗄 air conditioning in all rooms
🏋 gym/fitness facilities available in hotel
🏊 swimming pool in hotel
💼 business facilities: these include message-taking service, fax service, desk and telephone in each room, and meeting room within the hotel
🧒 caters for children
♿ wheelchair access
🛗 lift
🐕 pets allowed in bedrooms
P hotel parking available
🌳 garden or grounds
🍷 bar
🍴 restaurant
💳 credit cards accepted:
AE American Express
DC Diners Club
MC Mastercard/Access
V Visa

Price categories for hotels are based on a standard double room per night in high season, including tax and service. As most hostel accommodation is dormitory-style, prices are based on the the cost of a single bed in a dormitory.

€ up to €62
€€ €62–112
€€€ €112–174
€€€€ €174–248
€€€€€ over €248

Choosing a Hotel

THE HOTELS AND HOSTELS on the following pages have all been inspected and assessed specifically for this guide. This chart highlights some of the factors that may affect your choice. During the week, Brussels is Europe's top business destination, and hotels with office facilities are included here; but sight-seeing travellers may find weekend discounts useful. For more information on each entry, see pp 130–35. They are listed by area and appear alphabetically within their price categories.

	Price	Number of Rooms	Business Facilities	Restaurant	Garden	Quiet Location	Period Decor	Weekend Discounts
THE LOWER TOWN (see pp130–32)								
Barry	€	32						●
Les Eperonniers	€	21					▪	
Auberge Saint-Michel	€€	15					▪	●
George V	€€	16						
Hilton Brussels City	€€	285					▪	
Ibis Brussels City	€€	236	▪					
La Légende	€€	26				●	▪	
La Madeleine	€€	52						●
Matignon	€€	37		●				
Mozart	€€	47					▪	●
Noga	€€	19	●			●		
Orion	€€	169			▪			●
Queen Anne	€€	60						
Welcome	€€	10		●			▪	
Windsor	€€	24	▪					●
Arenberg NH	€€€	155	▪	●		●		
Art Hotel Siru	€€€	101	▪	●			▪	
Atlas	€€€	88	▪					
Crowne Plaza	€€€	356		●		●	▪	●
Dome	€€€	125	▪	●			▪	
Ibis off Grand Place	€€€	184			▪			
Vendôme	€€€	106	▪	●				●
Aris	€€€€	55						●
Bedford	€€€€	319	▪	●				●
Novotel off Grand Place	€€€€	136	▪	●				●
Amigo	€€€€€	182	▪				▪	●
Carrefour de L'Europe	€€€€€	63	▪	●				●
Métropole	€€€€€	410	▪	●	▪		▪	●
Plaza	€€€€€	193	▪	●			▪	●
Radisson SAS	€€€€€	281	▪	●				●
Sheraton Towers	€€€€€	533	▪	●	▪			●
THE UPPER TOWN (see pp132–33)								
Les Bluets	€	10						
Argus	€€	41	▪			●		●
Sabina	€€	24				●	▪	
Alfa Sablon	€€€	32				●		●
Dixseptième	€€€	24	▪		▪	●	▪	●
Hilton	€€€€	434	▪	●	▪			●
Sofitel	€€€€	175	▪		▪		▪	●
Stanhope	€€€€	50	▪	●	▪	●	▪	●
Astoria	€€€€€	118	▪	●			▪	●
Dorint	€€€€€	212	▪	●	▪			●
Jolly Grand Sablon	€€€€€	193	▪	●			▪	●
Méridien	€€€€€	224	▪	●				●
Renaissance Brussels Hotel	€€€€€	257	▪	●		●		●
Royal Windsor	€€€€€	266	▪	●			▪	●

	Price category	NUMBER OF ROOMS	BUSINESS FACILITIES	RESTAURANT	GARDEN	QUIET LOCATION	PERIOD DECOR	WEEKEND DISCOUNTS

Price categories for a double room (not per person), including service:

€ up to €62
€€ €62–112
€€€ €112–174
€€€€ €174–248
€€€€€ over €248

WEEKEND DISCOUNTS
Substantial drops in the room rate at weekends.

RESTAURANT
Hotel contains a dining room or restaurant serving lunch and dinner for hotel guests.

BUSINESS FACILITIES
Conference rooms, desks, fax, internet and computer service for guests.

PERIOD DECOR
Historic features, furniture and art decorate the public and private rooms.

QUIET LOCATION
Quiet residential neighbourhood or quiet street in a busy area.

	Price	Rooms	Business	Restaurant	Garden	Quiet	Period	Weekend
GREATER BRUSSELS *(see pp 134–35)*								
De Boeck's	€€	36			●	●		●
Les Tourelles	€€	21	■			●	■	●
Sun	€€	22				●		
Abbey	€€€	47	■					
Alfa Louise	€€€	40			■			
Château Gravenhof	€€€	26	■		■	●	■	
Holiday Inn City Centre	€€€€	201	■	●				●
Hyatt Regency Barsey	€€€€	99	■				■	●
Manos Stéphanie	€€€€	55			■	●		●
NH Brussels City Centre	€€€€	246	■	●				●
President WTC	€€€€	302	■	●	■	●		●
Sofitel	€€€€	125	■	●	■	●		●
Bristol Stéphanie	€€€€€	142	■	●			■	●
Conrad International	€€€€€	269	■	●	■			●
Gresham Belson	€€€€€	135	■					●
Montgomery	€€€€€	63	■	●		●	■	●
Sheraton	€€€€€	304	■	●				●
ANTWERP *(see p135)*								
Firean	€€€	15		●				
Hilton	€€€€€	211		●				●
BRUGES *(see p135)*								
de Pauw	€€	8		●				
't Bourgoensch Hof	€€€	22		●				
Hotel de Tuilerieen	€€€€	45						
GHENT *(see p135)*								
Erasmus	€€	11						
Gravensteen	€€€	49						●

Amigo

Rue de l'Amigo 1–3, 1000 Brussels.
Map 1 C3. ((02) 547 4747.
FAX (02) 513 5277.
W www.hotelamigo.com
Rooms: 182. 🛏 1 🛗 24 TV Y
🗘 🗐 🗄 🛗 👤 🗠 👤 🍽
🗲 AE, DC, MC, V. €€€€€

This elegant six-storey hotel
occupies the site of a 16th-century
prison, only a minute's stroll from
the Grand Place. The luxurious
rooms, recently renovated, are
decorated in the style of the
Spanish Renaissance, which was
popular during the reign of the
French king Louis XV. The Amigo
offers excellent facilities and an
extremely friendly, helpful service
in what is primarily a business
hotel. The marble bathrooms are
suavely charming if slightly
cramped. There is also a good
choice of restaurants. Breakfast
is included in the price of the
room. Rates from Friday through
Sunday nights inclusive are
reduced by half.

Carrefour de l'Europe

Rue du Marché-aux-Herbes 110,
1000 Brussels. **Map** 2 D3.
((02) 504 9400. FAX (02) 504
9500. W www.carrefoureurope.net
Rooms: 63. 🛏 24 TV 🗘 Y
🗐 🗄 🗘 Y 🍽 🗲 AE, DC, MC,
V. €€€€€

This business-oriented hotel is in a
modern building near the Grand
Place and the Gare Centrale. The
rooms are uniformly decorated
but comfortable; the triple glazing,
important in this busy city, ensures
that the worst of the city's noise is
kept at bay.

Métropole

Place de Brouckère 31, 1000 Brussels.
Map 1 D2. ((02) 217 2300.
FAX (02) 218 0220.
W www.metropolehotel.be
Rooms: 410. 🛏 1 🛗 24 TV
Y 🗘 🗐 🛗 🗘 🗠 Y 🍽
🗲 AE, DC, MC, V. €€€€€

Located on the busy, crowded
but central Place de Brouckère,
this Belle Epoque masterpiece
dates from 1895 and inside recalls
the city in its Art Nouveau heyday.
The period lift offers a wonderful
view of the richly decorated lobby
with its high ceilings, gilt cornices
and crystal chandeliers. The
modern rooms are comfortable
if a touch less characterful. The
bar is splendidly decorated with
Corinthian columns, palm plants
and roomy sofas. The room price
includes a good continental
breakfast.

Plaza

Boulevard Adolphe Max 118–126,
1000 Brussels. **Map** 2 D1. ((02)
227 6740. FAX (02) 223 7929. W
www.leplaza-brussels.be *Rooms:* 193.
🛏 1 🛗 TV 🗘 Y 🗲 🗐 🗄 🗘
🛗 P Y 🍽 🗲 AE, DC, MC, V.
€€€€€

The quarters of choice for senior
German officers during World
War II, this classic 1930s building on
a rather downbeat street off Place
de Brouckère has been resurrected
after a 20-year closure. Combining
old-fashioned style with state-of-the-
art facilities, period features include
chandeliers and Murano glassware.
Several rooms are tailored to busi-
nesswomen, and have been decorated in a gently relaxing pastel
pale turquoise with hairdryers
and extra-special toiletries.

Radisson SAS Hotel

Rue du Fossé-aux-Loups 47, 1000
Brussels. **Map** 2 D2. ((02) 219
2828. FAX (02) 219 6262.
W www. radisson.com *Rooms:* 281.
🛏 1 🛗 TV 🗘 Y 🗲 🗐 🛗
🗄 🗘 🛗 P Y 🍽 🗲 AE, DC,
MC, V. €€€€€

Built around a 12th-century
section of the city walls, this
Art Deco-inspired hotel near the
Galéries St-Hubert is among
the city's most impressive, with
comfortable rooms tastefully
decorated in Asian, Italian or
Scandinavian styles. Services for
guests include a personal answer-
phone and free mobile phones.
Tours of the city, as well as golfing
trips, can be organized by the
hotel. The hotel's 2-star Michelin
Sea Grill restaurant is among
Brussels' finest *(see p153)*.

Sheraton Towers

Place Rogier 3, 1210 Brussels. **Map** 2
D1. ((02) 224 3111. FAX (02) 224
3456. W www.sheraton.com/brussels
Rooms: 533. 🛏 🛗 24 TV Y
🗲 🗐 🗄 🗘 🗠 🛗 Y
P Y 🍽 🗲 AE, DC, MC, V.
€€€€€

Even among the looming sky-
scrapers that rear over Place
Rogier, there is no mistaking the
twin towers of the capital's biggest
hotel. The emphasis is firmly
on comfort, with large rooms decorated in understated brown and
deep red tones. This is a luxurious
and relaxing environment for
businesspeople to work, rest or
play with ease. Some rooms have
private offices, and all have well-
equipped work stations. The indoor
swimming-pool on the 30th floor
has spectacular views over the city.

Les Bluets

Rue Berckmans 124, 1060 Brussels.
((02) 534 3983. FAX (02) 543
0970. W www.geocities.com/
les_bluets/angl1/html *Rooms:* 10.
🛏 TV 🗄 🗲 🗲 AE, DC, MC, V. €

This charming late-19th-century
hotel is non-smoking throughout.
The decor features antique
furniture, lots of plants and caged
birds. Rooms are simply furnished
and breakfast is included in the
already reasonable price.

Argus

Rue Capitaine Crespel 6, 1050
Brussels. **Map** 2 D5. ((02) 514
0770. FAX (02) 514 1222.
W www.hotel-argus.be *Rooms:* 41.
🛏 1 TV Y 🗘 P 🗲 AE, DC,
MC, V. €€

Handily placed between the
Porte de Namur and Place Louise,
this tasteful, quiet hotel makes
a good base for exploring the
whole city. The rooms are clean
and comfortable. Prices drop
further at weekends and throughout July and August.

Sabina

Rue du Nord 78, 1000 Brussels.
Map 2 F2. ((02) 218 2637.
FAX (02) 219 3239. W www.hotel
sabina.be *Rooms:* 24. 🛏 1 TV
🗘 🛗 P Y 🗲 AE, DC. €€

This friendly and well-kept hotel
occupies an elegant 19th-century
building. Inside, authentic wood
panelling and fireplaces enhance
the peaceful atmosphere. The
hotel is located on a quiet street
in the residential area around
Place Madou. It is also close to
Brussels' main attractions and the
European government institutions.

Alfa Sablon

Rue de la Paille 2–8, 1000 Brussels.
((02) 513 6040. FAX (02) 511
8141. W www.alfahotels.com
Rooms: 32. 🛏 1 TV Y 🗲 🗐
🛗 🗘 🗠 🗲 AE, DC, MC, V.
€€€

This calm, refined hotel boasts a
great location near the Place du
Grand Sablon, which is noted for
its appealing antique shops and
enticing cafés. An attractive late
19th-century façade houses a light,
inviting contemporary interior.
There is a garden and a sauna,
and the four large, split-level
suites are particularly comfortable.

Dixseptième

Rue de la Madeleine 25, 1000 Brussels. **Map** 2 D3. (02) 502 5744. FAX (02) 502 6424. @ info@ledixseptieme.be W www.ledixseptieme.be **Rooms:** 24. AE, DC, MC, V. €€€

Built in the 17th century as the home of the Spanish ambassador, this small, peaceful hotel offers a calming break from the bustling Ilôt Sacré. Each room is named after a Belgian artist, and enthusiasts can refresh their painting knowledge thanks to the art library in the lounge. Many of the rooms are authentically decorated in Baroque style with parquet flooring throughout, and flamboyant crystal chandeliers in the public areas. A splendid Louis XIV staircase connects some of the rooms, several of which look out over a private courtyard.

Hilton

Boulevard de Waterloo 38, 1000 Brussels. **Map** 2 E5. (02) 504 1111. FAX (02) 504 2111. W www.hilton.com **Rooms:** 434. AE, DC, MC, V. €€€€

In addition to the usual features – crisp service, business facilities and large, comfortable rooms – the Hilton offers personal security guards and such facilities for Japanese visitors as Japanese speakers, newspapers and kimonos. The lobby is decorated with a large golden frieze depicting the Grand Place. The hotel also houses the Michelin-starred restaurant Maison de Boeuf.

Sofitel

Avenue de la Toison d'Or 40, 1050 Brussels. **Map** 2 E5. (02) 514 2200. FAX (02) 514 5744. W www. accorhotels.com **Rooms:** 175. AE, DC, MC, V. €€€€

Dwarfed by the looming 1960s-built Hilton on the opposite side of the street, this relatively discreet branch of the upmarket French chain easily holds its own in terms of elegance. The most impressive features are the English-style bar and library with its comfortable leather chairs. It is also possible to escape from the bustle of the city in the Sofitel's beautiful garden, with its statues by Belgian sculptor Jean Cayette. Inside the rooms, king-size beds and a quiet, comfortable atmosphere attract plenty of admirers. The hotel does not have its own restaurant but is within five minutes' walk of a selection of Brussels' finest.

Stanhope

Rue du Commerce 9, 1000 Brussels. **Map** 2 F4. (02) 506 9111. FAX (02) 512 1708. W www.summit hotels. com **Rooms:** 50. AE, DC, MC, V. €€€€

The Stanhope represents a luxurious Belgian vision of traditional upper-class historic British hospitality. The hotel has taken over three adjacent townhouses to deliver its elegant old-world service, which includes chauffeur-driven cars, afternoon tea and newspapers pushed under the door in the mornings. The rooms have marble bathrooms, handmade furniture and paintings on the walls. Breakfast is included. There are very good rates at weekends.

Astoria

Rue Royale 103, 1000 Brussels. **Map** 2 E2. (02) 227 0505. FAX (02) 217 1150. W www.sofitel.com **Rooms:** 118. AE, DC, MC, V. €€€€

This opulent Belle Epoque masterpiece recalls the capital's glory days of the early 20th century, when such famous statesmen as Eisenhower and Churchill were among its most distinguished guests. The lobby, staircase, wood-panelled lift and furnishings are all original. The recently renovated rooms retain their individual character, and each is triple-glazed. The Pullman bar is in a former Orient Express carriage.

Dorint

Boulevard Charlemagne 11–19, 1000 Brussels. **Map** 3 B2. (02) 231 0909. FAX (02) 231 3371. W www.dorint.be **Rooms:** 212. AE, DC, MC, V. €€€€

Situated near the European government complex, the Dorint is favoured by visiting journalists, diplomats and politicians. The hotel offers ISDN lines, translation cabins and a bar with a Reuters terminal updating news 24 hours a day. Try the fitness club with its Turkish bath, sauna and solarium, or take a stroll in the tranquil Oriental garden. For a taste of Brussels' culture, contemporary works by local photographers hang in the rooms.

Jolly Grand Sablon

Rue Boedenbroeck 2–4, 1000 Brussels. **Map** 2 D4. (02) 512 8800. FAX (02) 512 6766. W www.jollyhotels.it **Rooms:** 193. AE, DC, MC, V. €€€€

With an unbeatable location on the southern edge of the Place du Grand Sablon, this Italian chain's flagship Brussels hotel offers impeccable service and grand rooms. The façade is an unobtrusive addition to the wonderful Baroque masterpieces all around it. Good weekend rates.

Méridien

Carrefour de l' Europe 3, 1000 Brussels. (02) 548 4211. FAX (02) 548 4080. W www.meridien.be **Rooms:** 224. AE, DC, MC, V. €€€€€

This luxurious modern hotel is very close to the Grand Place but is also opposite the Gare Centrale, which can be, to some tastes, a slightly seedy area. The hotel is decorated in modern style and has a plush lobby featuring a large brass chandelier; this is a popular meeting place with a comfortable atmosphere that is enhanced by a regular pianist. The rooms are furnished in English Victorian style. The hotel manages to cater to both business travellers and families, with corporate facilities such as multilingual staff.

Renaissance Brussels Hotel

Rue de Parnasse 19, 1050 Brussels. (02) 505 2929. FAX (02) 505 2555. **Rooms:** 257. AE, DC, MC, V. €€€€€

The first luxury hotel to establish itself near the European Parliament, just a few minutes from the Palais Royal, the former Archimède was taken over by Renaissance in 2001. Each bedroom is large and well equipped. Guests also have access to the world-class Academy Gym next door.

Royal Windsor

Rue Duquesnoy 5, 1000 Brussels. **Map** 2 D3. (02) 505 5555. FAX (02) 505 5500. W www.warwickhotels.com/brussels **Rooms:** 266. AE, DC, MC, V. €€€€€

This characterful deluxe hotel near the Grand Place has small but exquisite facilities. The sumptuous French-styled bedrooms are reckoned to be Brussels' most expensive per square metre. However, the wonderful marble bathrooms make up for the lack of space. Other facilities include a restaurant with a glorious circular stained-glass window in its ceiling.

WHERE TO EAT

Thai chef in Brussels

IT IS ALMOST impossible to eat badly in Brussels. Some say one can eat better here than in Paris, and even meals in the lower- to mid-price bracket are always carefully prepared and often innovative. Venues range from top gastronomic restaurants to unpretentious local taverns where you can find generous servings of local specialities. If you tire of Belgian fare, try the variety of excellent local seafood and the range of ethnic cuisine that reflects the city's lively cultural diversity. The listings on pp146–53 give a detailed description of all the selected restaurants and the key features of each restaurant are summarized on pp144–5.

Brasserie Horta in Centre Belge de la Bande Dessinée *(see p146)*

WHERE TO EAT

THE BELGIAN love affair with dining out makes for an astonishing concentration of restaurants and eateries: a 10-minute stroll from almost anywhere in Brussels should bring you to a decent, and often almost undiscovered, tavern or brasserie. However, superb dining is to be had without leaving the Ilôt Sacré, the area around the central Grand Place, where many very good and surprisingly reasonable restaurants abound. Beware the tourist traps around the Grand Place that make their living from gulling unwary visitors into spending far more than they intended to. The impressive displays of seafood adorning the pavements of Rue des Bouchers northwest of the Grand Place and Petite Rue des Bouchers can promote rather touristy restaurants, but those on pp146–7 are recommended.

TYPES OF CUISINE

ELSEWHERE IN the city centre is a wealth of quality fish restaurants, especially around the former fish market at Place Ste-Catherine, while the city's trendiest eateries can be found on Rue Dansaert and in the Place Saint-Géry district. If you are planning to explore other parts of Brussels, or if you are staying outside the city centre, you will find plenty of good Belgian fare on offer in the southern communes of Ixelles and Saint-Gilles, and in Etterbeek, where the European Commission buildings are located. Ixelles also boasts the largest concentration of Vietnamese and Southeast Asian cuisine, especially around Chaussée de Boondael. This student area in the Matonge district is also home to several African restaurants, serving food from the Congo (formerly Zaire), Senegal and Rwanda.

North of the city centre, in the communes of Schaerbeek and Saint-Josse, Turkish and North African communities have sprung up, and excellent Moroccan and Tunisian cuisine is commonplace. There is also a growing trend for "designer couscous", with Belgian restaurateurs exploiting the popularity of North African food in spectacularly ornate venues, often featuring ethnic music in the evenings.

Spanish and Portuguese restaurants can be found in the Marolles district and in Saint-Gilles, reflecting the wave of immigration in the 1950s and 1960s when many southern Europeans chose to settle in Brussels. The city is also liberally sprinkled with Greek restaurants, although many veer on the over-touristy side. A better bet are the modern Latin American eateries.

VEGETARIANS

DESPITE A MARKED upturn in recent years, Brussels is far from being a vegetarian-friendly city, since there are only a handful of specialist vegetarian restaurants *(see p153)*. However, those who eat fish will find mainstream restaurants cater generously to their needs; Brussels is very strong on fish and seafood. Also, the traditional dish, *stoemp*, mashed potatoes

Façade of the popular brasserie La Belle Epoque *(see p147)*

mixed with root vegetables, is a classic vegetarian speciality. North African restaurants usually offer vegetarian couscous options, and there are plenty of Italian options for cheese-eaters. Indian restaurants are few and far between, but most offer vegetable curries. Vegans may struggle, particularly in European restaurants.

HOW MUCH TO PAY

MOST RESTAURANTS, taverns and cafés display a menu in the window and the majority take credit cards. Prices usually include VAT (21 per cent) and service (16 per cent), although it is worth checking the latter before you tip. A meal at the city's most luxurious restaurants can cost up to €150 per head, but you can eat superbly for around €50 per head (including wine) and a hearty snack in a tavern should cost no more than €15. The mark-up level on wine can be very high, especially in most Mediterranean restaurants and in obviously touristic areas, but most taverns do a reasonable *vin maison* and serve myriad varieties of beer.

Service in all but the most expensive restaurants can be erratic by British and US standards. But beneath the sometimes grumpy exterior, you will often find warmth and an earthy, cheerfully self-deprecating sense of humour that is unique to Belgium. There are no hard and fast rules, but some diners leave an additional tip of up to 10 per cent if they are especially

The exotic interior of the Blue Elephant, Thai restaurant *(see p151)*

satisfied with the quality of the meal and the service. Note that some restaurants cannot take service on a credit card slip, and this, plus the tip, will have to be paid in cash, as do other gratuities in the city.

Stall selling freshly made snacks in Saint-Gilles at the weekend

DINING ON A BUDGET

MANY RESTAURANTS offer bargain, fixed-price or rapid lunchtime menus for under €12.50, plus reasonably priced dishes of the day. Even the city's most expensive

eateries have similar deals, meaning you can sample haute cuisine for less than €37. In the evening, look out for set menus with *vin compris* (wine included), which are often a way to save a large part of the dining bill.

At the other end of the scale, Brussels has most of the usual fast-food outlets, and sandwiches are sold at most butchers or delicatessens *(traiteurs)*, usually with tuna, cheese or cold meat fillings. Some of the latter offer sit-down snacks too. Alternatively, take advantage of Belgium's national dish, *frites/frieten* (French fries, hand-cut and double-fried to ensure an even crispiness). There are *Friteries/Frituurs* all over town, serving enormous portions of French fries with mayonnaise and dozens of other sauces, plus *fricadelles* (sausages in batter), lamb kebabs, fish cakes or meatballs. Inevitably, these establishments vary in quality; one sure bet is Maison Antoine on Place Jourdan in Etterbeek, where they have been frying for over half a century.

Brussels' sizeable Turkish community means that kebab, gyros and pitta restaurants are ubiquitous, especially in Saint-Josse and on the gaudy Rue du Marché aux Fromages, just off the Grand Place. Perhaps a better bet is the nearby L'Express, a Lebanese take-away specializing in chicken and felafel pittas, generously crammed with fresh salad.

Most cafés and taverns offer *petite restauration* (light meals) on top or instead of

Interior of Scheltema, a Belle Epoque brasserie *(see p153)*

**Entrance of the historic tavern
In 't Spinnekopke *(see p146)***

a regular menu. These simple,
traditional snacks include
croque monsieur, shrimp
croquettes, chicory baked
with ham and cheese, salads,
spaghetti bolognaise and
américain (raw minced beef
with seasoning). Do not be
fooled by the word "light" –
most of these dishes will keep
you going from lunchtime
well into the evening.

Healthy breakfasts and light
lunches with an emphasis on
organic food are the staple
of Le Pain Quotidien/Het
Dagelijks Brood *(see p155)*,
a fashionable Belgian chain
where customers are seated
all together around a large
wooden table: trying this out
is highly recommended if
breakfast is not included in

your hotel accommodation.
For snackers who are sweet-
toothed, waffle stands or vans
appear on almost every corner,
while cafés and taverns offer
a tempting variety of waffles
(topped with jam, cream or
chocolate). Pancakes *(crêpes)*
are just as popular – and
filling – although you can
cut down the calories with a
savoury wholewheat pancake
at one of the city's crêperies.

Ethnic food can also work
out at a very reasonable price;
large portions of couscous,
pizzas and African specialities
are often to be found at good
rates in student areas and at
stands throughout the city.

**Open-air tables outside fish
restaurants in Rue des Bouchers**

OPENING TIMES

S INCE time-consuming
business lunches are still
very much part of the culture
in Belgium, most restaurants
are open for lunch from noon

until 2 or 3pm. Dinner is
generally served from 7pm
onwards and last orders are
taken as late as 10pm. You
are more likely to find late-
night restaurants, serving until
midnight, in the side streets of
downtown Brussels; only a
handful provide meals after
1am. Breakfast bars usually
open around 7am. For details
of café and bar opening
times, see pp154–5.

MAKING A RESERVATION

W HEN VISITING one of the
city's more celebrated
restaurants, it is always wise
to book in advance. The
listings indicate where
booking is advisable. If you
are planning to go to the
legendary Comme Chez Soi,
you should reserve weeks
ahead rather than hope for a
last-minute cancellation.
Trendy designer restaurants
are often crowded in the
evening, but usually take
reservations well in advance.

READING THE MENU

M ENUS AT most restaurants
are written in French,
sometimes in Flemish and
French. Some, especially in
tourist areas, may have explanations in English. Dishes of
the day or suggestions are
often illegibly scribbled on

The Art Nouveau interior of Comme Chez Soi, often praised as Brussels' best restaurant *(see p149)*

The 16th-century cellar of 't Kelderke in the Grand Place (see p147)

blackboards. Fortunately, most waiters speak at least a little English. You may find a food dictionary useful. For details of some of the most popular Belgian specialities, see pp140–41. The phrasebook on pp189–91 also gives translations of many menu items.

ETIQUETTE

BRUSSELS IS LESS relaxed than, say, Amsterdam and, although casual or smart-casual dress is acceptable in most restaurants, you will probably feel more at home dressing up for upmarket places. A few formal restaurants will insist on a jacket and tie for men. The dress code for women is more flexible, but smartness is appreciated.

CHILDREN

IN GENERAL, Brussels is family-oriented and child-friendly, perhaps because Belgian children tend to be restrained and well behaved in restaurants. Many establishments have children's menus, although they are not always a bargain, and several offer free meals for children under 12. High-chairs should be available on request, and some restaurants have inside play areas, including some of the big hotels, where children are usually welcome. On the outskirts of Brussels or near one of the city's many parks, eateries can offer extensive outside playgrounds. Ethnic restaurants, in particular Vietnamese, Greek and the

less formal Italian ones, tend to be especially accommodating. They do not always have children's menus, but are happy for adults to share their meal with youngsters. Children are usually allowed in cafés and in bars although they are forbidden to drink alcohol. Some restaurants may be too formal for children to feel comfortable.

SMOKING

BRUSSELS IS STILL very much a smokers' city. Although a new law requests all but the smallest establishments to provide non-smoking areas plus ventilation, many do not conform to this regulation. If you are truly averse to cigarette smoke, make sure you ask about arrangements when reserving, or before you take a seat. Many cafés and taverns can be very smoky, and some locals do not take kindly to

Place settings at the restaurant La Truffe Noire (see p149)

being asked to put out a cigarette. Smokers should know that most restaurants do not sell cigarettes.

DISABLED FACILITIES

FACILITIES FOR the disabled are poor in Brussels, although there have been some recent improvements. The cobbled streets and hilly areas may well be difficult to negotiate, but most people are very helpful and will go out of their way to help those with difficulty walking or in a wheelchair. There is a limited number of restaurants with ramps and ground-floor bathrooms, so do check the extent of the access before making a reservation or taking a seat. A list of restaurants and cafés with disabled facilities is published by a Flemish charity; contact AWIPH at Rue de la Rivelaine 21, 6061 Charleroi (071 205 711).

USING THE LISTINGS

Key to symbols in the listings on pp144–53:

|●| fixed price menu, either at lunch or for dinner.

V vegetarian dishes a speciality

♟ childrens' portions

♿ wheelchair access to all or part of the restaurant

▦ outdoor eating

♟ good wine list

♫ live music on some nights of the week

★ highly recommended

✇ credit cards accepted

AE American Express

DC Diners Club

MC Master Card/Access

V VISA

Price categories for a three-course meal for one, including cover charge, service and half a bottle of wine or other drinks:

€ up to €25

€€ €25–37

€€€ €37–50

€€€€ €50–62

€€€€€ over €62

A Glossary of Belgian Dishes

French fries served with mayonnaise

BELGIANS LOVE food, and the quality of their cooking is matched only by the vast size of their portions. The Flemish and the Walloons each have their own style of cooking, both readily available in Brussels. With its lively history of invasions from around Europe, the culinary traditions of Holland, Spain and Austria have occasionally filtered into both cuisines. Walloon (Belgian-French) food is similar to French provincial cuisine – hearty and spicy, with rich dishes throughout the menu. Flemish cuisine is often simpler, featuring some substantial stews and traditional cooking. Many regions of Belgium have their specialities, such as Ardennes pâté and Liège sausage, but Brussels is truly the culinary heart of the country, and the city contains many fine restaurants to suit every budget. Most menus in the tourist areas will offer explanations in English but if not, usually the waiter will try to assist.

Steaming waffles freshly made on a stand, a familiar scent in the city

SNACKS

SOME OF THE most famous Belgian food is snack food, and with the amount of chip vans and waffle stands dotted around Brussels, you need never go hungry. Perhaps not appealing to all taste buds, but authentically Belgian, are the *caricole* stands, offering steaming hot, ready to eat buttered sea snails.

Frites
Thinly cut potato chips (French fries) are twice-fried and usually served in a cardboard cone, accompanied by a dollop of mayonnaise.

Gaufres
Waffles made of sweet batter, "toasted" in a waffle iron and served with syrup, chocolate or dusted with icing sugar.

Speculoos
Sugared ginger biscuits, often baked in patron saint-shaped moulds, served with coffee.

Smoutebollen
Sugared doughnuts.

Caricoles
Salted, boiled and buttered sea snails wrapped in paper.

Pistolets
Round oval-shaped bread breakfast rolls, with a hard crust and fluffy white interior.

SOUPS

SOUP IN BELGIUM is often a hearty meal in itself, served in large tureens accompanied by freshly baked bread. Vegetable soups with a stock base are particularly common, using ingredients such as carrot, cauliflower, cabbage or green peas, often mixed. Vegetarians, however, should be warned; green pea soup often includes pork and spicy sausage as well as potatoes.

Waterzooi
A stew of chicken or fish simmered in their stock, with cream and often white wine, and served with puréed vegetables.

Bisque de homard
Lobster poached in reduced seafood stock with brandy.

FISH AND SEAFOOD

MOST OF THE FISH served in Brussels comes straight from the Ostend coast, which, on a direct route less than 90 km (55 miles) away, means that it is fresh every day. At

Moules marinières, sweated in wine and onion, served in a tureen

the turn of the 20th century, the port of Brussels extended as far north as the Eglise Ste-Catherine, with a huge covered fish market behind the church. This area is still the centre of a bustling trade in seafood; although the market has long since vanished, the surrounding streets and alleys are filled with terraced fish restaurants.

The Belgians' love of seafood extends further than the national dish, *moules et frites*. Ostend sole, eels in green sauce, lobster in season and crispy shrimp croquettes are just some of the favourites. While the city's more formal establishments tend to be expensive, there are plenty of simple eateries offering the day's catch at very low prices.

Moules
Mussels, traditionally served in copper tureens, cooked in white wine and onions, with a side order of *frites*.

Hareng
Herring, prepared in a variety of ways: roll-mop, fried, steamed, marinated in vinegar or smoked.

Langouste
Spiny lobster, brought in fresh from Ostend; when it is available much will be made of it in lavish seafood displays and on daily "specials" menu boards.

Marinated herring

Huîtres
Oysters, swallowed raw or served *au gratin*; covered with breadcrumbs, bacon, herbs and cheese and grilled.

Anguilles au vert
Eels, commonly served with green herbs such as thyme or parsley, and cooked in butter.

Sole Ostendaise
Fresh sole fillet served with lemon and butter.

MEAT

ALTHOUGH HAPPY to use poultry in soups and lighter dishes, Belgians use their abundant supplies of red meat to create hearty main meals, often marinated in cream sauces or alcohol.

Choesels
Very fresh sweetbreads in cream sauces are a Brussels speciality.

Carbonnade of beef

Ragôut d'agneau
Lamb braised for hours with chicory, onions and herbs.

Gentse stoverij
Ghent's long-standing culinary legacy takes the form of a beer and beef stew with mustard.

Ardennes pâté
A coarse pork pâté often flavoured with garlic.

Bloedpens
Black pudding with chopped bacon.

Lapin
Rabbit will be seen in many guises, but it is most traditionally served with prunes soaked in brandy, or with beer and mustard.

Profiteroles

Carbonnades flamandes
A popular Flemish dish for centuries, fillets of beef are braised very slowly in gueuze beer, or occasionally kriek, cherry fruit beer.

Faisan à la Brabançonne
Pheasant roasted with braised chicory, herbs and bacon.

VEGETABLES

VEGETABLES are often treated as accompaniments to the main meat or fish course, although some can be served as dishes in their own right.

Witloof, chicory wrapped in ham and braised *au gratin*

Choux de Bruxelles
The Brussels sprout is served young, fresh and dripping with crispy lardons and butter.

Witloof/Chicon
Chicory, a favourite vegetable all over Brussels, is often served with ham and cheese.

Jets de houblon
Young Belgian hop shoots are braised to make a tender side dish.

Stoemp
Coarse mash of potatoes and vegetables (usually carrots or cabbage) served with sausage.

DESSERTS

ALMOST ANY DESSERT wished for can be found in restaurants in Brussels, from chocolate cake, mousses and profiteroles, to the classic French dishes, *tarte tatin* (upside-down apple cake) and *crème caramel*. Second only to the reputation of Belgium's chocolatiers is that of its pastry- and cakemakers. Using the same fine ingredients, and techniques honed since the 18th century, pastry chefs create concoctions as breathtakingly good-looking as they are delicious to eat.

Shelves of fresh cream and chocolate cakes in a pâtisserie

A common way to finish off a meal, however, is with cheese, served before or instead of dessert. Often mild and un-cured, local cheeses are made in the damp, fertile, cattle-grazing land of Wallonia and delivered fresh to the city.

Herve
A soft runny cheese, often served in bowls, with bread.

Tartine de fromage blanc
This soft cheese open sandwich is eaten with radishes.

Tarte tatin, upside-down apple cake made with fresh fruit

BELGIAN CHOCOLATE

Belgian chocolate is considered by many to be the finest in the world. The chocolate manufacturing industry took off during the 1880s, aided by the acquisition of the Belgian Congo *(see p36)*, which meant easy access to Africa's cocoa plantations. Traditionally Belgian chocolates, known as *pralines*, are filled with cream, nuts or a high-quality rich dark chocolate and covered with milk or white chocolate. Plain chocolate has a high cocoa content, usually at least 70 per cent. Belgian chocolate houses have passed down their recipes over generations, the contents of which are highly guarded and secret. Some of the renowned *"grandes maisons de chocolat"* include Mary, Neuhaus, Godiva, Léonidas and Wittamer. Ideal for a gift, buying chocolates is a treat; individually picked, they are often packaged in crêpe tissue in a finely decorated box.

Belgian chocolates wrapped in a typical luxury gift box

Belgian Beer

Gambrinus, legendary Beer King

BELGIUM MAKES MORE beers, in a greater mix of styles and flavours, than any other country in the world. The Belgian citizen drinks on average 100 litres (200 pints) a year, and even small bars will stock at least 20 varieties. The nation's breweries produce over 400 different beers. The cheerful peasants in Brueghel the Elder's 15th-century medieval village scenes would have been drinking beer from their local brewery, many of which had been active since the 11th century, as every small town and community produced its own beer. By 1900 there remained 3,000 private breweries throughout Belgium. Today, more than 100 still operate, with experts agreeing that even large industrial concerns produce a fine quality beer.

Detail from *The Wedding Dance* by Pieter Brueghel the Elder

TRAPPIST BEERS

Chimay label with authentic Trappist mark

Label for Westmalle Trappist beer

THE MOST REVERED of refreshments, Belgium's Trappist beers have been highly rated since the Middle Ages when monks began brewing them. The drink originated in Roman times when Belgium was a province of Gaul, Gallia Belgica. Beer was a private domestic product until the monasteries took over and introduced hops to the process. Today's production is still controlled solely by the five Trappist monasteries, although the brewers are mostly laymen. Trappist beers are characterized by their rich, yeasty flavour. They are very strong, ranging from 6.2 to 11 per cent in alcohol content by volume. The most celebrated of the 20 brands is Chimay, brewed at Belgium's largest monastic brewery in Hainaut. This delicate but potent bottled beer has three different strengths, and is best kept for many years before drinking. The strongest Trappist beer is Westvleteren, from Ypres.

Chimay served in its correct glass

LAMBIC BEERS

MADE FOR CENTURIES in the Senne Valley around Brussels, the unique family of lambic beers are made using yeasts naturally present in the air to ferment the beer, rather than being added separately to the water and grain mix. Containers of unfermented wort (water, wheat and barley) are left under a half-open roof in the brewery and wild airborne yeasts, only present in the atmosphere of this region of Belgium, descend to ferment it. Unlike the sterility of many breweries and officially exempt from EU hygiene regulations, lambic cellars are deliberately left dusty and uncleaned in order for the necessary fungal activity to thrive. Matured in untreated wooden casks for up to five years, the lambic is deliciously sour to drink, with a moderate strength of 5 per cent alcohol.

Young and old lambic beers are blended together to produce the variant of gueuze. A tiny bead, distinctive champagne mousse and a toasty, slightly acid flavour, are its main characteristics. Bars and restaurants lay down their gueuze for up to 2 years before it is drunk.

Lambic cherry beer

Brewer sampling beer from the vat at a brewery outside Brussels

SPECIALITY BELGIAN BEERS

| Duvel | Chimay | Brugse Tripel | De Verboden Frucht | Kwak |

SPECIALITY BEERS are common in Belgium, where the huge variety of brands includes unusual tastes and flavours. Fruit beers are a Brussels speciality but are available throughout the country. The most popular, kriek, is traditionally made with bitter cherries grown in the Brussels suburb of Schaerbeek; picked annually, these are added to the lambic and allowed to macerate, or steep. The distinctive almond tang comes from the cherry stone. Raspberries are also used to make a framboise beer, or frambozen.

For a characterful amber ale, Kwak is good choice. Strong beers are also popular; apart from the Trappist beers, of which Chimay is a popular variety, the pilseners De Verboden Frucht (meaning "forbidden fruit") and Duvel ("devil") are both as strong as red wine. Brugse Tripel, from Bruges, is also popular. Even Belgium's best-sellers, Jupiler and Stella Artois, are good quality beers.

Fruit beer mat of Chapeau brewery

The façade of a beer emporium in Brussels

BLANCHE BEERS

BELGIUM'S REFRESHING wheat beers are known as "blanche", or white beers, because of the cloudy sediment that forms when they ferment. Sour, crisp and light, they are relatively low in alcohol at 5 per cent. Blanche is produced in the western region of Hoegaarden, after which the best-known blanche is named. Many people now serve them with a slice of lemon to add to the refreshing taste, especially on warm summer evenings.

Hoegaarden

HOW TO DRINK BELGIAN BEER

THERE ARE NO snobbish distinctions made in Belgium between bottled and casked beer. Some of the most prestigious brews are served in bottles, and, as with casks, bottles are often laid down to mature. The choice of drinking glass, however, is a vital part of the beer-drinking ritual. Many beers must be drunk in a particular glass, which the barman will supply, ranging from goblets to long thin drinking tubes. Beers are often served with a complementary snack; cream cheese on rye bread and radishes are a popular accompaniment

The traditional drinkers' snack of *fromage blanc* on rye bread

Choosing a Restaurant

THE RESTAURANTS IN THIS GUIDE have been selected for their good value, exceptional food and interesting location. This chart highlights some of the factors which may influence your choice. Entries are listed in alphabetical order within price category, starting with the least expensive. The more detailed listings on pp146–53 are arranged by type of cuisine. Information on cafés and bars is on pp154–55.

Restaurant	Price	PAGE	CREDIT CARDS	HIGHLY RECOMMENDED	TABLES OUTSIDE	CHARACTER SETTING	ETHNIC	FIXED-PRICE MENU	CHILD FRIENDLY
THE LOWER TOWN									
Brasserie Horta (Belgian)	€	146	●			●			●
Chez Léon (Belgian)	€	146	●		●	●		●	●
Chez Patrick (Belgian)	€	146	●	●		●			
El Papagayo (Latin American)	€	152			●	●			
La Grande Porte (Belgian)	€	146	●						
Le Petit Chou de Bruxelles (Belgian)	€	146			●	●			
Al Barmaki (Lebanese)	€€	151	●				●		
Auberge des Chapeliers (Belgian)	€€	146	●			●			
Aux Paves de Bruxelles (Belgian)	€€	146	●		●				
Bij den Boer (Seafood)	€€	153	●					●	●
Brasserie de la Roue d'Or (Belgian)	€€	146	●	●		●			
Cantina Cubana (Latin American)	€€	152	●	●			●	●	●
Casa Manuel (Portuguese)	€€	152	●		●			●	
Domaine de Lintillac (French)	€€	148				●			
In't Spinnekopke (Belgian)	€€	146	●		●	●			
L'Achepot (Seafood)	€€	153	●		●				●
La Marée (Seafood)	€€	153	●	●					
La Rose Blanche (Belgian)	€€	147	●		●				
Rugantino (Italian)	€€	149	●	●	●				
't Kelderke (Belgian)	€€	147	●	●					
Aux Armes de Bruxelles (Belgian)	€€€	147	●		●			●	
Aux Marches de la Chapelle (French)	€€€	148	●			●		●	
Bonsoir Clara (French)	€€€	148	●			●			
La Taverne du Passage (Belgian)	€€€	147	●	●		●			●
Le Pou qui Tousse (Sardinian)	€€€	150	●				●		
La Truite d'Argent (Seafood)	€€€€	153	●	●		●		●	
L'Ogenblik (French)	€€€€	149	●		●	●			
Scheltema (Seafood)	€€€€	153	●		●				
Comme Chez Soi (French)	€€€€€	149	●	●		●			●
Sea Grill (Seafood)	€€€€€	153	●	●					
THE UPPER TOWN									
La Pirogue (African)	€	150			●		●		
Le Dieu des Caprices (Belgian)	€	146	●		●	●		●	●
Entrée des Artistes (French)	€€	148	●		●	●		●	●
Au Vieux Saint-Martin (Belgian)	€€€	147	●						●
La Porte des Indes (Indian)	€€€	151	●	●		●	●	●	
L'Estrille du Vieux Bruxelles (Belgian)	€€€	147	●			●			
Chez Moi (Belgian)	€€€€	147	●		●			●	
L' Ecailler du Palais Royal (Seafood)	€€€€€	153	●	●					
GREATER BRUSSELS									
Dolma (Vegetarian)	€	153	●					●	●
Gri Gri (African)	€	150	●	●	●		●	●	●
Hông Hoa (Vietnamese)	€	150				●	●	●	●
La Cantonnaise (Chinese)	€	151		●			●		●
Le Pacifique (Vietnamese)	€	151	●	●			●		●

Price categories for a three-course meal for one, including cover charge, service and half a bottle of wine or other drinks:
€ up to €25
€€ €25–37
€€€ €37–50
€€€€ €50-62
€€€€€ Over €62

CREDIT CARDS
Establishment accepts a combination of major credit cards.

HIGHLY RECOMMENDED
The quality of the dishes, decor and service are especially highly commended.

TABLES OUTSIDE
Outdoor dining facilities and service in summer.

CHARACTER SETTING
Unusually attractive interior decor and/or street setting and atmosphere.

ETHNIC
Exotic world cuisine of a high standard from outside Europe.

		PAGE	CREDIT CARDS	HIGHLY RECOMMENDED	TABLES OUTSIDE	CHARACTER SETTING	ETHNIC	FIXED-PRICE MENU	CHILD FRIENDLY
L'Ouzerie (Greek)	€	151	●						
L'Ouzerie du Nouveau Monde (Greek)	€	151	●	▣	●				
Poussières d'Etoiles (Vietnamese)	€	151			●		●	▣	●
Shanti (Vegetarian)	€	153	●	▣			●	▣	
Tsampa (Vegetarian)	€	153	●		●			▣	
Au Brabançon (Belgian)	€€	146	●	▣					
Aux Anges (Italian)	€€	149	●			●	▣		
El Yasmine (African)	€€	150	●				▣	●	
Ile de Gorée (African)	€€	150			●			●	●
Kocharata (Bulgarian)	€€	152	●						
La Belle Epoque (Belgian)	€€	147	●		●			▣	
La Citronnelle (Vietnamese)	€€	151	●		●		●	▣	
La Danse des Paysans (Belgian)	€€	147	●	▣	●				
Le Grain de Sel (French)	€€	148	●	▣	●	▣		▣	
Les Ateliers de la Grande Ile (Russian)	€€	152	●						
La Maison de Thailande (Thai)	€€	151	●	▣	●		●	▣	
Medina (African)	€€	150	●				▣	●	●
Mon Village (Belgian)	€€	147	●						●
Sahbaz (Turkish)	€€	151	●						
Tierra del Fuego (Latin American)	€€	152	●		●	▣	●		
Amadeus (French)	€€€	148	●		●	▣			●
A'mbriana (Italian)	€€€	149	●					▣	
La Brouette (Belgian)	€€€	147	●					▣	
La Fin de Siècle (Italian)	€€€	149	●	▣		●		▣	
La Scala (Italian)	€€€	149	●						
Le Doux Wazoo (French)	€€€	148	●					▣	
Le Fils de Jules (French)	€€€	148	●			●	▣		
Le Forcado (Spanish)	€€€	152	●	▣	●			▣	
Le Pain et le Vin (French)	€€€	148	●		●				
Les Amis du Cep (French)	€€€	149	●		●			▣	
Les Brasseries Georges (French)	€€€	149	●	▣	●				●
Les Jardins de Bagatelle (African)	€€€	150	●		●	▣	●	▣	
Osteria delle Stelle (Italian)	€€€	150	●	▣		▣			
Blue Elephant (Thai)	€€€€	151	●	▣			●	▣	●
La Truffe Noire (French/Italian)	€€€€€	149	●			●	▣	▣	
ANTWERP									
't Zolderke (French)	€€	148	●					▣	
De Matelote (Seafood)	€€€€€	153	●					▣	
BRUGES									
Den Dyver (Belgian)	€€€	147	●	▣	●			▣	
de Karmeliet (Belgian)	€€€€	147	●	▣	●			▣	
't Bourgoensche Hof (Belgian)	€€€€	148	●	▣	●			▣	
GHENT									
Pakhuis (French)	€€	148	●					▣	
't Buikske Vol (Belgian)	€€€	147	●	▣				▣	

BELGIAN

Although Belgium is a relatively new European state, its culinary traditions date back to the Middle Ages, when the dukes of Burgundy ruled over the Low Countries. To this day Burgundian is a synonym for hearty extravagance, of which the Belgians are inordinately fond. Authentic Belgian cooking is very rooted in peasant traditions, including warming winter stews such as *waterzooi* (chicken or fish stewed with cream), or *carbonnades* (beef casseroled in beer) as well as the national vegetable, chicory. Slow cooking is also an integral part of Belgian cuisine. Dieting is not, and never will be, compatible with rich Belgian food.

Most of the restaurants in this section offer authentic versions of Belgian dishes, usually at relatively affordable prices. While some pay great attention to presentation, lesser establishments are often more rewarding; this is a cuisine robust enough to cope with a few rough edges and dated decor.

Brasserie Horta

Rue des Sables 20. **Map** 2 E2.
[(02) 217 7271. **☑** AE, DC, MC, V.
◯ 10am–6pm daily. **ⓧ ⓖ €**

The Comic Strip Centre's restaurant is worth a visit to see the airy, high-ceilinged Art Nouveau brasserie designed by Victor Horta. Admire the cartoons of Tintin, the Smurfs and Lucky Luke while sampling cheap, hearty portions of chicken-stuffed vol-au-vents, spicy meatballs, *waterzooi*, beef stewed in beer and home-made *frites*. The bar is open during restaurant hours.

Chez Léon

Rue des Bouchers 18. **Map** 2 D2. **[**
(02) 511 1415. **☑** AE, DC, MC, V.
11:30am–11pm daily. **ⓧ 🔳 �"◉" €**

It may be more a fashionable factory-style diner than an intimate dining experience, but this casual haunt near the Grand Place provides unquestionable value for money in an expensive area (and has been doing so since 1893). It also offers a wide range of *moules-frites* dishes and a free menu for children under 12.

Chez Patrick

Rue des Chapeliers 6. **Map** 2 D3. **[**
(02) 511 9815. **★ ☑** AE, DC, MC, V.
◯ noon–3pm, 6–10pm Tue–Sat. **ⓖ**
"◉" €

Despite its popularity with tourists and expats, the family-run Chez Patrick has remained quintessentially Bruxellois since it opened in 1931. Wooden benches and white

tiles give the dining room a spartan, functional feel and the daily specials are scribbled on to mirrors on the walls. Beer cuisine figures large, but you can also tuck into *choucroute* (cabbage and sausage hotpot) or chicken *waterzooi*.

La Grande Porte

Rue Notre-Seigneur 9. **Map** 1 C4.
[(02) 512 8998. **☑** MC, V.
◯ noon–3pm, 6pm–2am Tue–Fri;
6pm–2am Sat. **ⓖ €**

This late-night spot in the Marolles area combines French *chanson* background music and an artfully chaotic interior adorned with finds from the flea market on Place du Jeu de Balle. Enjoy quality versions of basic Belgian fare such as *stoemp*, meatballs in tomato sauce or the traditional chicory grilled with cheese and, in winter, onion soup.

Le Dieu des Caprices

Rue Archimède 51. **Map** 3 B2.
[(02) 736 4116. **☑** AE, DC, MC, V.
◯ noon–3pm, 6:30–11pm Mon–
Fri; 6:30–11pm Sat. **ⓧ 🔳 "◉" €**

Nestling in the shadow of the European institutions, this traditional restaurant is going from strength to strength, thanks to a prize-winning young chef. The decor has an antiques market feel, and you can devour monkfish *waterzooi* and rabbit with plums and *foie gras* to the sound of 1960s background music.

Le Petit Chou de Bruxelles

Rue du Vieux-Marché-aux-Grains 2.
Map 1 C2. **[** (02) 502 6037.
◯ noon–10pm daily. **● Wed &**
Thu in winter. **🔳 €**

Despite the dingy glass-fronted interior and non-existent decor, this café near Place Ste-Catherine is well worth the visit, especially for a full meal outside normal eating hours. Old-fashioned cooking includes home-made pork rillettes and horse steaks. In summer, the renovated outdoor terrace is pleasant.

Auberge des Chapeliers

Rue des Chapeliers 3. **Map** 2 D3.
[(02) 513 7338. **☑** AE, DC, MC, V.
◯ noon–2pm, 6:30–11pm daily
(until midnight on Sat). **€€**

This 17th-century building near the Grand Place houses a cosy, split-level eatery with several dining sections and, unusually, a non-smoking area. The menu features sizeable helpings of classic Belgian dishes: mussels in a variety of preparations, black pudding Brussels-style *(boudin)*, salmon steak cooked in white beer and marinated herring fillets.

Au Brabançon

Rue de la Commune 75. **Map** 3 A1.
[(02) 217 7191. **★ ☑** AE, MC, V.
◯ noon–2:30pm, 7–9:30pm
Mon–Sat. **● Sun. "◉" €€**

This tiny St-Josse restaurant is a haven for lovers of authentic Belgian specialities. The formidable septuagenarian owner loves to cook offal, including brains and sweetbreads. The faint-hearted can opt for creamy chicken *waterzooi* or Marolles-style meatballs once they have deciphered the handwritten menu. As with much Belgian food, this is not an establishment for slimmers or vegetarians.

Aux Paves de Bruxelles

Rue Marché-aux-Fromages 1–3.
Map 2 D3. **[** (02) 502 0457.
☑ AE, DC, MC, V. **◯** noon–2:30pm,
7–11pm Mon–Fri; 7pm–midnight Sat.
● Sun. 🔳 €€

At this old-fashioned eatery in a 17th-century house near the Grand Place, good prices and a sturdy emphasis on red meat keep the place packed for lunch and dinner. While Argentine steaks and spare ribs are house specialities, the mussel dishes should satisfy non-carnivores and fish-eating vegetarians.

Brasserie de la Roue d'Or

Rue des Chapeliers 26. **Map** 2 D3.
[(02) 514 2554. **★ ☑** AE, DC,
MC, V. **◯** noon–12.30am daily.
● mid-Jul– mid-Aug. €€

This upmarket Art Nouveau brasserie with Surrealist murals excels in modernism. The great-value menu blends Belgian and French cuisine: eel in mustard sauce, pig's trotter vinaigrette, prawn croquettes, snails in garlic butter and home-made *frites*. Pierre Wynants, the chef of Michelin three-star Brussels restaurant Comme Chez Soi, is an enthusiastic visitor.

In 't Spinnekopke

Place du Jardin aux Fleurs 1. **Map** 1
B2. **[** (02) 511 8695. **☑** AE, DC,
MC, V. **◯** noon–3pm, 6–11pm Mon–
Fri; 6pm–midnight Sat. **ⓖ 🔳 €€**

This former coaching inn at the end of Rue Chartreux is popular with canny tourists and local politicians alike. Enjoy Belgian fare and creative beer cuisine in 18th-century decor: the restaurant's name means "In the spider's head" and, while spider is not on the menu, exotic dishes include guinea-fowl in raspberry beer and calf's head with vinaigrette. There is a huge choice of small cottage-industry beers.

La Belle Epoque

Avenue Houba de Strooper 188. 🄲
(02) 478 9647. 🄴 *AE, DC, MC, V.*
🄾 *noon–11pm Sun–Thu; noon–mid-night Fri & Sat.* 🄷 🄳 🄵 🄵🄸 €€

One of the best restaurants near the Atomium, this hospitable 1920s brasserie offers French and Italian cuisine as well as Belgian classics. Dishes include eels in herbs, rabbit in gueuze beer, *osso bucco* (stewed veal in wine and tomatoes) and veal kidneys in cider. Wash it all down with a reasonably priced selection of New World wines.

La Danse des Paysans

Chaussée de Boondael 441. 🄲 *(02) 649 8505.* ★ 🄴 *MC, V.* 🄾 *noon–3pm, 6:30–11:30pm Mon–Fri; 6:30–11:30pm Sat.* 🄵 €€

In the heart of the university area, this rustic restaurant is a perfect spot to sample authentic beer cooking such as scampi stew with white beer and lamb in pastry with mint and the blanche beer Duvel.

La Rose Blanche/ De Witte Roos

Grand Place 11. **Map** 2 D3.
🄲 *(02) 513 6479.* 🄴 *AE, DC, MC, V.*
🄾 *10am–11pm daily.* 🄵 €€

One of the best places for tradi-tional Belgian beer cuisine, this Baroque tavern serves mussels in beer, roast salmon in beer, chicken in kriek and even waffles with an Ardennes brew called La Chouffe. The popular three-course menu is centred around three dif-ferent types of beer, with a bottle of each included in the set price.

Mon Village

Rue Champ de la Couronne 6.
🄲 *(02) 478 3579.* 🄴 *AE, DC, MC, V.*
🄾 *noon–3pm, 7–11:30pm Tue–Sat.*
€€

At this informal restaurant close to Parc de Laeken, the owner also does the cooking, and favourites include chicken cooked in strong Duvel beer and rillettes prepared with white beer.

't Kelderke

Grand Place 15. **Map** 2 D3. 🄲 *(02) 513 7344.* ★ 🄴 *AE, DC, MC, V.*
🄾 *noon–2am daily.* €€

This reasonably priced restaurant in a 17th-century cellar feels genuine despite its commercial location. Speedy waiters proffer huge pots of mussels and good-sized portions of traditional Belgian food. Waffles and whipped cream make a fine ending. No reservations are accep-ted, so queues are not uncommon.

Au Vieux Saint-Martin

Place du Grand Sablon 38. **Map** 2 D4.
🄲 *(02) 512 6476.* 🄴 *MC, V.* 🄾
noon–midnight daily. 🄷 🄵 €€€

A truly professional establishment with crisp modern decor, swift and courteous waiters, this restaurant also boasts a contemporary art collection. The accomplished menu features regional specialities like *stoemp*, rabbit in kriek and *filet américain*, prepared to a recipe conceived by the restaurant's founder in the 1920s.

Aux Armes de Bruxelles

Rue des Bouchers 13. **Map** 2 D2.
🄲 *(02) 511 5550.* 🄴 *AE, DC, MC, V.*
🄾 *noon–11pm Tue–Sun.* 🄵 *mid-Jun–mid-Jul.* 🄵 🄵🄸 €€€

This friendly restaurant was a favourite of Belgian chanson legend Jacques Brel. Some critics complain that its charm has faded a little in recent years, but the restaurant still offers classic, high-quality cuisine including lobster, mussels, poached cod, veal and, in season, game. The freshly made shrimp croquettes are a must. It is important to reserve in advance.

Den Dyver

Dijver 5, Bruges. 🄲 *(050) 33 6069.* ★
🄴 *AE, V.* 🄾 *noon–2pm, 6:30–9pm Thu–Tue.* 🄵 *Thu lunch.* 🄵 🅅 🄵🄸
€€€

This excellent restaurant, located close to the Markt, specializes in Flemish beer cooking. There is no drinks list, and diners are automatically served a glass of the beer that features in their dish.

La Brouette

Boulevard Prince de Liège 61,
Anderlecht. 🄲 *(02) 522 5169.*
🄴 *DC, MC, V.* 🄾 *noon–2:30pm, 7–9:30pm Tue–Sun.* 🄵 *Sat lunch, Sun eve.* 🄵 🄴 *DC, MC, V.* 🄵🄸 €€€

A restaurant with a well-deserved Michelin star, La Brouette is a jewel off the beaten track. Chef Hermann Dedapper, a top sommelier, provides gourmet food and an innovative menu in an unpretentious setting.

La Taverne du Passage

Galerie de la Reine 30. **Map** 2 D2. 🄲 *(02) 512 3731.* ★ 🄴 *AE, DC, MC, V.* 🄾 *noon–midnight daily.* 🄵 *Jun–Jul: Wed & Thu.* 🄵 🄵 €€€

This Belgian brasserie has an alluring Art Deco interior and 70 years' worth of culinary expertise. Housed in the elegant Galerie de la Reine, between Rue des Bouchers and Rue du Marché aux Herbes, it features roasts carved at your table, as well as shrimp croquettes, steak tartare and mussels. The waiters are helpful and efficient; this is a popular choice with families. Relax on the terrace in the arcade and watch the world go by under the Art Deco roof.

L'Estrille du Vieux Bruxelles

Rue de Rollebeek 7. **Map** 2 D4.
🄲 *(02) 512 5857.* 🄴 *AE, DC, MC, V.* 🄾 *noon–2pm, 6:30–10pm Mon–Fri; noon–3pm, 6:30–10:30pm Sat & Sun.* 🄵 *Sun lunch.* €€€

Just off the Place du Grand Sablon and housed in an elegant 16th-century building, this cosy tavern specializes in meat grilled over an open fire in the main room. Homely dishes include beef stew, rabbit with plums and gueuze beer, eel in herbs and, in season, game. The background music is usually classical or jazz.

't Buikske Vol

Kraanlei 17, Ghent. 🄲 *(09) 225 1880.* ★ 🄴 *AE, V.* 🄾 *noon–2pm, 7–9:30pm Mon, Tue, Thu; 7–9:30pm Fri & Sat.* 🅈 🄵🄸 €€ €€

The trendy Patershol district is home to many upscale restaurants, and this is one of the best. The beautifully prepared dishes range from river fish *waterzooi* to sweetbreads with rabbit.

Chez Moi

Rue du Luxembourg 66. 🄲 *(02) 280 2666.* 🄴 *DC, MC, V.* 🄾 *noon–3pm, 7–10pm Mon–Fri.* 🄵 🄵🄸
€€€€

Close to the European Parliament, this welcoming restaurant is popular with Eurocrats at lunch, but quieter and more romantic in the evening. The menu offers fish and game with good vegetable side dishes.

de Karmeliet

Langestraat 19, Bruges. 🄲 *(09) 33 8259.* ★ 🄴 *AE, DC, MC, V.* 🄾 *noon–1:30pm, 7–9:30pm Tue–Sun.* 🄵 *Tue lunch, Sun eve.* 🅈 🅅 🄵
🄵 🄵 🄵🄸 €€€€

Impeccable service, lavish surroundings in the centre of town and exquisite Belgian/French cuisine have earned this restaurant in the heart of historical Bruges three Michelin stars. Try the rabbit with Rodenbach beer and the delicious thin omelettes.

't Bourgoensche Hof

Wollestraat 41, Bruges. █ (050) 33 7926. ★ 🔲 AE, MC, V. ☐ noon–2pm, 7–9:15pm Thu–Mon. 🍽 🔳
🍷 V 🔳 €€€€

This 19th-century wooden building is the ideal place for a romantic, canalside meal. The perfect setting is matched by superior cuisine, especially the seafood dishes.

FRENCH

Perhaps unsurprisingly given its proximity to France, Brussels has a large number of extremely good French restaurants, from grand Parisian-style brasseries to modern establishments serving nouvelle cuisine. While the brasserie menus sometimes overlap with their Belgian counterparts, the nouvelle cuisine places offer a lighter option for those fed up with frites. Many of the city's great French restaurants are expensive, but there are plenty of bargains to be had, especially at lunchtime or following the set menus. Value for money is almost universally guaranteed.

Domaine de Lintillac

Rue de Flandre 25. **Map** 1 B1.
█ (02) 511 5123. ☐ noon–2pm, 7:30– 10pm Tue–Sat. 🔳 €€

This small restaurant serves nothing but duck: wine-soaked pâté, sliced breasts, *rillettes* cooked in lard and pounded to a fine paste, confit, as well as the gourmet *foie gras*. Each of the tables has a toaster to ensure your pâté toast is cooked to perfection. The main courses include a marvellous cassoulet, with duck, pork and goose cooked for hours in duck fat, a rich wine tomato sauce and haricot beans. For dessert, try the excellent crème brulée. The rich fare is not for those on a diet, but is delicious for a special occasion.

Entrée des Artistes

Place du Grand Sablon 42. **Map** 2 D4.
█ (02) 502 3161. 🔲 AE, MC, V. ☐ 8am–2am daily. 🎄 🍽 €€€

The Grand Sablon can be an unsatisfyingly expensive place to eat, but this unassumingly trendy brasserie is a happy exception. Cinema posters and licence plates decorate the walls and the well-judged brasserie fare includes toast with mushrooms, salmon steaks and lobster. A *plat du jour* at lunchtime costs around €7.

Le Grain de Sel

Chaussée de Vleurgat 9. █ (02) 648 1858. ★ ☐ noon– 3:15pm, 7:30–10:30pm Tue–Fri; 7:30–10pm Sat.
🍽 V 🔳 €€

Tucked away in a townhouse near Place Eugène Flagey in Ixelles, this exquisite eatery is one of Brussels' best-kept secrets. Book in advance to ensure a spot on the rambling rose-filled patio at the back, then settle down to a selection of light, fresh dishes: cannelloni with goat's cheese and spinach, scampi in creamy curry sauce, crispy roast duck, pan-fried beef with rocket and exquisite home-made ice cream. The three-course menu offers a wide selection of regular dishes as well as daily suggestions.

Pakhuis

Schuurkensstraat 4, Ghent. █ (09) 223 5555. 🔲 AE, DC, MC, V. ☐ noon–2:30pm, 6:30pm–midnight Mon–Sat. V 🍽 🍷 🍽 €€

This popular brasserie occupies a huge, early-19th-century converted warehouse. Its special attractions are the oyster bar and the fresh shellfish served daily.

't Zolderke

Hoofdkerkstraat 7, Antwerp. █ (03) 233 8427. ★ 🔲 MC, V. ☐ 6–11pm Mon–Fri, noon–midnight Sat & Sun.
🔳 🍽 V 🍽 €€

The menu at this light and airy French restaurant features old classics such as steak in peppercorn and roquefort sauce with fries, and meats such as boar and deer when in season.

Amadeus

Rue Veydt 13. █ (02) 538 3427.
🔲 AE, DC, MC, V. ☐ noon–3pm, 6:30pm–midnight Tue–Fri, Sun; 6pm–12:30am Mon & Sat. V 🎄
🔳 🍷 €€€

Near the Place Stephanie, off Chaussée de Charleroi, this romantic candle-lit restaurant and wine bar was once the studio of 19th-century French sculptor Auguste Rodin. Diners come more for the ornate mirrors and intimate corners than the brasserie fare, which is adequate but unremarkable by Brussels standards. The wine list, however, is top quality, and the view of the entrance hall alone is worth the trip.

Aux Marches de la Chapelle

Place de la Chapelle 5. **Map** 1 C4.
█ (02) 512 6891. 🔲 AE, MC, DC, V. ☐ noon–2:30pm, 6–11pm Mon–Fri; 7pm–midnight Sat; noon–2:30pm, 7–10pm Sun. 🔳 🍽 €€€

A Brussels institution, this stylish restaurant with opulent Belle Epoque decor and chandeliers is

a favoured gourmet haunt. Try the excellent sauerkraut, poached egg with grey shimps, or eel dishes.

Bonsoir Clara

Rue Antoine Dansaert 22. **Map** 1 B2.
█ (02) 502 0990. 🔲 AE, MC, V. ☐ noon–2:30pm, 7–11:30pm Mon–Fri; 7–midnight Sat & Sun.
🎄 🍷 €€€

Like most of the restaurants started by young restaurateur Frederic Nikolay, Bonsoir Clara is a great place to eat in, rather than a great place to eat. The city's fashionable crowd are drawn by the prime location on Brussels' trendiest street, by the extravagant decor, a confection of multicoloured quilting and garish mirror walls, and by the chance to see and be seen. The food is upmarket brasserie cooking, with dishes including seared tuna and caramelized duck among the regular specialities.

Le Doux Wazoo

Rue du Relais 21. █ (02) 649 5852.
🔲 AE, DC, MC, V. ☐ noon–2:30pm, 7–11pm Mon–Fri; 7–11:45pm Sat. ● Mon pm. 🍷 🍽 €€€

A small, cheerful turn-of-the-century bistro in the university district, where the owners' bohemian philosophy is applied to the atmosphere rather than the service. Confit of duck, roast lamb with pepper purée or duck stew are on the menu, all made with quality local produce. The restaurant's name translates as "the sweet bird", although non-natives might find this hard to work out.

Le Fils de Jules

Rue du Page 35. █ (02) 534 0057.
🔲 AE, DC, MC, V. ☐ noon–2:30pm, 7–11pm Mon–Fri; 7pm–midnight Sat. 🔳 🍷 🍽 €€€

Brussels' only Basque restaurant offers rich, imaginative cuisine and fine wines from southwest France in a plum spot near Ixelles' busy Place du Châtelain. Dishes include spiced squid, *foie gras* with a compote of figs, and duck breast in walnut sauce. While the cooking is clearly Mediterranean, the setting is a stylishly minimal blend of Art Deco and the French modernist designer Philippe Starck, who has designed many of Europe's top restaurants including the London Conran chain. Reserve in advance.

Le Pain et le Vin

Chaussée d'Alsemberg 812a. █ (02) 332 3774. 🔲 AE, MC, V. ☐ noon–2:30pm, 7–10:30pm Mon–Fri; 7–10:30pm Sat. 🔳 🍷 €€€

Eric Boschman is one of Belgium's most talented sommeliers, so it is no surprise that his restaurant on the southern tip of Brussels offers a splendid selection of French and New World wines at extremely reasonable prices. The good news is that it also offers light, imaginative French and modern Mediterranean cuisine, with an emphasis on fish, and a candle-lit garden.

Les Amis du Cep

Rue Theodore Decuyper 136. **(** (02) 762 6295. **🍽** AE, MC, V. **◯** noon–2pm, 7–10pm Tue–Sat. **🏧 🍴**

€€€

This refined restaurant housed in a Thirties villa in the residential Woluwe-Saint-Lambert district offers classic and modern French food. Most people choose the four-course "surprise menu" for two, but some may prefer to stick to the à la carte menu, which includes quail stew with *foie gras*, and *scallop tartare*. The lunch menu is fantastic value.

Les Brasseries Georges

Ave Winston Churchill 259. **(** (02) 347 2100. ★ **🍽** AE, DC, MC, V. **◯** 11:30am–midnight Sun–Thu; 11:30am–1am Fri & Sat. **🏧 🍴 👤**

€€€

The first thing to notice here is the ostentatious pavement stall, piled high with tubs of oysters and lobsters. Inside, the brash, bustling brasserie has become one of southern Brussels' landmarks. The service is professional if a little brusque, which is understandable given the volume of custom. The extensive wine list includes several vintages by the glass, and menu staples vary from grilled tuna with herb butter to kidneys in mustard sauce, although the Georges' fame depends partly on the exquisitely fresh seafood platters.

L'Ogenblik

Galerie des Princes 1. **Map** 2 D2. **(** (02) 511 6151. ★ **🍽** AE, MC, DC, V. **◯** noon–2:30pm, 7pm–midnight Mon–Thu; 7pm–12:30am Fri & Sat. **🏧 €€€€**

In a little side street off the Rue des Bouchers, this classy but informal establishment masks its quality behind artfully faded Parisian-style bistro decor. The creative dishes, among them fillet of sea bass with aubergine caviar and calf sweetbreads with cheese-topped courgette, are prepared with impeccably fresh ingredients. Despite the central location, the lively crowd is mostly composed of well-heeled locals.

Comme Chez Soi

23 Place Rouppe. **Map** 1 C4. **(** (02) 512 2921. ★ **🍽** AE, DC, MC, V. **◯** noon–1:30pm, 7–9:30pm Tue–Sat. **🏧 🍷 🍴 €€€€€**

Brussels' best restaurant works hard to maintain its three Michelin stars, with head chef Pierre Wynants continually creating adventurous market-based dishes for those not satisfied by his legendary sole fillet with Riesling mousse. The game, *foie gras* and caviar are superlative, as is the Art Nouveau decor, although the intimacy can border on the cramped. Tables must be booked weeks in advance.

La Truffe Noire

Boulevard de la Cambre 12. **(** (02) 640 4422. **🍽** AE, DC, MC, V. **◯** noon–2pm, 7–10pm Mon–Fri; 7–10pm Sat. **V 🏧 🍷 🍴 €€€€€**

This gourmet restaurant is seventh heaven for truffle-lovers. The location – a townhouse on a quiet street near Bois de la Cambre – has a discreetly exclusive feel, heightened by the fresh, modern interior and the classical background music. Indulge in truffle-stuffed pigeon, truffle carpaccio, truffle purée or the extravagant six-course menu, which takes in all aspects of this delicious fungus.

ITALIAN

Belgium has a sizeable Italian community, most of whom arrived in the 1950s to work in the mines of Wallonia. Many moved to Brussels, where they opened unpretentious trattorias or pizzerias. The bulk of the capital's Italian restaurants fall into this category, and are often unremarkable, though handy for those on a budget. Brussels also has several upmarket Italian restaurants, serving more accomplished and authentic food. These establishments tend to be rather formal, and booking is always advisable.

Aux Anges

Rue Diderich 33–35. **(** (02) 539 3906. **🍽** MC, V. **◯** noon–2pm Mon; noon–2pm, 7–11pm Tue–Sat. **V 🏧 €€**

This small hideout in the backstreets of St-Gilles is a must for couples, not least because of the half-veiled corner niche designed especially for two. The decor features statuettes of angels and Raphael reproductions, while the menu offers modern, sophisticated pasta dishes such as penne with *foie gras* and truffle oil. Light modern cuisine is also represented in the use of grilled polenta and macerated olive oils.

Rugantino

Blvd Anspach 184–186. **Map** 1 C3. **(** (02) 511 2195. ★ **🍽** AE, MC, V. **◯** noon–3pm, 6:30pm–midnight Mon–Fri; 6:30–11:45pm Sat. **V 🏧 €€**

A short walk from the Grand Place, this airy, high-ceilinged trattoria has cream-coloured walls and flamboyant Art Deco motifs. The owner is from Abruzzi in Italy and the menu reflects his origins, with signature dishes including beef topped with rocket and Parmesan, rosemary roast lamb and pasta with spinach and ricotta.

A'mbriana

Rue Edith Cavell 151. **(** (02) 375 0156. **🍽** AE, DC, MC, V. **◯** noon–2:30pm, 7–10:30pm Wed–Mon; 7–10:30pm Sat. **V 🏧 🍴 €€€**

Exquisite Italian food and wine and a warm welcome have earned this slick modern eatery near Parc Montjoie a fine reputation, helped by the low prices of the fixed and lunch-time menus. Classic dishes include *carpaccio* of swordfish, beef with rocket and black lasagne with seafood and leeks. Much favoured by Eurocrats, the menu changes often but manages to stay both fresh and modern. Booking in advance is recommended.

La Fin de Siècle

Avenue de l'Armée 3. **Map** 4 F4. **(** (02) 732 7434. ★ **🍽** V. **◯** noon–2:30pm, 7–10:30pm Mon–Sat. **🏧 €€€**

Younger Eurocrats get business off their mind in this restfully Baroque restaurant, where candles and classical music ensure a harmonious ambiance. The creative, contemporary Italian menu includes linguine with scallops and truffle oil or smoked salmon with saffron and mascarpone. Its sister restaurant, Fin de Siècle, occupies a townhouse on Avenue Louise, with similar setting and dishes, but improved facilities for disabled travellers.

La Scala

Chaussée de Wavre 132. **Map** 2 F5. **(** (02) 514 4945. **🍽** AE, DC, MC, V. **◯** noon–2:30pm, 7–10pm Mon–Fri; 7–11pm Sat. **🎵 €€€**

One of the best Italian deals in town, this upbeat eatery has a popular fixed menu, which includes wine and coffee. Classical dishes include veal kidneys, *foie gras* with wild mushrooms and duck ravioli. Candle light and the owner's occasional tinklings on the piano provide plenty of romantic atmosphere.

Le Pou qui Tousse

Vieille Halle aux Blés 49. **Map** 1 C3.
[(02) 512 2871. **[]** AE, DC, MC, V.
[] noon–2pm, 6:30–10pm Mon,
Tue, Thu–Sat; noon–2pm Wed.
[] Sun. **€€€**

Le Pou qui Tousse (the coughing
flea) is a pleasant, family-run
Sardinian restaurant just off Rue
de Lombard, where you can watch
the chefs prepare risotto with cut-
tlefish ink, grill Mediterranean fish
or toss seafood salad in an open-
plan kitchen. The walls are hung
with contemporary European art.

Osteria delle Stelle

Avenue L. Bertrand 53–61.
[(02) 241 4808. **★ []** AE, DC,
MC, V. **[]** noon–3pm, 7–11pm
Mon–Sat. **[] €€€**

A hundred years ago, the northern
commune of Schaerbeek was one
of Brussels' most elegant districts,
and the splendid Art Nouveau
interior of this Italian brasserie
provides a poignant reminder of
former glories. A delightful place
to dine, fresh octopus salad, or sea
bass caught on a line accompany
gorgonzola polenta on the wide
menu. The all-you-can-eat buffet
of antipasti costs around just €15.
It is wise to reserve.

NORTH AFRICAN AND CENTRAL AFRICAN

Whether the sharp, nutty tastes of
central Africa or a spicy couscous
from Morocco appeal, African
cooking is among the world's most
vibrant, and the sizeable communities from the Democratic Republic
of Congo and North Africa have
brought plenty of flavour to
Brussels' dining scene. The city's
more enterprising entrepreneurs
have opened lavishly decorated
"designer couscous" eateries,
although many feel these are not
entirely authentic. Central African
food can vary sharply, and
although the quality of the cooking is not always consistent, dishes
such as the peanut-based chicken
moambe and chicken yassa, made
with limes, are deliciously simple.
The relaxed atmosphere is great.

Gri Gri

Rue Basse 16. **[** (02) 375 8202.
★ [] AE, DC, MC, V. **[]** 6:30–
11pm Mon; noon–3pm, 6:30–11pm
Tue–Fri; 6:30–11pm Sat. **[] [] []**
[] €

South of the city centre in the
district of Uccle, this small, brightly
decorated restaurant is an education
for those unfamiliar with central

African cooking. The starters
include spicy cod croquettes and
crispy meat samusas (deep-fried
mince-filled filo parcels) with a
sweet sauce. Kenyan-style scampi
with sweet curry and crocodile,
chicken yassa (in a lime sauce) or
stuffed crab are among the main
courses. On occasion, the owner
plays the drums for his customers.

La Pirogue

Rue Sainte-Anne 18. **Map** 2 D4.
[(02) 511 3525. **[]** noon–2:30pm
7–10:30pm Tue–Sun. **[] €**

If you find the cafés and restaurants on Place du Grand Sablon too
formal, then this is the perfect anti-
dote. Tucked away at the end of a
nearby quiet alley, it has an extensive and secluded outdoor seating
area where you can sip home-made
ginger beer or tamarind juice into
the early hours, or enjoy chicken
yassa (made with onions and lime),
spicy mutton chops or chicken in
peanut sauce. Given the location,
the prices are very low.

El Yasmine

Rue Defacqz 7. **[** (02) 647 5181.
★ [] AE, MC, V. **[]** 7–10:30pm
Mon–Sat. **[] [] €€**

This excellent restaurant specializes in refined Moroccan and
Tunisian cooking at reasonable
prices. The tent-like azure canopy
is reminiscent of Arabian legends,
and the eight-course gourmet
menu offers an excellent all-round
sample of authentic cuisine. The
quality of produce is much better
than in many of the city's couscous haunts, and the owner's
relaxed but attentive attitude –
not to mention his vast collection
of traditional music – create a
welcoming atmosphere.

Ile de Gorée

Rue Saint-Boniface 28. **Map** 2 E5.
[(02) 513 5293. **[]** noon–2:30pm,
4–11pm Mon–Sat. **[] [] €€**

One of the legacies of Belgium's
colonial occupation of central
Africa is an abundance of
Congolese, Senegalese and
Rwandan bars and eateries in
the capital. This upmarket, cosy
restaurant near Porte de Namur
boasts traditional music, decor and
cuisine, including smoked turkey
wings, generous portions of couscous and spicy lamb. The service
is leisurely and relaxed.

Medina

Avenue de la Couronne 2.
[(02) 640 4328. **[]** AE, DC, MC, V.
[] noon–2:30pm, 6pm–10:30pm
Tue–Sun. **[] [] €€**

Moorish arches, high ceilings and
blue-and-white tiles give this popular Moroccan restaurant in Ixelles
a bright, airy feel. Lift the funnelled
clay tajine lid that arrives over your
food and the aroma of lemons,
onions and fruit floods out, adding
considerably to the appeal of the
couscous and tajines that are the
menu's mainstays. Other specialities include pigeon-stuffed
pastries and orange and cinnamon
salad. A belly-dancer performs at
the weekend, much to the delight
of local patrons and their families.

Les Jardins de Bagatelle

Rue du Berger 17. **Map** 2 E5. **[** (02)
512 1276. **[]** AE, DC, MC, V.
[] noon–2pm, 7–11:30pm Tue–Sat.
[] Sat lunch. **[] [] [] €€€**

A turn-of-the-century Ixelles
townhouse houses one of the
capital's most eclectic restaurants,
where the leopard-skin chairs and
tropical plants are offset by stately
English porcelain. Equally lively,
the kitchen bursts with flavours
from across the globe. African and
French influences predominate,
with Congolese chicken, Louisana-
style prawns or salmon tartare
with a creamy lemon sauce.

ASIAN AND PACIFIC RIM

Brussels has an enormous number
of both Chinese and Vietnamese
restaurants, ranging from drop-in
snack bars to veritable miniature
palaces. The Chaussée de Boondael
student area in Ixelles has the best
choice, with over 20 good restaurants. Lighter and more pungent
than Chinese cuisine, Vietnamese
food is simpler and more homely
than Thai. Its emphasis on spicy
soups and pancakes can be a
diversion in a city of such rich food.
Brussels' Chinese restaurants may
not be entirely exceptional, but the
city's Thai restaurants, especially
the more expensive ones, are of
high quality. Those keen on low-
priced Indian food may be disap-
pointed, but, again, the more lavish
dining locations are excellent.

Hông Hoa

Rue du Pont de la Carpe 10.
Map 1 C2. **[** (02) 502 8714.
[] noon–11pm daily. **[] [] €**

There are only eight tables in this
cosy, crimson-walled restaurant
near the Halles St-Géry. Service
is fast and friendly and the food
includes pancakes stuffed with
pork and prawns, diced beef with
onions and crispy duck with fresh
slices of ginger.

La Cantonnaise

Rue Tenbosch 110. 📞 (02) 344 7042.
🕐 11:30am–3pm, 7–11pm Mon–Fri;
5–11pm Sat & Sun. ★ 🏠 ¶€¶ €

The owner of this deceptively plain little restaurant off Chaussée de Waterloo once ran a more formal establishment, but realized that, by reducing the number of tables and dishes on offer, he could slash his prices without compromising on quality. The result is a restaurant and take-away offering some of the capital's tastiest Chinese food: freshly cooked dim sum and spicy beef and pork dishes are prepared following recipes by the owner's mother, who is a professional cook.

Le Pacifique

Boulevard du General Jacques 115.
📞 (02) 640 5259. ★ 🍽 MC, V.
🕐 noon–3pm, 6:30–11pm
Wed–Mon. 🏠 ¶€¶ €

Le Pacifique is an unpretentious, hospitable Vietnamese restaurant in the bustling Chaussée de Boondael area of Ixelles, near the university. The prices are geared to the student market, but the cooking is subtle and makes considerable use of fresh herbs. Try clear, spicy soup with scampi and lemon, chicken and beansprout salad with mint or the restaurant's signature dish, pork-and-scampi stuffed pancakes.

Poussières d'Etoiles

Chaussée de Boondael 437. 📞 (02)
640 7158. 🕐 noon–2:30pm, 6:30pm–
11:30 daily. 🏠 🍽 ¶€¶ €

Despite the kitschy decor – starry skylights, twinkling twigs and fluffy, feather-fringed lanterns – this newish Vietnamese restaurant near the university is a welcome addition to the city's low-cost culinary scene, attracting a trendy but laid-back crowd. The range of dishes is unusually small, with the emphasis on quality produce rather than diversity: fragrant seafood stew with ginger and lime, caramelized langoustines and chicken with mushrooms and tangy ginger. Portions are on the delicate side.

La Citronnelle

Chaussée de Wavre 1377. 📞 (02)
672 9843. 🍽 AE, DC, MC, V.
🕐 noon–2:30pm, 6:30–10:30pm
Tue–Fri & Sun; 6:30–10:30pm Sat.
🏠 ¶€¶ €€

This Vietnamese restaurant in Auderghem oozes charm whether you sit in the plant-filled interior or the pretty garden. Traditional music plays in the background, and the delicate dishes include crispy duck with ginger, grilled scampi with lemongrass and braised beef.

La Maison de Thailande

Rue Middelbourg 22. 📞 (02) 672
2657. ★ 🍽 AE, DC, MC, V.
🕐 noon–2pm, 7–10pm Tue–Fri.
🕐 Tue lunch. ¶€¶ 🏠 €€

Lauded for its refined, delicious Thai cuisine, this restaurant in leafy Watermael-Boitsfort is run by a Thailand-obsessed Belgian photographer and his Thai wife. The "discovery menu" offers five starters and four main courses, offering a surprising array of delicate dishes, including fish and duck recipes.

La Porte des Indes

Avenue Louise 455. **Map** 2 D5. 📞
(02) 647 8651. ★ 🍽 AE, DC, MC, V.
🕐 noon–2:30pm, 7–10:30pm daily.
🕐 Sun lunch. ¶€¶ 🍽 €€€€

Brussels is something of a wilderness for curry-lovers, but this upmarket Indian eatery provides considerable consolation. Lavishly decorated with antiques collected by owner Karl Steppe, who also runs the Blue Elephant, La Porte des Indes serves delicate traditional cuisine from the Pondicherry region. Both exotic and traditional dishes are on offer, including Parsee fish with mint and coriander wrapped in banana leaf parcels and beef Pondicherry-style. Choose the "Brass Plate" menu if you want to sample several dishes. Traditional drinks, including Indian beers, are also on offer as well as the ubiquitous sweet and sour lassi and various native lager beers.

Blue Elephant

Chaussée de Waterloo 1120. 📞 (02)
374 4962. ★ 🍽 AE, DC, MC, V. 🕐
noon–2:30pm, 7–10:30pm Sun–Fri;
7–11:30pm Sat. ¶€¶ 🏠 €€€€

This high-dining experience at the Bois de la Cambre end of Chaussée de Waterloo shares an owner with the famous British restaurant of the same name; both are run by the Belgian nomad and antiques collector Karl Steppe. Thai paraphernalia and exotic plants fill the dining room without cluttering it, and the subtly spicy food has the same admirable clarity, combining sweet, hot, sour and bitter tastes without blurring them. The lunch menu, at around €13, is wonderful.

MEDITERRANEAN AND MIDDLE EASTERN

Like most European cities, Brussels has some authentic Mediterranean restaurants dotted about town. Considering the size of the city's Turkish population, Turkish restaurants have yet to make their mark, but the number of good Lebanese establishments is growing. Many specialize in meze and Lebanese kebabs, a quick way to eat well. Greek restaurants have also had a loyal following for decades.

L'Ouzerie

Chaussée d'Ixelles 235. **Map** 2 E5.
📞 (02) 646 4449. 🍽 AE, MC, V. 🕐
7pm–midnight, Mon–Sat. 🍽 🖥 €

This informal eatery stands out for the quality of its dishes and service. The decor is refreshingly simple, as is the menu, which avoids clichéd moussaka or grilled lamb, focusing instead on such traditional dishes as spinach and cheese stuffed pastries, grilled peppers and aubergine salad. L'Ouzerie can get crowded, so is worth booking in advance.

L'Ouzerie du Nouveau Monde

Chaussée de Boondael 290. 📞 (02)
649 8588. ★ 🍽 AE, DC, MC, V.
🕐 noon–3pm, 6pm–midnight Sun–
Fri; 6pm–1am Sat. 🍽 🖥 €

Along with L'Ouzerie, this authentic Greco-Cretan restaurant has breathed fresh life into Brussels' Greek restaurant scene, with low prices, delightful food and a warm welcome. The emphasis is on meze starters: grilled pepper salad, char-grilled ribs, stuffed vine leaves, spicy sausages, and Cypriot goat's cheese; around four per person should satisfy most appetites.

Al Barmaki

Rue des Eperonniers 67. **Map** 2 D3.
📞 (02) 513 0834. 🍽 MC, V.
🕐 7pm–midnight Mon–Sat.
🍽 ¶€¶ €€

A short walk from the Grand Place, this cavernous eatery is probably Brussels' best Lebanese restaurant. Al Barmaki specializes in meze, an assortment of small dishes that include tabouleh (a pungent mint, parsley and Bulgur wheat salad), felafel and hummus, as well as spicy sausages or chicken kebabs.

Sahbaz

Chaussée de Haecht 102–104. 📞 (02)
217 0277. 🍽 MC, V. 🕐 11:30–3pm,
6pm–midnight Mon–Tue, Thu–Sun.
🍽 🖥 🎵 €€

Brussels' oldest Turkish restaurant opened in 1980, when a wave of migrants from Turkey arrived in the city. Now quite an institution, a mixed crowd flocks to the little restaurant to sample sheep's head soup, oven-baked lamb, minced meat in aubergine parcels and, for vegetarians, crispy rolls stuffed with sour goat's cheese. Turkish-style omelettes and vegetable pizzas are on offer for the more budget-conscious.

Cafés and Bars

WITH A WATERING hole on almost every street offering world-famous quality ales, Brussels fully deserves its reputation as a paradise for beer-lovers. Taverns, cafés and bars all serve a range of at least twenty beers, as well as a handsome variety of continental coffees, herbal teas, fruit juice and spirits. Most establishments stay open from morning to midnight, and often later at weekends.

CLASSIC CAFES

A DRINK ON the Grand Place is an essential part of any visit to Brussels, although costs can be high. Perhaps the best, and one of the best priced, is **Le Roy d'Espagne** (see p43), a huge two-tiered bar housed in the bakers' guildhouse with prime views from its terrace. The terraces at neighbouring La Brouette offer similar views, as does Le Cygne, where Karl Marx worked on *The Communist Manifesto* during the early 1840s.

Moments from the Grand Place lies **Au Bon Vieux Temps**, a quiet bar in a 17th-century building with the homely feel of an English pub. **Le Cirio**, near the Bourse, is a quintessential café from the 1900s, beloved by fans of Belle Epoque decor. Close by is **A la Mort Subite**, one of the capital's most celebrated establishments. Immense wooden tables, peeling mirrors and brusque service add to the appeal. Moving eastward to Place de Brouckère, the Hôtel Métropole contains a fabulous, opulent Belle Epoque bar, **The 19th**, as well as a heated outdoor terrace.

The Place du Grand Sablon is a favourite area for café-goers and those who want to catch the feel of the bustling city. The most upmarket spot here is **Au Vieux Saint-Martin**. **Les Salons du Sablon**, nearby, is a luxurious tea-room run by top chocolatiers Wittamer. This family-run business uses a century's worth of skill to create delicious confections.

SPECIALIST BEER BARS

B EER BUFFS should head to **Chez Moeder Lambic**, near the town hall in St-Gilles. A small and chaotic bar with a few tables tottering outside on the pavement, it serves over 1,000 beers. The choice covers most of Belgium's 400 or so varieties, as well as exotic brews from overseas, many customers cope with the choice by picking a letter from the alphabetized menu.

ART NOUVEAU

A FORMER haunt of Surrealist painter René Magritte, **Le Greenwich** is now the city's premier venue for chess enthusiasts; matches run around the clock. Also celebrated is **Les Fleurs en Papier Doré**, the meeting point for Belgian Surrealists in the late 1920s and still lively. **Café Falstaff**, opened in 1903 by the Bourse, has original Horta-designed furniture. South of Place du Grand Sablon, **Le Perroquet** attracts a young crowd, keen on its filled pittas. The best-known Art Nouveau bar, **De Ultieme Hallucinatie**, is nearby.

COSMOPOLITAN

B RUSSELS HAS A thriving social scene for the young and fashionable, most of which takes place around Place St-Géry in the Lower Town. Trendy, but not pretentious or stuffy, the clutch of bars here are mostly modernist in design, with some restored historic features. **Zebra** is a tastefully minimal bare brick and metal bar with a huge terrace that attracts crowds on warm evenings. Opposite Zebra is **Mappa Mundo**, a two-storey oak-panelled drinking spot which offers light meals and a good beer selection. Nearby the cavernous **Beurs Café** attracts the artistic crowd with its DJ sets and hip sounds. **L'Archiduc** boasts a breathtaking Art Deco interior and live jazz performances (see p159).

Light Meals and Snacks

BESIDES ITS TRADITIONAL taverns, luxurious patisseries and lively cafés, not to mention the celebrated chip and sticky waffle stands, Brussels is home to a growing number of fashionable quick lunch venues. Several ethnic restaurants also offer hearty, inexpensive snacks.

BREAKFASTS

BRUSSELS WAS the birthplace of **Le Pain Quotidien,** the designer breakfast phenomenon, which now boasts chic outlets in New York, Munich and Paris. Wholesome breakfasts and lunches, featuring organic yogurt and wholemeal breads, are served around communal wooden tables. Founded in 1829, speculoo biscuit specialist **Dandoy** is an institution, popular with locals and visitors alike for coffee and homemade waffles. **La Maison de Paris** has delicious croissants.

TAVERNS

THE TRADITIONAL refreshment of Belgian beer and shrimp or cheese croquettes can be found in the city's historic taverns. **Le Paon Royal** is an insight into true Brussels style. **Plattesteen** serves steaks and salads. Nearby **Mokafe** is an elegant café, perfect for a bowl of pasta or a *croque monsieur.*

CHIP AND WAFFLE SHOPS

THE WARM SMELL of *frites* and sweet waffles is part of Brussels life. **Maison Antoine**, whose clients have included Johnny Hallyday and the Rolling Stones, is the most renowned *friterie*. **Fritland**, near the Grand Place, is also something of an institution.

SANDWICHES AND SNACKS

MOST TAVERNS and butchers offer straightforward cheese, ham and salami sandwiches, but for *tartines* (British-style sandwiches) or baguettes (French bread), try the elegant **Lunch Company**. Belgian action star Jean-Claude van Damme favours the downtown **Au Suisse**, which has been in the business since 1873 and offers a large choice of fillings, plus its popular double hot-dog. The Flemish Cultural Centre, **De Markten**, sells filling and wholesome snacks.

TEA ROOMS

BELGIUM IS NOTED for top-quality pastries and cakes, which easily rival its celebrated chocolates. **Au Flan Breton** has been baking fruit-filled cream pastries for nearly a century. Uptown, **Passiflore** serves heavenly chocolate concoctions. Ice-cream enthusiasts should head south to **Zizi's**, a family-run, traditional parlour.

ETHNIC

MIDDLE EASTERN snacks and take-away food are very well priced at **Orientalia**. Lebanese **L'Express** is often lauded as the best pitta joint in Brussels. **L'Orfeo** has a good selection of pittas and fresh salads. Downtown, Chinese restaurant **Chaochow City** has a bargain lunch room. The Italian bistro **Intermezzo** serves excellent Italian pasta, with many non-meat sauces.

VEGETARIAN

THE DELICIOUS quiches and salads at **Arcadi**, near the Galéries Saint-Hubert, are largely vegetarian. For organic vegan fare, **Den Teepot** is recommended; it offers a good daily dish or soup of the day, and vegan fruit tarts.

DIRECTORY

BREAKFASTS

Dandoy
Rue Charles Buls 14–18.
[(02) 512 6588.

La Maison de Paris
Rue de Namur 89. **Map** 2
E4. [(02) 511 1195.

Le Pain Quotidien
Rue Antoine Dansaert 16.
Map 1 B1. [(02) 502 2361.

TAVERNS

Mokafe
Galerie du Roi 9.
[(02) 511 7870.

Le Paon Royal
Rue du Vieux Marché aux Grains 6. **Map** 1 C2.
[(02) 513 0868.

Plattesteen
Rue du Marché au Charbon 41. **Map** 1 C3. [(02) 512 8203.

CHIP AND WAFFLE SHOPS

Fritland
Rue Maus.

Maison Antoine
Place Jourdan 1. **Map** 3 B4. [(02) 230 5456.

SANDWICHES AND SNACKS

Au Suisse
73–75 Blvd Anspach.
[(02) 512 9589.

Orientalia
129 Ch de Mons. **Map** 1 A3. [(02) 520 7575.

The Lunch Company
Rue de Namur 16. **Map** 2 E4. [(02) 502 0976.

TEA ROOMS

Au Flan Breton
Chaussée d'Ixelles 54. **Map** 2 E5. [(02) 511 8708.

Passiflore
Rue du Bailli 97.
[(02) 538 4210.

Zizi's
Rue de la Mutualité 57a.
[(02) 344 7081.

ETHNIC

Chaochow City
Boulevard Anspach 89.
Map 1 C3. [(02) 512 8283.

De Markten
Passage du Marché aux Grains. [(02) 512 3425.

L'Express
Rue des Chapeliers 8. **Map** 2 D3. [(02) 512 8883.

Intermezzo
Rue des Princes 16.
[(02) 218 0311.

L'Orfeo
Rue Haute 18. **Map** 1 C4.
[(02) 512 6041.

VEGETARIAN

Arcadi
Rue d'Arenberg 1b. **Map** 2 D2. [(02) 511 3343.

Den Teepot
Rue des Chartreux 66.
Map 1 C2. [(02) 511 9402.

SHOPPING IN BRUSSELS

BRUSSELS IS an ideal place to shop for luxury goods, from its glorious chocolate shops to quirky market finds and cutting-edge fashion. Street markets are popular year round, or, if your tastes are more glitzy, head for Avenue Louise and Boulevard de Waterloo, where top designers are represented; for the original creations

Belgian chocolates

of the Antwerp Six and new-wave fashions, try Rue Antoine Dansaert. For specialist stores, including home decoration, go to rues Haute and Blaes. Many mainstream stores are located on Brussels' longest pedestrian shopping street, Rue Neuve. Other pockets of interest lie a short detour from downtown, in Uccle, St-Gilles and Ixelles.

A colourful designer fashion boutique on Rue Neuve

OPENING HOURS

THERE ARE NO set opening times in Brussels, but most places are open at least between 10am and 5pm.

Mainstream shops in arcades, malls and the Rue Neuve area typically open at 9.30am and close between 6 and 7pm. Late-night shopping runs at some places until 8pm on Friday. Otherwise it depends on where the shop is located and what it is selling.

Mondays and Wednesday or Saturday afternoons are the likeliest times for smaller shops to close (some shut for lunch daily), while many now open for part of Sunday (not supermarkets). For late-night purchases, the White Night chain stays open until 1am. From mid-July to mid-August, many specialist shops, cafés and restaurants close.

HOW TO PAY

CASH IS THE preferred method of payment, and a surprising number of shops will not accept credit cards, including most supermarkets and many smaller establishments.

At small shops discounts are sometimes given on the more expensive items when they are paid for in cash.

VAT EXEMPTION

NON-EU residents visiting Belgium are entitled to VAT refunds on purchases of over €124 spent in one store. Deducting VAT from the selling price gives a saving of 5.6 to 17.35 per cent. When shopping, look for the "Tax-Free Shopping" logo. After purchase ask for a Global Refund or Tax-Free Shopping Cheque. This will be stamped by customs on your way out of the EU, and refunds made on the spot at the airport. Customs often ask to see goods, so carry them as hand luggage.

SALES

SALES DATES IN Belgium are fixed by law. The summer sales run from July 1 to 31 and the January sales from the first weekday after New Year's Day until the end of the month. Discounts start at 10 per cent and gradually drop, reaching 40–50 per cent in the last week.

DEPARTMENT STORES AND SHOPPING ARCADES

THE MAIN department store in the city is **Inno**. It is not spectacular by British and American standards. Brussels' equivalent to Harrods toy department is Serneels on Place Louise, in the luxury Wiltshire shopping complex. Traditional men's outfitter Degand has recently started selling luxury gift items.

Rue Neuve contains mainstream stores, including popular Dutch stores – We for clothes and Blokker and Hema for household goods and toys – and French cut-price store Tati. There are three shopping malls at either end of the road: the Anspach and Monnaie Centres at Place de la Monnaie and City 2 at Place Rogier.

Window shopping in the city's numerous boutiques or arcades is a popular Sunday pastime. The best arcade is the recently renovated

Galéries Saint-Hubert historic 19th-century shopping arcade

Browsers enjoying the Place du Jeu de Balle market in the sunshine

Galéries Saint-Hubert which dates from 1847 *(see p47)*. It houses several jewellers, and luxury leather bag maker Delvaux, as well as chocolate shops and smart boutiques, including popular women's fashion designer Kaat Tilley.

Less conservative is the **Galéries d'Ixelles** to the north of the city centre, where a bustling collection of cafés and tiny ethnic shops thrives in the city's trendy Matonge district. A stone's throw away, Galéries Toison d'Or and the adjacent Galéries Louise are mostly full of chain and adults' high-street European fashion boutiques.

Downtown towards the Grand Place is the quaint **Galérie Bortier**, the place to visit for collectors of antiquarian books and maps.

MARKETS

A TRIP TO Brussels must include the city's fabulous street markets, which offer anything from cheap flowers and food to second-hand bicycles and fine antiques.

Good for unusual fine antiques and a pleasant stroll is the weekend market on Place du Grand Sablon (from 9am, Saturday and Sunday). In the ancient Marolles district, the flea market on the Place du Jeu de Balle (daily, 7am to 1pm) is a colourful, eclectic affair.

Most spectacular is the huge vibrant market around Gare du Midi (Sundays, 6am to 1pm) with its mix of North African and home-grown delicacies.

It has a staggering blend of Moroccan and southern European treats, including oils, spices, and exotic herbs.

BEST BUYS AND SPECIALIST SHOPS

F OR CHOCOLATE, choose from **Pierre Marcolini**'s edible sculptures and gateaux, or the internationally known fine chocolatiers **Wittamer** and **Godiva**. Their flagship stores are in the Place du Grand Sablon. Fine biscuit specialist **Dandoy** can be found just behind the Grand Place.

Serious collectors of comic-strip memorabilia should visit **Little Nemo** and **La Bande des Six Nez**.

Elvis Pompilio's hats and bags

At **Beer Mania**, speciality beers can be bought on the spot or delivered.

Milliner **Elvis Pompilio** produces hand-made hats at his pilot store. The best of Belgian fashion, including Dries Van Noten and Ann Demeulemeester, is on offer at upmarket store **Stijl**.

BOOKSHOPS AND MAGAZINES

A BRANCH OF English bookstore Waterstone's *(see p163)* sells English-language magazines, fiction and reference material. Nijinsky (15 Rue de Page) is great for second-hand English-language fiction. French store Fnac at the City 2 mall also has a good English-language section. For international papers, go to Librairie de Rome, 50 Avenue Louise.

DIRECTORY

DEPARTMENT STORES AND SHOPPING ARCADES

Inno
Rue Neuve 111. **Map** 2 D2.
Avenue Louise 12. **Map** 2 D5.
((02) 211 2111.

Galéries d'Ixelles
Chaussée d'Ixelles. **Map** 2 E5.

Galérie Bortier
Rue de la Madeleine 17–19.
Map 2 D3.

BEER

Beer Mania
Chaussée de Wavre 174–178.
Map 2 E5.
((02) 512 1788.

CHOCOLATE

Pierre Marcolini
Place du Grand Sablon 39.
Map 2 D4.
((02) 514 1206.

Godiva
Grand Place 22.
Map 2 D3.
((02) 511 2537.

Wittamer
Place du Grand Sablon 6–12.
Map 2 D4.
((02) 512 3742.

Dandoy
Rue au Beurre 31. **Map** 2 D3.
((02) 511 0326.

FASHION

Elvis Pompilio
Rue du Lombard 18. **Map** 1 C3.
((02) 511 1188.

Stijl
Rue Antoine Dansaert 74.
Map 1 B2.
((02) 512 0313.

CARTOONS

Little Nemo
Boulevard Lemonnier 25.
((02) 514 6804.

La Bande des Six Nez
Chaussée de Wavre 179.
Map 2 E5.
((02) 513 7258.

ENTERTAINMENT IN BRUSSELS

WITHIN EASY REACH of London, Paris and Amsterdam, Brussels is an established stop on the international touring circuit, with regular visits from the world's best orchestras, soloists, rock bands and dance troupes. It is also a great place to experience Belgium's thriving cultural scene, which is especially distinguished in the fields

Ecran Total Cinema poster

of medieval music, jazz and contemporary dance. Brussels has several cinemas showing a wide range of films, including movies from the US and Europe (many in English). Professional theatre here is mostly performed in French or Flemish. Outside the city's major venues, the quality of entertainment can vary, but jazz and blues bars offer good free gigs.

The 19th-century interior of La Monnaie Opera House

OPERA, CLASSICAL MUSIC AND DANCE

BRUSSELS' OPERA HOUSE, **La Monnaie**, has a unique claim to fame: on August 25, 1830, an aria in Auber's opera *La Muette de Portici* provoked the capital's citizens into rioting against their Dutch rulers, setting the country on the road to independence *(see pp34–5)*. Now the house is among Europe's finest venues for opera. Its current artistic director Antonio Pappano will join London's Royal Opera House when his contract runs out in 2003. The season runs from September to June, with tickets starting at €7.50. Most productions are sold out many months in advance.

Designed by Victor Horta in 1928, the **Palais des Beaux-Arts** is the capital's flagship cultural venue, with an exhibition space, a theatre, film archives, a small cinema and Brussels' largest auditorium for classical music *(see p60)*. Following sustained criticism

of the accoustics, the Art Nouveau hall has recently been renovated. The venue is home to the Belgian National Orchestra, which has grown in stature under Russian conductor Yuri Simonov. Again, the season runs from September to June, with tickets costing from €7.50 to €75.

In March, the city hosts a trend-making contemporary classical festival, *Ars Musica*, with an emphasis on new works and an impressively avant-garde feel. In the holiday season, the Brussels' Summer

Festival offers concerts on the Grand Place as well as informal events in the Town Hall and the Palais des Beaux-Arts (see pp 62–7) nearby. In September and October, the Festival of Flanders is a gala-heavy event showcasing top Belgian artists as well as world-famous singers and conductors.

Over the past 15 years Belgium has won a reputation for being on the cutting edge of contemporary dance. Anne Teresa De Keersmaeker and her company Rosas put on regular performances, as do several other major Belgian companies, at the beautiful Art Deco **Kaaitheater** or the **Halles de Schaerbeek**, a 19th-century former market. Although Brussels has no ballet company of its own, it attracts major European touring companies including Jiri Kylian's outstanding Nederlands Dans Theater.

ROCK AND JAZZ

ANTWERP MAY be the centre of Belgium's alternative rock scene, but Brussels has several superb venues for rock gigs. Big names such as Aerosmith and Céline Dion

Le Botanique cultural centre in Brussels' Rue Royale

perform at **Forest-National**, a modern arena southeast of the city centre. The **Ancienne Belgique** downtown is a medium-sized venue hosting hip or up-and-coming guitar bands, folk, Latin and techno acts; **Le Botanique**, the French-speaking Community's cultural centre, has a strong if intermittent roster of rock and electronic music, including a marvellous ten-day festival, *Les Nuits Botanique*, held at the end of September.

The best places to catch good jazz acts are **Travers**, a cramped, intimate bar frequented by most of the country's top players, and **Sounds**, a larger venue which places an equal emphasis on blues music. On Saturday and Sunday afternoons, it is worth stopping by **L'Archiduc**, a refurbished Art Deco bar in the centre of town where you can find jazz musicians in relaxed, informal mood.

CINEMA

NORTH OF THE CITY, by the Heysel exhibition centre, the **Kinepolis** cinema is a state-of-the-art 28-screen multiplex which rivals US giants for consumer comfort. It screens all the Hollywood blockbusters and major French and British releases; one IMAX screen shows a selection of nature and adventure films. Parking is free.

In the centre of Brussels, the major cinema is **UGC/De Brouckère**, a modern 12-screen complex with a standard programme of mainstream releases. A second, smaller UGC is in Avenue de la Toison d'Or.

The **Arenberg/Galeries**, in the Galéries Saint-Hubert, is another quality cinema with comfortable auditoriums and an arthouse slant. From late June to September, it hosts "Ecran Total", a festival combining as yet unreleased films from around the world with established classics, often in remastered or "director's" versions. Perhaps the best of Brussels' cinemas is the Musée du Cinema, part of the Palais des Beaux-Arts complex. Home to one of the world's largest film archives, the museum shows classics, from Chaplin to Tarantino, for just €2.30. Silent films are accompanied by live piano music.

Tickets for most cinemas are around €6.20. Visit www.cinebel.be to find out which film is playing where.

INFORMATION

THE PRINCIPAL source of entertainment information in English is *The Bulletin* magazine, which has comprehensive listings of forthcoming events in Brussels and the rest of Belgium. The magazine is published weekly and is available at newsstands throughout the country. Costing around €2.30, it has excellent coverage of news, travel ideas and a pot-pourri of information about life in the capital. The magazine's listings section, *What's On*, is also distributed free to hotels in the capital.

The company that publishes *The Bulletin* also owns an English-language website (www.xpats.com). The portal includes cultural information, news, weather reports and useful links for expats. The central **Tourist Information Office** (*see p162*) offers free maps, as well as information about arts and entertainment events, and publishes a calendar of major events. Advisors will assist in the booking of tickets.

French-speakers should try the monthly *Kiosque*, which offers capsule roundups of major arts events and a regular coupon with a variety of free ticket offers. Two daily papers, *Le Soir* and *La Libre Belgique*, publish cultural supplements on Wednesdays, with detailed arts and cinema listings. For Flemish-speakers, *Humo* or the daily newspaper *De Morgen*, also offer information on events and exhibitions.

Magazines on sale in Brussels

SURVIVAL GUIDE

PRACTICAL INFORMATION

ALTHOUGH COMFORTABLE with its status as a major political and business centre, Brussels has sometimes struggled with its role as a tourist destination. It can be hard to find all but the most obvious sights: the same goes for inexpensive hotels. Both the Upper and Lower Town can easily be negotiated on foot, which might be a relief to those visitors reluctant to take

Guided tour walking group

on the challenging Belgian drivers and roads. Brussels is a very cosmopolitan city, and its residents, many of whom are foreigners themselves, are usually charming and friendly, with most speaking English. The tourist office goes out of its way to help travellers enjoy the city and provides help with everything from finding hidden sights to medical and financial information.

CUSTOMS AND IMMIGRATION

BELGIUM IS ONE of the 11 EU countries to have signed the 1985 Schengen agreement, which means travellers moving from one Schengen country to another are not subject to border controls. If you enter Belgium from France, Luxembourg, Germany or the Netherlands, you will not have to show your passport, although it is wise to carry it in case of trouble. Bear in mind that it is a legal requirement in Belgium to carry ID on the person at all times. Britain does not belong to Schengen, so travellers coming from the UK must present a valid passport and hold proof of onward passage when entering Belgium. This also applies to US, Australian, Canadian and other Commonwealth citizens.

British travellers no longer benefit from duty-free goods on their journey. Travellers from non-EU countries are still entitled to refunds of VAT (21 per cent on most products) if they spend more than €127 in a single transaction.

TOURIST INFORMATION

BRUSSELS IS RARELY crowded, so you should not expect to queue at major attractions and museums unless a special event or show is taking place. If you are planning to do extensive sightseeing, the one-day tram and bus pass *(see pp168–9)* is a must. Better still, pick up a "tourist passport" from the tourist office *(see below)*. Drivers should avoid rush hour (Monday to Friday

from 8am to 9:30am and 5pm to 7pm), although public transport is manageable throughout the day. Many of the city's prestige hotels slash their rates at weekends, when business custom slacks off, so it can be worthwhile timing a short visit around this. Although Brussels' reputation as a rainy city is overplayed, bring a raincoat or waterproof jacket in summer and warm clothing for winter.

The Tourist and Information Office publishes a variety of maps, guides and suggested walks and tours. It offers a tourist passport for €7.44, which includes a one-day tram and bus pass, discounts on train tickets countrywide as well as reductions on museum daily admission prices worth over €50.

OPENING HOURS

MOST SHOPS AND businesses are open Mondays to Saturdays from 10am to 6pm, with some local shops closing for an hour during the day.

Supermarkets are usually open from 9am to 8pm. For late-night essentials and alcohol, "night shops" stay open to 1am or 2am. Banking hours usually run on weekdays from 9am to 1pm and 2 to 4pm. Most branches have 24-hour ATMs, and many have Visa or Euro points with Maestro, where foreign cashcards can be used. Many sights are closed on Mondays. Public museums are usually open on Tuesdays to Sundays from 10am to 5pm.

MUSEUM ADMISSION CHARGES

THERE WAS MUCH controversy when the city's major museums, including the Musées des Beaux-Arts and the Musées Royaux d'art et d'histoire introduced a €3.70 admission charge in the mid-1990s, but so far the money seems to have been well spent, with the Cinquantenaire Museum in particular undergoing much-needed layout improvements. Elsewhere, admission charges

The sculpture court in the Musées Royaux des Beaux-Arts in summer

Visitors taking a break from sightseeing in a pavement café

range from free entry to a daily tariff starting at €5. Reductions for students, children, the unemployed and senior citizens are always given.

TIPPING

A SERVICE CHARGE OF 16 per cent as well as VAT of 21 per cent are included in restaurant bills (this is marked on the menu as *"Service et TVA compris"*), but most diners round up the bill or add about 10 per cent if the service has been particularly good. Service is also included in taxi fares, although a 10 per cent tip is customary. Some theatre and cinema ushers expect €0.25 per person. You should pay nightclub doormen around €1 if you plan to go back. In hotels, a small tip for the chambermaid and porter should be given personally to them or left in your vacated room, and expect to pay railway porters €1 per bag. Finally, many public toilets – including those in bars, restaurants and even cinemas – have attendants who should be given €0.25.

DISABLED TRAVELLERS

B RUSSELS IS NOT the easiest city for the disabled traveller, but the authorities are beginning to recognize that there is room for improvement. Most of the more expensive hotels have some rooms designed for people with disabilities, and most metro stations have lifts.

There are designated parking spaces for disabled drivers, and newer trams have wheelchair access. The Tourist Office provides information and advice about facilities within the city.

Façade of the Sterling bookshop

NEWSPAPERS, TV AND RADIO

M OST BRITISH AND American daily newspapers produce international editions, which are on sale at major newsstands. The *Financial Times*, the *International Herald Tribune* and the *Wall Street Journal* are widely available. **Librairie de Rome, Waterstone's** or **Sterling Books** sell English magazines.

Belgium has one of the world's most advanced cable TV networks, with access to more than 40 channels, including BBC 1 and 2, CNN, NBC, MTV and Arte. Belgian channels include RTL and RTBF 1 and 2 (French-speaking) and VTM and Ketnet/Canvas (Flemish-speaking). TV listings are in the English-language magazine *The Bulletin*. Classical music stations include Musique 3 (91.2 FM), Studio Brussel (100.6 FM), or Radio 3.

Personal Security and Health, Banking and Communications

BRUSSELS IS ONE OF Europe's safest capitals, with street crime against visitors a relatively rare occurrence. The poorer areas west and north of the city centre, including Anderlecht, Molenbeek and parts of Schaerbeek and St-Josse, have quite a bad reputation, but these areas are perfectly safe during the daytime for everyone except those who flaunt their wealth. After dark, it is sensible not to walk around on your own in these areas. Public transport is usually safe at all hours. Banking follows the European system and is straightforward. In addition, there are hundreds of 24-hour cashpoints located around the city.

LAW ENFORCEMENT

BELGIUM HAS A complex policing system, whose overlapping and often contradictory mandates have been criticized in the past. Calls have been made to simplify the judicial structure, a process that is still slowly taking place. Major crimes and motorway offences are handled by the national gendarmerie. However, visitors are most likely to encounter the communal police, who are responsible for law and order in each of the capital's 19 administrative districts. All Brussels police officers must speak French and Flemish.

The main police station for central Brussels is on Rue du Marché au Charbon, close to the Grand Place. If stopped by the police visitors will be asked for identification, so carry your passport at all times. Belgian law classes as a vagrant anyone carrying less than €15 cash. Not using road crossings correctly is also illegal here.

Female police officer

SAFETY GUIDELINES

MOST OF Brussels' principal tourist attractions are located in safe areas where few precautions are necessary. When driving, make sure car doors are locked and any valuables are kept out of sight. If you are sightseeing on foot, limit the amount of cash you carry and never leave bags unattended. Women should wear handbags with the strap across the shoulder and the clasp facing towards the body. Wallets should be kept in a front, not back, pocket. Hotel guests should keep rooms and suitcases locked and avoid leaving cash or valuables lying around. Rooms often come with a safe; if not, there should be one at reception.

At night, avoid the city's parks, especially at Botanique and Parc Josaphat in Schaerbeek, both of which are favoured haunts of drug-dealers.

LOST PROPERTY

CHANCES OF retrieving property are minimal if it was lost in the street. However, it is worth contacting the police station for the commune in which the article disappeared. (If you are not sure where that is, contact the central police station on Rue du Marché au Charbon.) Public transport authority **STIB/MIVB** operates a lost-and-found service for the metro, trams and buses. Report items lost in a taxi to the police station nearest your point of departure; quote registration details and the taxi licence number.

TRAVEL AND HEALTH INSURANCE

TRAVELLERS FROM Britain and Ireland are entitled to free healthcare under reciprocal agreements within the EU. British citizens need an E111 form from a post office, which should be validated before their trip. Europeans should make it clear that they have state insurance, or they may end up with a large bill. While generous, state healthcare subsidies do not cover all problems and it is worth taking out full travel insurance. This can also cover lost property.

DIRECTORY			
CRISIS INFORMATION	**Medigard Private Doctor Bureau** (02) 479 1818.	**Hôpital Universitaire Saint Luc** Ave Hippocrate 10, 1200 Brussels. (02) 764 1602.	**STIB/MIVB** Avenue de la Toison d'Or 15, 1050 Brussels. **Map 2** D5. (02) 515 2394. www.stib.be www.mivb.be
Police 101.	**Medigard Private Dentist Bureau** (02) 426 1026.	**Community Help Service** (02) 648 4014.	
Ambulance and fire services 100.	**EMERGENCY DEPARTMENTS**		**LOST CREDIT CARDS**
Central police station Rue du Marché au Charbon 30, 1000 Brussels. **Map 1** C3. (02) 279 7979.	**Institut Edith Cavell** Rue Edith Cavell 178, 1180 Brussels. (02) 340 4001.	**LOST PROPERTY** **Central police station** (02) 517 9611.	**American Express** (02) 676 2111. **MasterCard** (02) 205 8585. **Visa** (02) 205 8585.

MEDICAL MATTERS

WHETHER OR not you have insurance, doctors in Belgium will usually expect you to settle the bill on the spot – and in cash. Arrange to make a payment by bank transfer (most doctors will accept this if you insist).

Pharmacies are generally open Mondays to Saturdays from 8:30am to 6:30pm, with each commune operating a rota system for late-night, Sunday and national holiday cover. All pharmacies display information about where to find a 24-hour chemist.

Assistants at pharmacies may not speak good English, so when receiving a prescription, make sure the doctor goes through the details before you leave the surgery.

EMERGENCIES

FOR EMERGENCIES requiring police assistance, call 101; for medical or fire services, phone 100. Hospitals with emergency departments include **Institut Edith Cavell** and **Hôpital Universitaire Saint-Luc**. The Community Help Service's (CHS) 24-hour English-language help line is for expatriates, but it may be able to assist tourists.

CURRENCY

BELGIUM, together with 11 other countries, has replaced its traditional currency with the euro. Austria, Finland, France, Germany, Greece, Ireland, Italy, Luxembourg, Netherlands, Portugal and Spain also chose to join the new currency.

The euro came into circulation in Belgium on 1 January 2002. A transition period has allowed euros and Belgian francs (BF) to be used together, with the franc phased out by mid-2002.

The Euro bank notes have seven denominations. The 5-euro note (grey) is the smallest, followed by the 10-euro note (pink), 20-euro note (blue), 50-euro note (orange), 100-euro note (green), 200-euro note (yellow) and the 500-euro

note (purple). The euro has eight coin denominations: the 1 euro and 2 euros are both silver and gold in colour; the 50-, 20- and 10-cent coins are gold; and the 5-, 2- and 1-cent coins are bronze.

BANKING

MOST BANKS IN Brussels are open from 9am–1pm and 2–4pm; some open late on Friday until 4:30 or 5pm, and a few on Saturday mornings.

Banks often offer very competitive exchange rates, and most will happily serve non-clients. Many transactions (especially money transfers) are liable to banking fees, so ask in advance what these rates might be. Most banks will be able to cash traveller's cheques with the signatory's passport or other form of photographic identification. Visitors are usually able to exchange foreign currency, again with valid ID. Many bank attendants speak good English.

CREDIT CARDS

AMERICAN EXPRESS, Diners Club, Mastercard and Visa are widely accepted in Brussels, although it is wise to check in advance if booking a hotel or restaurant. Most hotels will accept a credit card booking. The cardholder may be asked for a credit card imprint at check-in.

BUREAUX DE CHANGE

IF YOU ARE unable to change money at a bank, you may be forced to rely on bureaux de change, which often charge commission of 3 to 4 per cent and may have uncompetitive exchange rates. There is a 24-hour automated exchange machine at Grand Place 7, while the streets around the square have several bureaux open until 7pm or later. There are also exchange booths at the city's major stations.

Travellers using currency from one of the countries which are members of the

European single currency have a rate of exchange fixed at constant rates. Commission for transactions between them should be 1.5 per cent. If a bureau does not honour these conditions, go elsewhere.

ATM machine in Brussels

AUTOMATED TELLER MACHINES

MOST BANK branches have 24-hour cashpoint facilities, with a lobby reserved for bank members and an ATM on the wall outside. Most ATMs will accept cards belonging to the Cirrus, Maestro, Plus and Star systems, as well as MasterCard and Visa cards.

POST AND COMMUNICATIONS

BRUSSELS' PUBLIC payphones are run by former state operator Belgacom. Public phone booths are plentiful but the service information can be difficult to understand; the operator can be contacted by dialling 1380 or directory enquiries in English on 1405. Payphones accept Belgacom phonecards, and most will take collect and calling-card calls. Both €5 and €10 Belgacom cards are sold at newsagents, post offices and train stations. Payphones in metro stations accept cash. When using the postal service, bear in mind that Belgium's service is automated, so addresses should be written in capital letters. A blue "A prior" sticker should ensure swifter delivery on international mail. Stamps are on sale in some supermarkets and post offices.

Red Belgian postbox

GETTING TO BRUSSELS

High-speed Thalys train

BRUSSELS IS WELL suited to both casual and business travellers, with abundant and excellent connections by air, rail and road. The increasing political significance of Brussels in its new role as the heart of Europe has led to greater competition between airlines, with many operators offering a variety of discounted fares. The Eurostar and Thalys high-speed trains link the city with London, Paris, Amsterdam and Germany, and compare favourably with flying in terms of time. British travellers can use the Channel Tunnel to bring their car with them.

An aeroplane from Belgian carrier SN Brussels Airlines' fleet

ARRIVING BY AIR

SITUATED 14 KM (8¾ miles) northeast of the city centre, Brussels National Airport is in the Flemish commune of Zaventem (the name by which it is known to most citizens, including taxi drivers). A centre for Belgian carrier SN Brussels Airlines, which replaced the bankrupt airline Sabena, the airport is also served by major carriers such as British Airways, American Airlines, Air Canada, Delta, Lufthansa and Air France. Among the low-cost operators flying to and from Zaventem are Virgin Express (for London and Europe) and City Bird (for US destinations). A typical journey from London takes 45 minutes. Costs for UK flights range from £60 for a student flight to £270 for a scheduled return flight. Fares are lower out of season, but tend to rise at the weekend.

Reaching Brussels from the US can be more expensive than reaching other major European cities. Return flights average US $700 for a charter return from New York. Prices from Canada are comparable.

The best-value flights from Australia and New Zealand include Alitalia, Lauda-air, and KLM, with fares from A$2,100.

Brussels South-Charleroi Airport has become a second important hub, since Ryanair has been operating scheduled flights from various European destinations, including the UK. It is 55 km (34 miles) from the centre of Brussels and can be reached by train or coach.

AIRPORT FACILITIES

BRUSSELS NATIONAL Airport has been extensively renovated over the past decade, with a new concourse for intra-EU travel due for completion by 2003. Brussels airport features baggage reclaim, customs, car-hire booths, tourist information and ground transport on the lower level. The departure lounge has check-in facilities, ticket and insurance counters and restaurants, bars and shops, before and after the security checkpoints. In addition, there are special lounges for busi-ness or first-class SN Brussels Airlines passengers, and a corporate meeting centre. On arrival, passengers will also find ATMs, foreign exchange booths and coin- and card-operated payphones.

GETTING INTO TOWN

THE CHEAPEST way of getting from Zaventem to the city centre is the express train from the airport to Gare du Nord, Gare Centrale or Gare du Midi. Tickets (about €2.50) are on sale in the airport complex or, for a small supplementary fee, on the train itself. Three trains run each hour, between 5am and midnight; the journey to Gare Centrale takes 20 minutes.

There is a taxi rank outside the arrivals hall. A one-way fare to the centre of Brussels will cost €25–€30 and should take around 20 minutes (longer at rush hour). If you plan to return by taxi, ask the driver about deals as some companies offer discounts on return fares.

An SNCB/NMBS train runs from Charleroi to Gare du Midi. It takes about 45 minutes to/from the station.

ARRIVING BY TRAIN

BRUSSELS IS AT the heart of Europe's high-speed train networks, connected to London by the Eurostar service and to Paris, Amsterdam and Cologne by the Thalys network. These trains have a top speed of 300 kph (186 mph) and have slashed journey times between northern Europe's major cities, making them a challenge to the supremacy of the airlines.

Eurostar passengers should book their tickets at least a week in advance, especially to take advantage of reduced

SN Brussels Airlines

Logo for SN Brussels Airlines

fares; they should also arrive at the terminal at least 20 minutes before departure to go through check-in and customs before boarding. You may be refused access to the train if you arrive after this, although you can often be transferred to the next service at no extra charge.

Trains run hourly between London's Waterloo station and Brussels via the Channel Tunnel; the journey takes 2 hours 40 minutes, arriving at the Gare du Midi. Return fares start at around £70/€87. The trains are comfortable, with plenty of legroom, and have two buffet cars, one of which is licensed; first-class passengers receive a meal, free drinks and the day's international newspapers.

Many visitors to Brussels arrive from mainland Europe. The high-speed train company Thalys offers a comfortable journey, with Paris accessible in 1 hour 25 minutes, Amsterdam in around two hours and Cologne in under three.

Eurostar train arriving at the Gare du Midi, Brussels

ARRIVING BY SEA

BELGIUM CAN easily be reached from the UK several times daily. Hoverspeed operates a catamaran service, the SeaCat, from Dover to Ostend. The crossing takes around two hours. Cross-Channel ferries run frequently from Dover to Calais, Felixstowe to Ostend and Hull to Zeebrugge. Foot

passengers do not usually need to book, but those with cars should always reserve a space and arrive promptly. Visitors with children should be aware that ferry companies have good child discounts, often with children under 14 years old travelling free.

ARRIVING BY CAR

THE OPENING of the Channel Tunnel has given drivers from Britain a new option for reaching mainland Europe: Le Shuttle. This is a car train that takes vehicles from the Tunnel entrance near Folkestone to Calais, with the journey taking around 35 minutes. From there, Brussels is a two-hour drive via the A16 motorway, which becomes the E40 when you cross the Franco-Belgian border. Follow signs to Brugge (Bruges), then Brussels. Those planning to ride Le Shuttle should book tickets in advance and try to arrive early. Three trains per hour run between 6:30am and midnight, with one train hourly from midnight to 6:30am. Standard fares start at £169 return per vehicle in low season, but rise for stays over five days and at popular times.

PASSPORTS AND ENTRY REQUIREMENTS

VISITORS FROM Britain will find that a passport is the only documentation required for a stay of up to 90 days. For a visit of the same length, European nationals should be prepared to produce their identity card. Travellers from the US and Canada need a full passport. All visitors should, if asked, be able to produce enough money, or proof of access to money, on arrival to pay for their entire stay as well as a return ticket to their home country.

DIRECTORY

BRUSSELS NATIONAL AIRPORT INFORMATION

(www.brusselsairport.be)

Flight Information
☏ (02) 753 3913.

Disabled Travellers and Special Needs
☏ (02) 723 6381.

Airport Police
☏ (02) 753 7000.

Customs
☏ (02) 753 4850.

AIRLINES

SN Brussels Airlines
☏ (020) 8780 1444 (UK).
🖳 www.brussels-airlines.com

Air Canada
☏ (0990) 247 226 (UK).

Air France
☏ (0845) 084 5111 (UK).

American Airlines
☏ (020) 8572 5555 (UK).
☏ (1 800) 433 7300 (US).
🖳 www.americanair.com

British Airways
☏ (020) 8759 5511 (UK).
🖳 www.britishairways.com

City Bird
☏ (212) 947 1408 (US).

Delta
☏ (0800) 414 767 (UK).
☏ (404) 765 5000 (US).

Lufthansa
☏ (0345) 737 747 (UK).

Ryanair
☏ (08701) 569 569 (UK).

Swissair
☏ (020) 7434 7300 (UK).

Virgin Express
☏ (020) 7744 0004 (UK).

TRAIN AND BOAT INFORMATION

Belgian & International Railway Info
🖳 www.b-rail.be

Belgian Transport
☏ (02) 515 2000.
🖳 www.stib.be

Eurostar
☏ (0870) 578 6186 (UK).

Eurotunnel
☏ (0990) 353 535 (UK).

Hoverspeed
☏ (0870) 240 8070 (UK).

Thalys
☏ (0900) 10366 (Belgium).

The Hoverspeed catamaran SeaCat crossing the Channel

Getting around Brussels

Metro station street sign

ALTHOUGH ITS public transport system is clean, modern and efficient, Brussels is a city best explored on foot. Most of the key attractions for first-time visitors are within a short walk of the Grand Place, and the Art Nouveau architecture in Ixelles and Saint-Gilles is also best enjoyed on a leisurely stroll. For those anxious to see the main sights in limited time, the tram and metro network covers most of the city at speed, while buses are useful for reaching more out-of-the-way areas. Although expensive, taxis are recommended for late-night journeys. Cycling can be hazardous for the inexperienced.

PLANNING YOUR JOURNEY

IF YOU ARE seeing Brussels by car, avoid its major roads during rush hours, which run on weekdays from 8–9:30am and 5–7pm as well as Wednesday lunchtimes during the school year, when there is a half day. Tram and bus services run frequently at peak time and are usually not too crowded. However, the small size of Brussels means that walking is usually a viable option.

WALKING IN BRUSSELS

THE SHORT distance between sights and the interest in every corner make central Brussels easy to negotiate on foot. Outside the city centre, walking is the only way to appreciate the concentration of Art Nouveau buildings on and around Square Ambiorix, around the district of Ixelles and near St-Gilles Town Hall.

Drivers in Brussels have a bad reputation, and it is important to be alert to traffic while crossing roads. Until 1996, motorists were not obliged to stop at pedestrian crossings: the laws came into effect on April 1 of that year and many drivers still treat them as a seasonal pleasantry. At traffic lights, motorists turning right or left may ignore the walkers' priority. It is essential to be careful even in residential areas.

Blue or white street signs are placed on the walls of buildings at one corner of a street, and can be somewhat hard to locate. Street names

are always in French first, then Flemish, with the name in capital letters and the street type in small letters to the top left and bottom right corners (for example, Rue STEVIN straat).

Mother and child seeing Brussels' historic architecture by bicycle

CYCLING

COMPARED TO THE cyclist-friendly cities of Flanders, Brussels can be a frustrating place for pushbike-riders. Car-free zones are few and far between, and cycle lanes are rare. However, on a trip to the suburbs or the Fôret de Soignes, bicycles are the best option and can be cheaply hired from most railway stations (non-Belgians must leave a small deposit).

TRAVELLING BY BUS, TRAM AND METRO

THE AUTHORITY governing Brussels' public transport is the bilingual **STIB/MIVB**, which runs buses, trams and metro services in the capital. Tickets are valid on all three services, which run between 5:30am and 12:30am on weekdays with shorter hours on Sundays and public holidays.

A single ticket, which allows the passenger an unlimited number of changes within one hour (excluding the Nato-Brussels Airport line 12), costs €1.40. You can also buy a ten-ticket card at €9 or a one-day pass costing €3.59. The five-ticket card, for €6.20, is not competitively priced but it can be convenient for avoiding repeated queues. There are also combined "STIB/MIVB + Taxi" tickets, a single ticket that offers a reduction on taxi rides.

Single tickets can be bought on buses and trams, and should be stamped in the orange machines next to the exits; you must restamp your ticket if the journey involves a change. On the metro, tickets must be bought and stamped before you reach the platform. Metro ticket offices and most private newsagents sell 10-ticket cards and one-day passes.

Bus at a stop in Brussels city centre

A city tram travelling down Rue Royale towards the city centre

Most stops have clear, comprehensible maps of the city's public transport system, with metros in orange, trams in blue and buses in red (see endpaper), and timetables mark all the stops on each route. Metro stations in the city centre have electronic displays showing where each train is in the system. Those unfamiliar with the tram system will notice the lack of on-board information; there is no indication of what the upcoming stop is, of which many are request stops. Request stops can be made by pressing the yellow buttons by each of the vehicle's exits. Ask the driver to call the relevant stop. Smoking is banned, as is playing music, although dogs are allowed on trams and buses.

A few bus services in the capital are run by the Walloon transport group (TEC) or the Flemish operator De Lijn. These services have lettered rather than numbered codes (for instance, the 60 bus is run by STIB/MIVB, the W by De Lijn), but most tickets are valid on all the services.

BRUSSELS BY CAR

IT MAY BE A small city, but Brussels has been known to reduce motorists to tears. The seemingly perverse one-way system in many sections of the city centre can swiftly confuse newcomers, while the network of tunnels that bisect the city are notoriously difficult to navigate even for city-dwellers. Belgian drivers, too, have been the butt of jokes from their fellow Europeans for decades. Nonetheless the city's systems are not difficult to learn, and a car is handy for planning day trips around the rest of Belgium.

Most international rental agencies have branches here, many at the National Airport in Zaventem or at the Gare du Midi, where the Eurostar and train services arrive.

Like the rest of mainland Europe, Belgium drives on the right, and the "priorité à droite" rule – which means that the driver coming from the right at junctions has absolute priority to pull out unless otherwise indicated – is enforced with sometimes startling regularity. Always watch for vehicles coming from the right, no matter how small the road; some drivers have been known to take their priority even though it means a crash, secure in the knowledge that they are legally correct. Verve and confidence are helpful when driving in a city where many motorists take a flexible approach to road rules. Essential safety precautions, however, should be adhered to at all times. Safety belts are obligatory in all seats, and children under 12 years old are not allowed in the front when other seats are free.

One-day travel pass

Cars and taxis threading their way through the main streets

Drink-driving is illegal (the limit in Belgium is currently 0.5g/l). Speed limits are 50 kph (30 mph) in built-up areas, 120 kph (75 mph) on motorways and dual carriageways and 90 kph (55 mph) on all other roads. Always give way to trams, who will ring their bells should a car be in the way. Street parking, usually by meter, is becoming increasingly difficult in the city centre.

TAKING A TAXI

BRUSSELS' TAXIS are among Europe's more expensive, but most journeys are short and cabs are the city's only 24-hour transport service. Service is generally efficient, with most drivers speaking at least a little English, although some people may be surprised at many drivers' lack of familiarity with sections of the city. All taxis have a rooftop sign which is illuminated when the vehicle is vacant. Most cars are either black or white, with Mercedes the make of choice for most companies. It is advisable to find a taxi rank or order a cab by phone, although occasionally drivers will stop if hailed on the street. Passengers ride in the back seat, with the fare meter on the dashboard or just behind the gear-stick. Fares should be posted inside the vehicle. Tips are included in the price, but an extra tip is usually expected.

To make a complaint, write to the **CCN-Service Régional des Taxis et Limousines**, Rue du Progrès 80, 1030 Brussels. Give the taxi's registration number, its make and colour when making the complaint.

Getting around Belgium

As you might expect from a country that is small, modern and predominantly flat, Belgium is an extremely easy place in which to travel. The toll-free motorways compare favourably with any in France, train travel is swift and competitively priced and there are good bus services in those areas not covered by the railway network. Public transport is clean and efficient and the range of touring tickets allows a great deal of freedom and the ability to see the whole country inexpensively. In the level Flemish countryside to the north, hiking and cycling are highly pleasant ways to get around.

Cyclists on a tour of the scenery of Durbuy in the Ardennes

TRAVELLING BY CAR

After the rather enervating traffic in Brussels, driving in the rest of Belgium comes a something of a relief. The motorways are fast, reasonably well maintained and toll-free, while major roads are also excellent. Drivers in cities outside the capital tend to be more relaxed, although the trend in Flanders for car-free city centres can make navigation demanding. The only difficulty most drivers encounter is an occasional absence of clear signs for motorway exits and junctions, which can necessitate taking extra care when approaching junctions (in Flanders, many drivers are confused by signs for "Uitrit". It means exit).

The road rules detailed in the Getting Around Brussels section (see p169) hold good for the rest of the country, with speed limits at 50 kph (30 mph) in built-up areas, 120 kph (75 mph) on motorways and dual carriageways and 90 kph (55 mph) on other national roads.

If you break down, three motoring organizations should be able to provide assistance: **Touring Club de Belgique, Royal Automobile Club de Belgique** and **Vlaamse Automobilistenbond** in Flanders. It is worth getting breakdown coverage before you leave, and you must have a valid driving licence (from the EU, US, Australia or Canada) or an International Driving Licence on your

person. It is also essential to have comprehensive insurance and/or a Green card, and visitors are expected to carry a first-aid kit and a warning triangle at all times.

All the major rental agencies operate in Belgium, although renting a car can be an expensive business. To rent a vehicle, you must be 21 or over, with a year's driving experience, and have a credit card. A week's rental with unlimited mileage will cost €370 or more but might be reduced on the regular special deals at the big firms. Local agencies may also be cheaper, but be sure to check the terms and conditions. Bicycle hire is available in most Flemish towns with a modest deposit of €15.

TRAVELLING BY TRAIN

Belgium's train network is a more than adequate means of getting to and from major towns and cities. From Brussels, there are direct links to Antwerp, Ghent, Bruges, Ostend, Liège, Mons, Namur and the Ardennes, and even journeys involving a change rarely take more than two hours in total.

Run by **Belgian National Railways** (Société Nationale Chemins de Fer Belges/ Belgische Spoorwegen), the system is clean, modern and efficient, although the quality of rolling stock varies somewhat: older carriages have a slightly drab feel, but new

FRENCH/FLEMISH PLACE NAMES

One of the most confusing aspects of travel in Belgium is the variation between French and Flemish spellings of town names. On road signs in Brussels, both names are given, while in Flanders only the Flemish and in Wallonia only the French are shown. The following list gives main towns:

French	Flemish	French	Flemish
Anvers	Antwerpen	Malines	Mechelen
Ath	Aat	Mons	Bergen
Bruges	Brugge	Namur	Namen
Bruxelles	Brussel	Ostende	Oostende
Courtrai	Kortrijk	Saint-Trond	Sint-Truiden
Gand	Gent	Tongrès	Tongeren
Liège	Luik	Tournai	Doornik
Louvain	Leuven	Ypres	Ieper

Train travelling through Belgium on a spring evening

models are spacious, very comfortable, and, typically Belgian, offer fine meals and light refreshments.

Fares for standard second-class tickets are calculated by distance, with 100 km (63 miles) costing around €9.40; first-class fares will set you back around 50 per cent more. Because distance is the determining factor in price, return tickets generally offer no saving and are valid only until midnight. Children aged under six travel free, with a maximum of four children allowed per adult, and those aged between six and 11 receive a 50 per cent discount. Several special tariffs are available, including discounts for young adults aged under 26, with weekend tickets and day returns

Train and motor tour logos

reducing the price by up to 40 per cent. The more people travelling, the larger the discount; family members may be eligible for discounts of up to 60 per cent.

A variety of rail passes are on offer for extensive travel. The Belgian Tourrail pass (approximately €52) allows unlimited travel on any five days within one month of purchase, while the Carte de reduction à prix fixe (at approximately €15) offers 50 per cent off all first- and second-class tickets for one month.

TRAVELLING BY BUS

WHILE SLOWER and less comfortable for travelling between major cities, buses come into their own in the more remote or rural areas of the rest of Belgium, as well as in city suburbs. In Flanders, buses are run by the **De Lijn** group; in Wallonia, the network is operated by **TEC**. Fares are calculated according to distance, and are bought from the driver. Bus stops and terminals are generally close to railway stations. Buses have priority on public roads, so journeys are often swift.

SPECIALIST TOURS

TOURING CAN BE a journey full of cultural variety in both Brussels and the rest of the country. In the capital, the Tourist Information Centre

(see p162) runs a series of over 40 walking and car day tours that cover all the capital and its 19 districts with topics as diverse as "Humanist Brussels" and "Industrial Belgium". The focus is largely on the city's exceptional range of art and architecture, but many diverse themes are covered.

In each major regional city, detailed, multi-lingual private tours are available in the historic town centre; contact the town's main tourist booth for full information.

Away from cities, Belgium also offers hiking and cycling excursions, ranging from one-day adventures to five-day hikes. The Ardennes is a popular destination for hikers, who can appreciate the area's flora and fauna as well as its dramatic history. First Travel Management (02 716 1870) will arrange tours.

DIRECTORY

TRAINS AND BUSES

SNCB/BS (Belgian National Railways)
(02) 555 2555, 555 2525.
www.sncb.be

TEC
(010) 235353.

De Lijn
(02) 526 2828.

MOTORING ORGANIZATIONS

Police Road Information
www.policefederale.be

Touring Club de Belgique
Rue de la Loi 44, 1040 Brussels.
Map 3 A2. (02) 233 2211.

Royal Automobile Club de Belgique
Rue d'Arlon 53, 1040 Brussels.
Map 3 A3. (02) 287 0911.

Vlaamse Automobilistenbond
Sint-Jacobsmarkt 45, Antwerp.
(03) 234 3434.

CAR RENTAL

Avis (02) 730 6211.
Budget (02) 646 5130.
Europcar (02) 640 9400.
Hertz (02) 513 2886.

A coach full of passengers travelling on a main bus route in Belgium

BRUSSELS STREET FINDER

THE PAGE GRID superimposed on the area by area grid below shows which parts of Brussels are covered in this *Street Finder*. The central Upper and Lower Town areas are marked in the colours that are also the thumbtab colours throughout the book. The map references for all sights, hotels, restaurants, shopping and entertainment

Nymph in Parc de Bruxelles

venues described in this guide refer to the maps in this section. A street index follows on pp178–81. The key, set out below, indicates the scales of the maps and shows what other features are marked on them, including transport terminals, emergency services and information centres. All the major sights are clearly marked so they are easy to locate. The map on the inside back cover shows public transport routes.

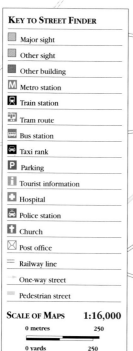

KEY TO STREET FINDER

	Major sight
	Other sight
	Other building
M	Metro station
	Train station
	Tram route
	Bus station
	Taxi rank
P	Parking
i	Tourist information
	Hospital
	Police station
	Church
✉	Post office
=	Railway line
→	One-way street
	Pedestrian street

SCALE OF MAPS   1:16,000

0 metres	250
0 yards	250

Façade of La Maison des Ducs de Brabant, Grand Place *(see pp42–3)*

The Triumphal arch in the
Parc du Cinquentenaire, built
in the 1880s *(see pp74–5)*

2

3

4

ARDIN BOTANIQUE
LAAN

KONINGSSTRAAT

L ROYALE

RUE DE LA LOI WETSTRAAT

AVE DE CORTENBERG

BVD BRAND WHITLOCK LAAN

RUE BELLIARD STRAAT

WATERLOO

Upper Town

AVE DE TERVUREN LAAN

RUE DU TRONE TROONSTRAAT

0 metres   500

0 yards   500

Cathédrale Sts
Michel et Gudule
(see pp70–71)

General Index

Acknowledgments

DORLING KINDERSLEY would like to thank the following people whose assistance contributed to the preparation of this book:

MAIN CONTRIBUTORS

ZOË HEWETSON is based in London but works in Brussels as a simultaneous translator for the European Commission. She is also a keen walker and has recently published a guide to walking in Turkey.

PHILIP LEE lives and works in Nottingham. A veteran travel writer, he has contributed to numerous *Rough Guide* and *Dorling Kindersley Travel Guide* publications, including the *Rough Guide to Belgium*. He frequently writes on travel for British newspapers and magazines.

ZOË ROSS is a London-based writer and editor. She has worked on several Dorling Kindersley travel guides, and is now a freelance author.

SARAH WOLFF has lived and worked in Brussels for several years. An editor and journalist, she is currently working for *The Bulletin*, Brussels' English-language newsweekly magazine.

TIMOTHY WRIGHT lived in Brussels for most of the 1990s. A successful journalist, he contributed to several English-language magazines published in Brussels and elsewhere in the Benelux countries.

JULIA ZYRIANOVA is a freelance journalist and translator. She lived in Brussels and Paris for several years and is now based in London.

FOR DORLING KINDERSLEY

Gillian Allan; Douglas Amrine; Louise Bostock Lang; Vivien Crump; Donald Greig; Marie Ingledew; Lee Redmond; Marisa Renzullo.

PROOFREADER

Sam Merrell.

INDEXER

Hilary Bird.

ADDITIONAL PHOTOGRAPHY

Steve Gorton, Ian O'Leary, Neil Mersh, David Murray, Tim Ridely, Jules Selmes, Clive Streeter, Matthew Ward.

SPECIAL ASSISTANCE

Many thanks for the invaluable help of the following individuals: Joanna at Belgo; Derek Blyth; Christiana Ceulemans at Institut Royal Du Patrimonie Artistique; Charles Dierick at Centre Belge de la Bande Dessinée; Anne at Gaspard de Wit; Elsge Ganssen and Georges Delcart at Rubenshuis; Doctor Janssens at the Domaine de Laeken; Leen de Jong at Koninklijk Museum Voor Schone Kunsten; Antwerpen; Noel at Leonidas; Chantal Pauwert at Stad Brugge Stedelijke Musea; Marie-Hélène van Schonbroek at Cathédrale Sts Michel et Gudule; Elaine de Wilde and Sophie van Vliet at Musées Royaux des Beaux-Arts.

PHOTOGRAPHY PERMISSIONS

Dorling Kindersley would like to thank all the cathedrals, churches, museums, hotels, restaurants, shops, galleries and sights too numerous to thank individually for their assistance and kind permission to photograph at their establishments.

Placement Key - t=top; tl=top left; tlc= top left centre; tc= top centre; trc= top right centre; tr= top right; cla= centre left above; ca= centre above; cra= centre right above; cl = centre left; c= centre; cr= centre right; clb= centre left below; cb = centre below; crb = centre right below; bl= bottom left; b= bottom; bc= bottom centre; bcl= bottom centre left; br= bottom right; d = detail.

Works of art have been produced with the permission of the following copyright holders: ©Casterman 19 br, Ted Benoit Berceuse Electrique 50clb; ©DACS 2000 16bl, 51t/cra/crb/b, 78tr/cl/cr; ©Dupuis 1999 18tr, 19ca; Sofa Kandissy ©Alessandro Medini 111c; Lucky Luke Licensing ©MORRIS 18br; @Moulinsart SA 4, 18tl/cr/cl/bl, 50tl/tr/cra/crb, 51cla/clb; ©Peyo 1999 - Licensed through I.M.P.S. (Brussels) 19bc; 50cla;

The publishers would like to thank the following individuals, companies, and picture libraries for their kind permission to reproduce their photographs:

AKG, LONDON: 31b, 34t, 36b, 37bl, 37br, 142tr; Galleria Nazdi Cupodimonte 20-1; Erich Lessing 28,/ Kunsthistoriches Museum 31t; Musée du Louvre 29b; Musée Royaux d'Arts et d'Histoire, Brussels 35c; Museo de Santa Cruz, Toledo 29t; Museum Deutsche Geschichte, Berlin 31c; Private Collection 142tl; Pushkin Museum 30c; Victoria and Albert Museum, London 32c.

DUNCAN BAIRD PUBLISHERS: Alan Williams 143br. CH. BASTIN & J. EVRARD: 16tr/cb/bc, 17tr/br, 82bl/br; 91t, 99t, 112b, 115br; BRIDGEMAN ART LIBRARY, LONDON: Christie's Images, London Peter Paul Rubens (1557–1640) *Self Portrait* 15t; Musée Crozatier, Le Puy-en-Velay, France designed by Berain (c.1725–1730) *Dawn*, Brussels lace 21bl; Private Collection/ Marie-Victoire Jaquotot (1778–1855) *Portrait of the Duke of Wellington* 35b./Max Silbert (b.1871) *The Lacemakers of Ghent* 1913 21t; Private Collection French School (19th century) Louis XIV (1638–1715) of *France in the costume of the Sun King in the ballet 'La Nuit' c.1665* (litho) 32br; Private Collection/Bonhams, London/Robert Alexander Hillingford (1825–1904) *The Turning Point at Waterloo* (oil on canvas) 34bl; STAD BRUGGE STEDELIJKE MUSEA: Groeninge-museum 118ca/cb/b, 119c/bl; Paul Delveaux *Serenity*, 1970 ©Foundation P. Delveaux – St Idesbald, Belgium 118t; Gruithuis 116t/cb/b, 117c; Gruuthusemuseum 30t.

CAFE COULEUR: 25t; CEPHAS: Nigel Blythe 122-3; TOP/A. Riviere-Lecoeur 142bl; CHIMAY: 142cr; DEMETRIO CARRASCO: 137b; ALAN COPSON: 13bl, 37c; CORBIS: David Bartruff 19cb, 140tr; Wolfgang Kaehler 167c; Patrick Ward 25b.

DAS PHOTO: 158c, 164c, 166t, 170.

ECRAN TOTAL©CINEDIT: 158t; ET ARCHIVE: Imperial War Museum, London 107b; EUROPEAN COMMISSION: 22b.

ROBERT HARDING PICTURE LIBRARY: Julian Pottage 77t, 169b; Roger Somvi 15b, 24t/c; HOVERSPEED: 167b; HULTON GETTY COLLECTION: 22c, 33t, 34c, 36c, 91b; Keytone 37t.

INSTITUT ROYAL DU PATRIMOINE ARTISTIQUE/KONINKLIJK INSTITUUT VOOR HET KUNSTPATRIMONIUM: 20tr, Societé des Expositions du Palais des Beaux-Arts de Bruxelles 53tr.

KONINKLIJK MUSEUM VOOR SCHONE KUNSTEN, ANTWERP: P. Delvaux *Pink's Bow* ©Foundation P. Delveaux – St Idesbald, Belgium/DACS, London 2000 95c; J. Jordaens *As the old sang, the young ones play pipes* 95tr; R. Magritte *Madame Recamier*©ADAGP, Paris and DACS, London 2000 95b; P.P. Rubens *Adoration of the Magi* 95tl; J. Van Eyck *Saint Barbara* 94c; R. Wouters *Woman Ironing* 94b.

MUSÉE DE L'ART WALLON DE LA VILLE DE LIÈGE: Legs M. Aristide Cralle (1884) 35tl; MUSÉES ROYAUX DES BEAUX-ARTS DE BELGIQUE, BRUXELLES-KONINKLIJKE MUSEA VOOR SCHONE KUNSTEN VAN BELGIË, BRUSSEL: photo Cussac 6–7, 14t, 34–5, 62clb, 63crb/bl, 64c/b, 65tl/tr, 66t, 67b, /©ADAGP, Paris and DACS, London 2000 65br, /© The Henry Moore Foundation 65c; photo Speltdoorn 14b, 15c, 20c, 63cr, 66b,/©ADAGP, Paris James Ensor *Skeletons Fighting Over a Pickled Herring*, 1891 ©DACS 2000 64t; and DACS, London 2000 67t.

DOCUMENT OPT: Alain Mathieu 171t.

PICTOR: 89t; ROBBIE POLLEY: 112b, 116ca, 117b, 119br, 162t, 163c, 165t, 168c/b, 171b; PRIVATE COLLECTION: 7, 34, 39, 85, 123, 161.

REX FEATURES: 22, 24b, 26c, Action Press 36t; Sipa Press/Vincent Kessler 23t.

SABENA: 166clb; SCIENCE PHOTO LIBRARY: CNES 1992 Distribution Spot Image 8; ©STANDAARD STRIPS: 19bl; NEIL SETCHFIELD: 20tl, 88t, 140c, 157t/c; SUNDANCER: © Moulinsart 18cl.

TELEGRAPH COLOUR LIBRARY: Ian McKinnell 84-5; ARCHIVES DU

THEATRE ROYAL DE LA MONNAIE: 35tr; TONY STONE IMAGES: Richard Elliott 27; Hideo Kurihara 2–3; ©TOERISME OOOST-VLAANDEREN: 99br; SERVICE RELATIONS EXTERIEURES CITY OF TOURNAI: 20b.

ROGER VIOLLET: 32t; Musee San Martino, Naples 33b.

WORLD PICTURES: 26b, 101b.

All other images ©Dorling Kindersley.
For further information see: www.dkimages.com

Jacket: All special photography except BRITSOCK: SEIP-BACH clb; ALAN COPSON: cra; ROBERT HARDING PICTURE LIBRARY: Roy Rainford t; Sofa Kandissy ©Alessandro Medini crb.

DORLING KINDERSLEY SPECIAL EDITIONS

Dorling Kindersley books can be purchased in bulk quantities at discounted prices for use in promotions or as premiums.
We are also able to offer special editions and personalized jackets, corporate imprints, and excerpts from all of our books, tailored specifically to meet your own needs.

To find out more, please contact:
(in the United Kingdom) – SPECIAL SALES, DORLING KINDERSLEY LIMITED, 80 STRAND, LONDON WC2R ORL;

(in the United States) – SPECIAL MARKETS DEPT., DK PUBLISHING, INC., 375 HUDSON STREET, NEW YORK, NY 10014.

Phrase Book

Tips for Pronouncing French

French-speaking Belgians, or Walloons, have a throaty, deep accent noticeably different from French spoken in France. Despite this, there are few changes in the vocabulary used in spoken and written language.

Consonants at the end of words are mostly silent and not pronounced. *Ch* is pronounced *sh*; *th* is *t*; *w* is *v*; and *r* is rolled gutturally. *Ç* is pronounced *s*.

In Emergency

Help!	**Au secours!**	oh sek**oor**
Stop!	**Arrêtez!**	aret-**ay**
Call a doctor!	**Appelez un medecin**	apuh-**lay** uñ meds**añ**
Call the police!	**Appelez la police**	apuh-**lay** lah pol-**ees**
Call the fire brigade!	**Appelez les pompiers**	apuh-**lay** leh poñ-**peeyay**
Where is the nearest telephone?	**Ou est le téléphone le plus proche**	oo ay luh tehleh**fon** luh ploo **prosh**
Where is the nearest hospital?	**Ou est l'hôpital le plus proche**	oo ay l'opeetal luh ploo **prosh**

Communication Essentials

Yes	**Oui**	wee
No	**Non**	noñ
Please	**S'il vous plait**	seel voo **play**
Thank you	**Merci**	mer-**see**
Excuse me	**Excusez-moi**	exkoo-**zay** mwah
Hello	**Bonjour**	boñz**hoor**
Goodbye	**Au revoir**	oh ruh-**vwar**
Good night	**Bonne nuit**	boñ-**swar**
morning	**Le matin**	mat**añ**
afternoon	**L'apres-midi**	l'apreh-**meedee**
evening	**Le soir**	swah
yesterday	**Hier**	eeyehr
today	**Aujourd'hui**	oh-zhoor-**dwee**
tomorrow	**Demain**	duhm**añ**
here	**Ici**	ee-**see**
there	**Là bas**	lah bah
What?	**Quel/quelle?**	kel, kel
When?	**Quand?**	koñ
Why?	**Pourquoi?**	poor-**kwah**
Where?	**Où?**	oo
How?	**Comment?**	kom-**moñ**

Useful Phrases

How are you?	**Comment allez vous?**	kom-moñ tal**ay** voo
Very well, thank you.	**Très bien, merci.**	treh byañ, mer-**see**
How do you do?	**Comment ça va?**	kom-moñ sah **vah**
See you soon	**A bientôt.**	byañ-toh
That's fine.	**Ça va bien.**	Sah vah byañ
Where is/are...?	**Où est/sont...?**	ooh ay/soñ
How far is it to...?	**Combien de kilomètres d'ici à...?**	kom-**byañ** duh keelo-**metr** d'ee-**see** ah
Which way to...?	**Quelle est la direction pour...?**	kel ay lah deer-ek-**syoñ** poor
Do you speak English?	**Parlez-vous Anglais?**	par-**lay** voo oñg-**lay**
I don't understand.	**Je ne comprends pas.**	zhuh nuh kom-**proñ** pah
Could you speak slowly?	**Vous puissez parler plus lentement?**	voo pwee-say par-lay ploos **loñ**tuh-moñ
I'm sorry.	**Excusez-moi.**	exkoo-**zay** mwah

Useful Words

big	**grand**	groñ
small	**petit**	puh-**tee**
hot	**chaud**	show
cold	**froid**	frwah
good	**bon**	boñ
bad	**mauvais**	moh-**veh**
enough	**assez**	assay
well	**bien**	byañ
open	**ouvert**	oo-**ver**
closed	**fermé**	fer-**meh**
left	**gauche**	gohsh
right	**droite**	drawh
straight on	**tout droit**	too drwah
near	**près**	preh
far	**loin**	lwañ
up	**en haut**	oñ oh
down	**en bas**	oñ bah
early	**tôt**	toh

late	**tard**	tar
entrance	**l'entrée**	l'on-**tray**
exit	**la sortie**	sor-**tee**
toilet	**toilette**	twah-let
occupied	**occupé**	o-koo-**pay**
free (vacant)	**libre**	leebr
free (no charge)	**gratuit**	grah-**twee**

Making a Telephone Call

I would like to place a long-distance telephone call	**Je voudrais faire un interurbain**	zhuh voo-dreh faire uñ añter-oorbañ
I'd like to call collect	**Je voudrais faire un communication PCV**	zhuh voo-**dreh** faire oon kom-oonikah-**syoñ** peh-seh-veh
I will try again later	**Je vais essayer plus tard**	zhuh vay ess-ay-eh ploo tar
Can I leave a message?	**Est-ce que je peux laisser un message?**	es-**keh** zhuh puh les-**say** uñ meh-sazh
Could you speak up a little please?	**Pouvez-vous parler un peu plus fort?**	poo-**vay** voo par-**lay** uñ puh ploo for
Local call	**Communication local**	komoonikah-**syoñ** low-**kal**

Shopping

How much does this cost?	**C'est combien?**	say kom-**byañ**
I would like....	**Je voudrais**	zhuh voo-**dray**
Do you have...	**Est-ce que vous avez...**	es-kuh voo zavay
I'm just looking	**Je regarde seulement**	zhuh ruhgar suhl-moñ
Do you take credit cards?	**Est-ce que vous acceptez les cartes de crédit**	es-**kuh** voo zaksept-ay leh kart duh kreh-**dee**
Do you take travellers' cheques?	**Est-ce que vous acceptez les chèques de voyage**	es-**kuh** voo zak-sept-**ay** lay shek duh vwayazh
What time do you open?	**A quelle heure vous êtes ouvert**	ah kel urr voo zet oo-**ver**
What time do you close?	**A quelle heure vous êtes fermé**	ah kel urr voo zet fer-**may**
This one	**Celui-ci**	suhl-wee see
That one	**Celui-là**	suhl-wee **lah**
expensive	**cher**	shehr
cheap	**pas cher, bon marché**	pah shehr, boñ mar-shay
size, clothes	**la taille**	tye
white	**blanc**	bloñ
black	**noir**	nwahr
red	**rouge**	roozh
yellow	**jaune**	zhownh
green	**vert**	vehr
blue	**bleu**	bluh

Types of Shops

shop	**le magasin**	le maga-**zañ**
bakery	**la boulangerie**	booloñ-**zhuree**
bank	**la banque**	boñk
bookshop	**la librairie**	lee-**brehree**
butcher	**la boucherie**	boo-**shehree**
cake shop	**la pâtisserie**	patec-**sree**
chocolate shop	**la chocolatier**	shok-oh-lah-tych
chip stop/stand	**la friterie**	free-tuh-ree
chemist	**la pharmacie**	farmah-**see**
delicatessen	**la charcuterie**	shah-koo-tuh-**ree**
department store	**le grand magasin**	groñ maga-**zañ**
fishmonger	**la poissonerie**	pwasson-**ree**
greengrocer	**le marchand des légumes**	mar-**shoñ** duh lay-**goom**
hairdresser	**le coiffeur**	kwafuhr
market	**le marché**	marsh **ay**
newsagent	**le magasin de journaux/tabac**	maga-**zañ** duh zhoor-**no**/ta-bak
post office	**le bureau de poste**	boo-**roh** duh pohst
supermarket	**le supermarché**	soo-pehr-**marshay**
travel agent	**l'agence de voyage**	azhons duh vwayazh

Sightseeing

art gallery	**le galérie d'art**	galer-**ree** dart
bus station	**la gare routière**	gahr roo-tee-yehr

cathedral	la cathédrale	katay-**dral**
church	l'église	ayg**leez**
closed on public holidays	fermeture jour ferié	fehrmeh-tur zhoor fehree-ay
garden	le jardin	zhah-**dañ**
library	la bibliothèque	beeb**leeo**-tek
museum	le musée	moo-**zay**
railway station	la gare (SNCF)	gahr (es-en-say-ef)
tourist office	les informations	layz uñ-for-mah-syoñ
town hall	l'hôtel de ville	oh**tel** duh vil
train	le train	trañ

STAYING IN A HOTEL

Do you have a vacant room?	est-ce que vous avez une chambre?	es-kuh voo z**avay** oon shambr
double room with double bed	la chambre à deux personnes, avec un grand lit	la shambr uh duh per-**son** uh-vek uñ groñ lee
twin room	la chambre à deux lits	la shambr ah duh lee
single room	la chambre à une personne	la shambr ah oon pehr-**son**
room with a bath	la chambre avec salle de bain	shambr ah-vek sal duh bañ
shower	une douche	doosh
I have a reservation	J'ai fait une reservation	zhay fay oon ray-zehrva-**syoñ**

EATING OUT

Have you got a table?	Avez vous une table libre?	avay-**voo** oon tahbl leebr
I would like to reserve a table.	Je voudrais réserver une table.	zhuh voo-dray rayzehr-**vay** oon tahbl
The bill, please.	L'addition, s'il vous plait.	l'adee-**syoñ**, seel voo **play**
I am a vegetarian.	Je suis végétarien.	zhuh swee vezhay-**tehryañ**
waitress/waiter	Garçon, Mademoiselle	gah-sohn/ mad-uh-mwah-zel
menu	le menu	men-**oo**
cover charge	le couvert	luh koo-**vehr**
wine list	la carte des vins	lah **kart**-deh vañ
glass	verre	vehr
bottle	la bouteille	boo-**tay**
knife	le couteau	koo-**toh**
fork	la fourchette	for-**shet**
spoon	la cuillère	kwee-**yehr**
breakfast	le petit déjeuner	puh-**tee** day-**zhuh-nay**
lunch	le déjeuner	day-**zhuh-nay**
dinner	le dîner	dee-**nay**
main course	le grand plat	groñ plah
starter	l'hors d'oeuvres	or duhvr
dessert	la dessert	duh-zehrt
dish of the day	le plat du jour	plah doo joor
bar	le bar	bah
cafe	le café	ka-**fay**
rare	saignant	say-nyoñ
medium	à point	ah **pwañ**
well done	bien cuit	byañ **kwee**

NUMBERS

0	zero	zeh-**roh**
1	un	uñ, oon
2	deux	duh
3	trois	trwah
4	quatre	katr
5	cinq	sañk
6	six	sees
7	sept	set
8	huit	weet
9	neuf	nerf
10	dix	dees
11	onze	oñz
12	douze	dooz
13	treize	trehz
14	quatorze	**katorz**
15	quinze	kañz
16	seize	sehz
17	dix-sept	dees-**set**
18	dix-huit	dees-**zweet**
19	dix-neuf	dees-**znerf**
20	vingt	vañ
21	vingt-et-un	vañ ay uhn
30	trente	tront
40	quarante	karoñt
50	cinquante	sañkoñt

60	soixante	swahsoñt
70	soixante-dix	swahsoñt-dees
80	quatre-vingt	katr-vañ
90	quatre-vingt-dix/ nonante	katr vañ dees/ nonañ
100	cent	soñ
1000	mille	meel
1,000,000	million	miyoñ

TIME

What is the time?	Quelle heure?	kel uhr
one minute	une minute	oon mee-**noot**
one hour	une heure	oon uhr
half an hour	une demi-heure	oon duh-**mee** uhr
half past one	une heure et demi	uhr ay duh-mee
a day	un jour	zhuhr
a week	une semaine	suh-mehn
a month	un mois	mwah
a year	une année	annay
Monday	lundi	luñ-**dee**
Tuesday	mardi	mah-**dee**
Wednesday	mercredi	mehrkruh-**dee**
Thursday	jeudi	zhuh-**dee**
Friday	vendredi	voñdruh-**dee**
Saturday	samedi	sam-**dee**
Sunday	dimanche	dee-**moñsh**

BELGIAN BEER AND FOOD

fish	poisson	pwah-**ssoñ**
bass	bar/loup de mer	bah/loo duh mare
herring	hareng	ah-**roñ**
lobster	homard	oh-ma
monkfish	lotte	lot
mussel	moule	mool
oyster	huitre	weetr
pike	brochet	brosh-ay
salmon	saumon	soh-moñ
scallop	coquille Saint-Jacques	kok-eel sañ jak
sea bream	dorade/daurade	doh-rad
prawn	crevette	kreh-vet
skate	raie	ray
trout	truite	trweet
tuna	thon	toñ

MEAT

meat	viande	vee-**yand**
beef	boeuf	buhf
chicken	poulet	poo-**lay**
duck	canard	kanar
lamb	agneau	ahyoñ
pheasant	faisant	feh-zoñ
pork	porc	por
veal	veau	voh
venison	cerf/chevreuil	surf/shev-roy

VEGETABLES

vegetables	légumes	lay-**goom**
asparagus	asperges	ahs-pehrj
Belgian endive /chicory	chicon	shee-koñ
Brussels sprouts	choux de bruxelles	shoo duh broocksell
garlic	ail	eye
green beans	haricots verts	arrykoh vehr
haricot beans	haricots	arrykoh
potatoes	pommes de terre	pom-duh **tehr**
spinach	epinard	aypeenar
truffle	truffe	troof

DESSERTS

pancake	crêpe	crayp
waffle	gauffre	gohfr
fruit	fruits	frwee

DRINKS

coffee	café	kah-**fay**
white coffee	café au lait	kah-**fay** oh lay
milky coffee	caffe latte	kah-**fay** lat-uh
hot chocolate	chocolat chaud	shok-oh-lah shoh
tea	thé	tay
water	l'eau	oh
mineral water	l'eau minérale	l'oh meenay-ral
lemonade	limonade	lee-moh-nad
orange juice	jus d'orange	zhoo doh-ronj
wine	le vin	vañ
house wine	vin maison	vañ may-sañ
beer	un bière	byahr

TIPS FOR PRONOUNCING FLEMISH

Flemish is a dialect of Dutch, with most of the language remaining the same, bar some regional differences. The language is pronounced in largely the same way as English, although many vowels, particularly double vowels, are pronounced as long sounds. *J* is the equivalent of the English *y*, *v* is pronounced *f*, and *w* is *v*.

IN EMERGENCY

Help!	**Help!**	help
Stop!	**Stop!**	stop
Call a doctor!	**Haal een dokter!**	Haal uhn **dok**-tur
Call the police!	**Roep de politie!**	Roop duh poe-**leet**-see
Call the fire brigade!	**Roep de brandweer!**	Roop duh **brahnt**-vheer
Where is the nearest telephone?	**Waar ist de dichtsbijzijnde telefoon?**	Vhaar iss duh **dikst**-baiy-zaiyn-duh-tay-luh-**foan**
Where is the nearest hospital?	**Waar ist het dichtsbijzijnde ziekenhuis**	Vhaar iss het **dikst**-baiy-zaiyn-duh **zee**-kuh-hows

COMMUNICATION ESSENTIALS

Yes	**Ja**	yaa
No	**Nee**	nay
Please	**Alstublieft**	ahls-tew-**bleeft**
Thank you	**Dank u or**	dhank-ew
Excuse me	**Pardon**	pahr-**don**
Hello	**Bedankt**	be-dunk
Goodbye	**Dag**	dahgh
Good night	**Slaap lekker**	slap **lek**-kah
morning	**Morgen**	**mor**-ghugh
afternoon	**Middag**	**mid**-dahgh
evening	**Avond**	**av**-vohnd
yesterday	**Gisteren**	**ghis**-tern
today	**Vandaag**	**van**-daagh
tomorrow	**Morgen**	**mor**-ghugh
here	**Hier**	heer
there	**Daar**	daar
What?	**Wat?**	vhat
When?	**Wanneer?**	vhan-**eer**
Why?	**Waarom?**	vhaar-**om**
Where?	**Waar?**	vhaar
How?	**Hoe?**	hoo

USEFUL PHRASES

How are you?	**Hoe gaat het ermee?**	Hoo ghaat het er-**may**
Very well, thank you	**Heel goed, dank u**	Hayl ghoot, dhank ew
How do you do?	**Hoe maakt u het?**	Hoo maakt ew het
See you soon	**Tot ziens**	Tot zeens
That's fine	**Prima**	**Pree**-mah
Where is/are...?	**Waar is/zijn...?**	vhaar iss/zayn
How far is it to...?	**Hoe ver is het naar...?**	Hoo vehr iss het nar
How do I get to...?	**Hoe kom ik naar...?**	Hoo kom ik nar
Do you speak English?	**Spreekt u engels?**	Spraykt uw **eng**-uhls
I don't understand	**Ik snap het niet**	Ik snahp het neet
Could you speak slowly?	**Kunt u langzamer praten?**	Kuhnt ew **lahng**-zarmer-praat-tuh
I'm sorry	**Sorry**	sorry

USEFUL WORDS

big	**groot**	ghroat
small	**klein**	klaiyn
hot	**warm**	vharm
cold	**koud**	khowt
good	**goed**	ghoot
bad	**slecht**	slekht
enough	**genoeg**	ghuh-**noohkh**
well	**goed**	ghoot
open	**open**	open
closed	**gesloten**	ghuh-**slow**-tuh
left	**links**	links
right	**rechts**	rekhts
straight on	**rechtdoor**	rehkht dohr
near	**dightbij**	dikht baiy
far	**ver weg**	vehr vhekh
up	**omhoog**	om-**hoakh**
down	**naar beneden**	naar buh **nay**-duh
early	**vroeg**	vrookh

late	**laat**	laat
entrance	**ingang**	**in**-ghang
exit	**uitgang**	**ouht**-ghang
toilet	**wc**	vhay-say
occupied	**bezet**	buh-**zett**
free (vacant)	**vrij**	vraiy
free (no charge)	**gratis**	**ghraah**-tiss

MAKING A TELEPHONE CALL

I'd like to place a long-distance telephone call	**Ik wil graag interlokal telefoneren**	ik vhil ghraakh **inter**-loh-kaal tay-luh-foh-**neh**-ruh
I'd like to call collect	**Ik wil "collect" bellen**	ik vhil "collect call" **bel**-luh
I will try again later	**Ik probeer het later nog wel eens**	ik pro-**beer** het laater nokh vhel ayns
Can I leave a message?	**Kunt u een boodschap doorgeven?**	kuhnt ew uhn **boat**-skhahp **dohr**-ghay-vuh
Could you speak up a little please?	**Wilt u vat harder praten?**	vhilt ew vhat **hahr**-der **praat**-ew
Local call	**Lokaal gesprek**	low-**kaahl** ghuh-**sprek**

SHOPPING

How much does this cost?	**Hoeveel kost dit?**	hoo-**vayl** kost dit
I would like...	**Ik wil graag...**	ik vhil ghraakh
Do you have...?	**Heeft u...?**	hayft ew
I'm just looking	**Ik kijk alleen even**	ik kaiyk alleyn **ay**-vuh
Do you take credit cards?	**Neemt u credit cards aan?**	naymt ew credit cards aan?
Do you take travellers' cheques?	**Neemt u reischeques aan?**	naymt ew **raiys**-sheks aan
What time do you open?	**Hoe laat gaat u open?**	hoo laat ghaat ew opuh
What time do you close?	**Hoe laat gaat u dicht?**	hoo laat ghaat ew dikht
This one	**Deze**	**day**-zuh
That one	**Die**	dee
expensive	**duur**	dewr
cheap	**goedkoop**	ghoot-**koap**
size	**maat**	maat
white	**wit**	vhit
black	**zwart**	zvhahrt
red	**rood**	roat
yellow	**geel**	ghayl
green	**groen**	ghroon
blue	**blauw**	blah-ew

TYPES OF SHOPS

antique shop	**antiekwinkel**	ahn-**teek**-vhin-kul
bakery	**bakker**	**bah**-ker
bank	**bank**	bahnk
bookshop	**boekwinkel**	**book**-vhin-kul
butcher	**slager**	slaakh-er
cake shop	**banketbakkerij**	bahnk-**et**-bahk-er-aiy
chip stop/stand	**patatzaak**	pah-**taht**-zak
chemist/drugstore	**apotheek**	ah-poe-**taiyk**
delicatessen	**delicatessen**	daylee-kah-**tes**-suh
department store	**warenhuis**	**vhaah**-uh-houws
fishmonger	**viswinkel**	**viss**-vhin-kul
greengrocer	**groenteboer**	**ghroon**-tuh-boor
hairdresser	**kapper**	**kah**-per
market	**markt**	mahrkt
newsagent	**krantenwinkel**	**krahn**-tuh-vhin-kul
post office	**postkantoor**	**pohst**-kahn-tor
supermarket	**supermarkt**	**sew**-per-mahrkt
tobacconist	**sigarenwinkel**	see-**ghaa**-ruh-vhin-kul
travel agent	**reisburo**	**raiys**-bew-roa

SIGHTSEEING

art gallery	**gallerie**	ghaller-ee
bus station	**busstation**	**buhs**-stah-shown
bus ticket	**strippenkaart**	**strip**-puh-kaart
cathedral	**kathedraal**	kah-tuh-**draal**
church	**kerk**	kehrk
closed on public holidays	**op feestdagen gesloten**	op **fayst**-daa-ghuh ghuh-slow-**tuh**
day return	**dagretour**	**dahgh**-ruh-tour
garden	**tuin**	towun
library	**bibliotheek**	bee-bee-yo-**tayk**
museum	**museum**	mew-**zay**-um

railway station	**station**	stah-**shown**
return ticket	**retourtje**	ruh-**tour**-tyuh
single journey	**enkeltje**	**eng**-kuhl-tyuh
tourist information	**dienst voor tourisme**	deenst vor **tor**-ism
town hall	**stadhuis**	**staht**-houws
train	**trein**	traiyn

STAYING IN A HOTEL

Do you have a vacant room?	**Zijn er nog kamers vrij?**	zaiyn er nokh **kaa**-mers vray
double room with double bed	**een twees persoons-kamer met een twee persoonsbed**	uhn **tvhay** per-**soans**-ka-mer met uhn **tvhay** per-**soans** beht
twin room	**een kamer met een lits-jumeaux**	uhn **kaa**-mer met uhn lee-zjoo-**moh**
single room	**eenpersoons-kamer**	**ayn**-per-**soans** **kaa**-mer
room with a bath/shower	**kaamer met bad/douche**	**kaa-mer** met baht/doosh
I have a reservation	**Ik heb gereserveerd**	ik hehp ghuh-ray-sehr-**veert**

EATING OUT

Have you got table?	**Is er een tafel vrij?**	iss ehr uhn **tah**-fuhl vraiy
I would like to reserve a table	**Ik wil een tafel reserveren**	ik vhil uhn **tah**-fel ray schr-**veer**-uh
The bill, please	**Mag ik afrekenen**	muhk ik **ahf**-ray-kuh-nuh
I am a vegetarian	**Ik ben vegetariër**	ik ben fay-ghuh-**taahr**-ee-er
waitress/waiter	**serveerster/ober**	schr-**veer**-ster/**oh**-ber
menu	**de kaart**	duh kaahrt
cover charge	**het couvert**	het koo-**vehr**
wine list	**de wijnkaart**	duh **vhaiyn**-kart
glass	**het glass**	het ghlahss
bottle	**de fles**	duh fless
knife	**het mes**	het mess
fork	**de vork**	duh fork
spoon	**de lepel**	duh **lay**-pul
breakfast	**het ontbijt**	het ont-**baiyt**
lunch	**de lunch**	duh lernsh
dinner	**het diner**	het dee-**nay**
main course	**het hoofdgerecht**	het **hoaft**-ghuh-rekht
starter, first course	**het voorgerecht**	het **vhor**-ghuh-rekht
dessert	**het nagerecht**	het **naa**-ghuh-rekht
dish of the day	**het dagmenu**	het **dahg**-munh-ew
bar	**het cafe**	het kaa-**fay**
café	**het eetcafe**	het **ayt**-kaa-**fay**
rare	**rare**	'rare'
medium	**medium**	'medium'
well done	**doorbakken**	door-**bah**-kuh

NUMBERS

1	**een**	ayn
2	**twee**	tvhay
3	**drie**	dree
4	**vier**	feer
5	**vijf**	faiyf
6	**zes**	zess
7	**zeven**	**zay**-vuh
8	**acht**	ahkht
9	**negen**	**nay**-guh
10	**tien**	teen
11	**elf**	elf
12	**twaalf**	tvhaalf
13	**dertien**	**dehr**-teen
14	**veertien**	**feer**-teen
15	**vijftien**	**faiyf**-teen
16	**zestien**	**zess**-teen
17	**zeventien**	**zayvuh**-teen
18	**achtien**	**ahkh**-teen
19	**negentien**	**nay-ghuh**-tien
20	**twintig**	**tvhin**-tukh
21	**eenentwintig**	**aynuh**-tvhin-tukh
30	**dertig**	**dehr**-tukh
40	**veertig**	**feer**-tukh
50	**vijftig**	**faiyf**-tukh
60	**zestig**	**zess**-tukh
70	**zeventig**	**zay**-vuh-tukh
80	**tachtig**	**tahkh**-tukh
90	**negentig**	**nayguh**-tukh

100	**honderd**	**hohn**-durt
1000	**duizend**	**douw**-zuhnt
1,000,000	**miljoen**	mill-**yoon**

TIME

one minute	**een minuut**	uhn meen-**ewt**
one hour	**een uur**	uhn ewr
half an hour	**een half uur**	een hahlf uhr
half past one	**half twee**	hahlf twee
a day	**een dag**	uhn dahgh
a week	**een week**	uhn vhayk
a month	**een maand**	uhn maant
a year	**een jaar**	uhn jaar
Monday	**maandag**	**maan**-dahgh
Tuesday	**dinsdag**	**dins**-dahgh
Wednesday	**woensdag**	**vhoons**-dahgh
Thursday	**donderdag**	**donder**-dahgh
Friday	**vrijdag**	**vraiy**-dahgh
Saturday	**zaterdag**	**zaater**-dahgh
Sunday	**zondag**	**zon**-dahgh

BELGIAN BEER AND FOOD

FISH

fish	**vis**	fiss
bass	**zeebars**	see-buhr
herring	**haring**	**haa**-ring
lobster	**kreeft**	krayft
monkfish	**lotte/zeeduivel**	lot/scafuhdul
mussel	**mossel**	**moss**-uhl
oyster	**oester**	**ouhs**-tuh
pike	**snoek**	snook
prawn	**garnaal**	gar-nall
salmon	**zalm**	sahlm
scallop	**Sint-Jacoboester/ Jacobsschelp**	**sind**-yakob-ouhs-tuh/yakob-scuhlp
sea bream	**dorade/zeebrasem**	doh-rard
skate	**rog**	rog
trout	**forel**	foh-ruhl
tuna	**tonijn**	tuhn-een

MEAT

meat	**vlees**	flayss
beef	**rundvlees**	**ruhnt**-flayss
chicken	**kip**	kip
duck	**eend**	aynt
lamb	**lamsvlees**	**lahms**-flayss
pheasant	**fazant**	**fay**-zanh
pork	**varkensvlees**	**vahr**-kuhns-flayss
veal	**kalfsvlees**	**karfs**-flayss
venison	**ree (bok)**	ray

VEGETABLES

vegetables	**groenten**	**ghroon**-tuh
asparagus	**asperges**	as-puhj
Belgian endive/ chicory	**witloof**	vit-lurf
Brussels sprouts	**spruitjes**	spruhr-tyuhs
garlic	**knoflook**	**knoff**-loak
green beans	**princesbonen**	prins-ess-buh-nun
haricot beans	**snijbonen**	snee-buh-nun
potatoes	**aardappels**	**aard**-uppuhls
spinach	**spinazie**	spin-a-jee
truffle	**truffel**	truh-fuhl

DESSERTS

fruit	**fruit/vruchten**	vroot/vrooh-tuh
pancake	**pannekoek**	**pah**-nuh-kook
waffle	**wafel**	vaff-uhl

DRINKS

beer	**bier**	beeh
coffee	**koffie**	coffee
fresh orange juice	**verse jus**	**vehr**-suh zjhew
hot chocolate	**chocola**	sho-koh-**laa**
mineral water	**mineraalwater**	meener-**aahl**-vhaater
tea	**thee**	tay
water	**water**	**vhaa**-ter
wine	**wijn**	vhaiyn